*f*P

OVERBLOWN

How Politicians and the Terrorism Industry
Inflate National Security Threats,
and Why We Believe Them

John Mueller

FREE PRESS

New York   London   Toronto   Sydney

FREE PRESS
A Division of Simon & Schuster, Inc.
1230 Avenue of the Americas
New York, NY 10020

Copyright © 2006 John Mueller
All rights reserved,
including the right of reproduction
in whole or in part in any form.

FREE PRESS and colophon are trademarks of Simon & Schuster, Inc.

For information about special discounts for bulk purchases,
please contact Simon & Schuster Special Sales at
1-800-456-6798 or business@simonandschuster.com

DESIGNED BY ERICH HOBBING

Manufactured in the United States of America

1   3   5   7   9   10   8   6   4   2

Library of Congress Cataloging-in-Publication data is available.

ISBN-13: 978-1-4165-4172-1

To JAM
To Karl, Michelle, Karen, Erik, Susan, and Kraig
To Timothy, Samuel, Clara, Kara, Malcolm, Atticus, and Lida
To Lois and Phyllis
And to the memory of
David Maki
and
Elsie S. Mueller

Contents

OVERBLOWN

Overblown

Upon discovering that Weeki Wachee Springs, his Florida roadside water park, had been included on the Department of Homeland Security's list of over 80,000 potential terrorist targets, its marketing and promotion manager, John Athanason, turned reflective. "I can't imagine bin Laden trying to blow up the mermaids," he mused, "but with terrorists, who knows what they're thinking. I don't want to think like a terrorist, but what if the terrorists try to poison the water at Weeki Wachee Springs?"

Whatever his imaginings, however, he went on to report that his enterprise had quickly and creatively risen to the occasion—or seized the opportunity. They were working to get a chunk of the counterterrorism funds allocated to the region by the well-endowed, anxiety-provoking, ever-watchful Department of Homeland Security.[1]

Which is the greater threat: terrorism, or our reaction against it? The Weeki Wachee experience illustrates the problem. A threat that is real but likely to prove to be of limited scope has been massively, perhaps even fancifully, inflated to produce widespread and unjustified anxiety. This process has then led to wasteful, even self-parodic expenditures and policy overreactions, ones that not only very often do more harm and cost more money than anything the terrorists have accomplished, but play into their hands.

The way terrorism anxiety has come to envelop the nation is also illustrated by a casual exchange on television's *60 Minutes*. In an interview, filmmaker-provocateur Michael Moore happened to remark, "The chances of any of us dying in a terrorist incident is very, very, very small," and his interviewer, Bob Simon, promptly admonished, "But no one sees the world like that." Remarkably, both statements are true—the first only a bit more so than the second. It is the thesis of this book that

1

our reaction against terrorism has caused more harm than the threat warrants—not just to civil liberties, not just to the economy, but even to human lives. And our reaction has often helped the terrorists more than it has hurt them. It is the reactive consequences stemming from Simon's perspective—or from what journalist Mark Bowden has characterized as "housewives in Iowa . . . watching TV afraid that al-Qaeda's going to charge in their front door"—that generate one of the chief problems presented by terrorism.[2]

International terrorism generally kills a few hundred people a year worldwide—not much more, usually, than the number who drown yearly in bathtubs in the United States. Americans worry intensely about "another 9/11," but if one of these were to occur every three months for the next five years, the chance of being killed in one of them is 0.02 percent. Astronomer Alan Harris has calculated that at present rates, the lifetime probability that a resident of the globe will die at the hands of international terrorists is 1 in 80,000, about the same likelihood that one would die over the same interval from the impact on the earth of an especially ill-directed asteroid or comet.[3]

Figure 1: Concerns about terrorism, 2001-2006

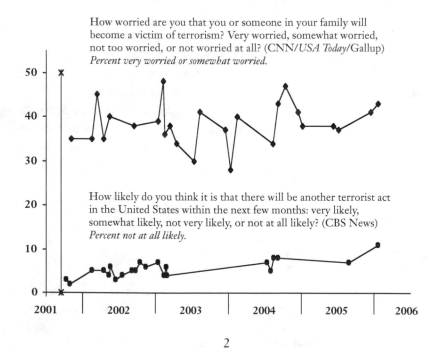

But such numbers are almost never discussed: Moore's outburst is exceedingly rare. Instead, most Americans seem to have developed a false sense of insecurity about terrorism.[4] Thus, since 9/11, over a period in which there have been no international terror attacks whatever in the United States and in which an individual's chances of being killed by a terrorist have remained microscopic even if one—or many—did occur, nearly half of the population has continually expressed worry that they or a member of their family will become a victim of terrorism, as Figure 1 shows. Moreover, when asked if they consider another terrorist attack likely in the United States within the next several months, fewer than 10 percent of Americans usually respond with what has proven to be the correct answer: "Not at all likely." Yet, this group has not notably increased in size despite continual confirmation of its prescience.

That the costs of terrorism chiefly arise from fear and from overwrought responses holds even for the tragic events of September 11, 2001, which constituted by far the most destructive set of terrorist acts in history and resulted in the deaths of nearly 3,000 people. The economic costs of reaction have been much higher than those inflicted by the terrorists even in that record-shattering episode, and considerably more than 3,000 Americans have died since 9/11 because, out of fear, they drove in cars rather than flew in airplanes, or because they were swept into wars made politically possible by the terrorist events.

Moreover, as terrorist kingpin and devil du jour Osama bin Laden has gleefully noted, fear, alarmism, and overreaction suit the terrorists' agenda just fine because they create the damaging consequences the terrorists seek but are unable to perpetrate on their own. As he put it mockingly in a videotaped message in 2004, it is "easy for us to provoke and bait. . . . All that we have to do is to send two mujahidin . . . to raise a piece of cloth on which is written al-Qaeda in order to make the generals race there to cause America to suffer human, economic, and political losses." His policy, he extravagantly believes, is one of "bleeding America to the point of bankruptcy," and it is one that depends on overreaction by the target: he triumphally points to the fact that the 9/11 terrorist attacks cost al-Qaeda $500,000, while the attack and its aftermath inflicted, he claims, a cost of more than $500 billion on the United States. Shortly after 9/11, he crowed, "America is full of fear from its north to its south, from its west ot its east. Thank God for that."[5]

PRESENTING AN UNCONVENTIONAL CONVENTIONAL WISDOM

In exploring these issues, this book develops three themes, in this order: (1) terrorism's threat, while real, has been much overblown, something that aids terrorist aims; (2) this process is a familiar one since, with the benefit of hindsight, we can see that many international threats have been considerably inflated in the past; and (3) applying these lessons, policy toward terrorism should very substantially focus on reducing the damaging fears and overreactions terrorism so routinely fosters.

In the process, I present a considerable number of propositions that, it seems to me, should be—but decidedly aren't—the conventional wisdom on this subject. These propositions are certainly susceptible to debate and to reasoned criticism, but it seems to me that they, rather than their hysterical if attention-grabbing opposites, ought to be the base from which the discussion proceeds. At the very least, they should be part of the policy discussion mix, but they seem almost entirely to have been ignored.

Among these propositions are the following:

- In general, terrorism, particularly international terrorism, doesn't do much damage when considered in almost any reasonable context.
- Although airplanes can still be blown up, another attack like the one on 9/11 is virtually impossible. In 2001 the hijackers had the element of surprise working for them: previous hijackings (including one conducted by Muslim terrorists six months earlier) had mostly been fairly harmless as the perpetrators generally landed the planes somewhere and released, or were forced to release, the passengers. After the 9/11 experience, passengers and crew will fight to prevent a takeover, as was shown on the fourth plane on 9/11.
- The likelihood that any individual American will be killed in a terrorist event is microscopic.
- Just about any damage terrorists are likely to be able to perpetrate can be readily absorbed. To deem the threat an "existential" one is somewhere between extravagant and absurd.
- The capacity of al-Qaeda or of any similar group to do damage in the United States pales in comparison to the capacity other dedicated enemies, particularly international communism, have possessed in the past.

- Lashing out at the terrorist threat is frequently an exercise in self-flagellation because it is usually more expensive than the terrorist attack itself and because it gives the terrorists exactly what they are looking for.
- Chemical and radiological weapons, and most biological ones as well, are incapable of perpetrating mass destruction.
- The likelihood that a terrorist group will be able to master nuclear weapons any time soon is extremely, perhaps vanishingly, small.
- Although murderous and dedicated, al-Qaeda is a very small and very extreme group, and it is unlikely by itself to have the capacity for taking over any significant government.
- Al-Qaeda's terrorist efforts on 9/11 and in the years since have been substantially counterproductive.
- Although additional terrorist attacks in the United States certainly remain possible, an entirely plausible explanation for the fact that there have been none since 2001 is that there is no significant international terrorist presence within the country.
- Policies that continually, or even occasionally, focus entirely on worst-case scenarios (or worst-case fantasies) are unwise and can be exceedingly wasteful.
- In fact, much, probably most of the money and effort expended on counterterrorism since 2001 (and before, for that matter) has been wasted.
- Seeking to protect all potential targets against terrorist attack is impossible and foolish. In fact, just about anything is a potential target.
- Terrorism should be treated essentially as a criminal problem calling mainly for the application of policing methods, particularly in the international sphere, not military ones.
- Because terrorism probably presents only a rather limited threat, a viable policy approach might center around creating the potential to absorb its direct effects and to mitigate its longer range consequences while continuing to support international policing efforts, particularly overseas.

THE ROLE OF THE TERRORISM INDUSTRY

One reason these propositions have gone almost entirely unconsidered is that the fears and anxieties created by the 9/11 experience have been so deftly orchestrated and overblown by members of the terrorism industry: politicians, experts, the media, academics, the bureaucracy, and risk entrepreneurs who profit in one way or another by inflating the threat international terrorism is likely to present. For example, in 2003, while Homeland Security czar Tom Ridge was bravely declaring that "America is a country that will not be bent by terror" or "broken by fear," General Richard Myers, chairman of the Joint Chiefs of Staff, was ominously suggesting that if terrorists were able to engineer an event that managed to kill 10,000 Americans, they would successfully "do away with our way of life."[6]

The sudden deaths of that many Americans—although representing fewer than 0.004 percent of the population—would indeed be horrifying and tragic, the greatest one-day disaster the country has suffered since the Civil War. But the United States is hardly likely to be toppled by dramatic acts of terrorist destruction, even extreme ones. The country can readily absorb considerable damage if necessary, and it has outlasted far more potent threats in the past. To suggest otherwise is to express contempt for America's capacity to deal with adversity.

The only way terrorist acts could conceivably "do away with our way of life" would be if, bent and broken, we did it to ourselves in reaction. As broadcaster Edward R. Murrow put it in a different context, "No one can terrorize a whole nation, unless we are all his accomplices." The process would presumably involve repealing the Bill of Rights, boarding up churches, closing down newspapers and media outlets, burning books, abandoning English for North Korean, and refusing evermore to consume hamburgers.

As it is now, terrorism policy constantly seeks to enhance this (rather unlikely) possibility by stoking fear and by engaging in costly, terrorist-encouraging overreaction. For example, the hastily assembled and massively funded Department of Homeland Security officially intones on the first page of its defining manifesto, "Today's terrorists can strike at any place, at any time, and with virtually any weapon." This warning may be true in some sense, of course (depending on how "virtually" is defined), but it is also fatuous and misleading. "Telling Kansan truck drivers to prepare for nuclear terrorism is like telling bullfighters to watch out for lightning. It should not be their primary concern," aptly notes analyst Benjamin Friedman. "For questionable gains in preparedness, we spread paranoia" and facilitate the bureaucratically and politically appealing notion that "if the threat is everywhere, you must spend everywhere," while developing and perpetrating the myth, or at least the impression, that the terrorists are omnipotent and omnipresent.[7]

The department has also urged people to stock up on duct tape and plastic sheeting so they can (almost certainly inadequately) seal off their homes in the wildly unlikely event that a significant chemical or biological attack happened to transpire in their neighborhood. Meanwhile, although it has yet to uncover a single true terrorist cell in the United States, the FBI has warned the citizenry, apparently seriously, to be wary of people bearing almanacs—which, they helpfully explain, contain information of great value to your average diabolical terrorist, such as the location of bridges.[8]

AN ALTERNATIVE APPROACH TO TERRORISM

By contrast, a sensible approach to terrorism would support international policing while seeking to reduce terrorism's principal costs—fear, anxiety, and overreaction—not to aggravate them. In the process it would stress that some degree of risk is an inevitable fact of life, that the country can, however grimly, absorb just about any damage terrorism can inflict (it now "absorbs" 40,000 traffic deaths per year, almost all of which could be prevented by imposing a thirteen-mile-per-hour speed limit), and that seeking to protect every imaginable terrorist target (such as Weeki Wachee Springs) is impossible and absurd.

Moreover, there are important economic benefits to such a policy. Effectively it can encourage people to get on airplanes and spend money while their terrified counterparts cower at home, decorate their cars with flag decals, and loudly, defiantly, and pointlessly bellow anthems about "the Home of the Brave." One day we might even begin to consider a heretical possibility, one that may or may not be true but that fits the evidence gathered so far: that the massive Homeland Security apparatus in the United States is persecuting some, spying on many, inconveniencing most, and taxing all to defend against an internal enemy that scarcely exists.

In my view, then, the focus should be on treating terrorism as a criminal activity of rather limited importance and on reducing anxieties and avoiding policy overreaction. These tasks, however, may be exceedingly difficult because fears, once embraced, are not all that susceptible to rational analysis and because the terrorism industry will likely continue assiduously to cultivate those fears.

LESSONS OVERLEARNED:
THE PERSISTENCE OF EXAGGERATION AND OVERREACTION

"At the summit of foreign policy," political scientist Warner Schilling once observed, "one always finds simplicity and spook."[9] This book deals with the results of that proposition as it pertains to American foreign policy over the past several decades: the tendency to exaggerate foreign threats and then, partly in consequence, to overreact to them. It then applies that experience to the current era, specifically to the extravagant, sometimes even hysterical fears international terrorism has fostered and to the expensive and sometimes counterproductive policies those fears have inspired. Analyzed are responses to Pearl Harbor (an event often compared to 9/11), anxieties over the threat presented by domestic and foreign communism, fears about the imminence of thermonuclear war, apprehensions over challenges posed by various "rogue states," most of which eventually faded into insignificance (remember Castro?), absurd insecurities engendered by the Iran hostage crisis and the Japanese economic challenge, and concerns about "ethnic warfare" that was supposed to engulf the world.

In all this, I do not wish to suggest that all fears are unjustified or that international threats are never *under*estimated. In fact, I suspect that some of the tendency to overestimate threats in the period after World War II derives from the fact that the dire threat presented by Adolf Hitler's Germany had been underappreciated in the period before it. This underestimate, however, was premised in part and in turn on an overestimate: the exaggerated supposition that the next major war would obviously lead to human annihilation, an assumption that led to the logical, but profoundly misguided, conclusion that Hitler could not possibly be willing to risk, much less start, such a war.[10] The postwar proclivity toward exaggeration and overreaction may also stem in part from the traumatic prewar experience with Japan, when there was a tendency to underestimate its capacity and, in particular, its willingness to take risks. Nor do I wish to argue that every overreaction is wasteful or foolish to the same degree; historical comparisons suggest that the inflation of the terrorist threat may be unusually excessive.

Political scientist Robert Jervis has suggested that "those who remember the past are condemned to making the opposite mistakes."[11] It is a central burden of this book that the prewar experience with Hitler and with Japan may have been too well remembered and that, despite the alarmism of prominent members of the terrorism industry, today's tiny bands of international terrorists hardly present a Hitlerian threat. Accordingly, our present anxieties are much inflated, and it is time to think again.

Judge Richard Posner notes that "when a nation is surprised and hurt there is a danger that it will overreact," but, he continues, "it is only with the benefit of hindsight that a reaction can be separated into its proper and excess layers."[12] It will be seen in this book that unpleasant surprises very frequently, though not always, lead to two responses that are serially connected and often prove to be unwise. First, the surprise is treated not as an aberration, but as a harbinger indicating that things have suddenly become much more dangerous and threatening, will remain so, and will become worse—an exercise that might be called "massive extrapolation." Second, there is a tendency to lash out at the threat without a great deal of thought about alternative policies, including and especially ones that might advocate simply letting it be.

Posner is certainly correct to argue that we can be sure only in hindsight about whether a reaction has been excessive, but very frequently that retrospective evaluation is never made. For example, now that we know how the cold war came out, it seems a reasonable, and potentially profitable, exercise to consider whether the fears, anxieties, reactions, and expenditures the Soviet challenge inspired were, in fact, wise and sensible, or perhaps even necessary. Moreover, even taking into consideration the emotions of the time and the limitations of knowledge and intelligence information that policymakers inevitably labor under, data interpretations and policy options that should at least have *occurred* to responsible decision makers at the time—if only to be rejected for one reason or another—often never percolated into their consciousness at all. In the case of terrorism, for instance, I just presented a substantial list of plausible interpretations and options that have been almost entirely ignored in the extensive public discussion on (or endless yammering about) terrorism that has taken place since September 11, 2001. Thus, simplicity and spook very frequently have prevailed in the past, and they seem to be doing so now.

Accordingly, this book liberally and unapologetically applies hindsight to evaluate reactions to such surprises as Pearl Harbor, the Korean War, *Sputnik*, hostage taking in the Middle East, and the eruption of ethnic conflict in Europe. Not all threats that could potentially have been seized upon have evoked anxiety and overreaction. For example, the American public and its leaders have remained remarkably calm about the potential damage that could be inflicted by the planet's intersection with large meteors or comets, and (perhaps more pertinently) they do not seem to be exercised all that much by advertised dangers stemming from global warming or genetically modified food.[13] But it does appear that every foreign policy threat in the past several decades that has come to be accepted as significant has then eventually been unwisely exaggerated.

It does not automatically and necessarily follow, of course, that because foreign policy threats have been inflated in the past, we are doing so now. However, this book finds a significant pattern of overextrapolation and overreaction, not to mention simplicity and spook, that has often led to policies that were unwise, costly, unnecessary, and sometimes massively counterproductive. And we seem to be at it yet again, perhaps now more than ever.

PART I

TERRORISM'S IMPACT

CHAPTER 1

The Limited Destructiveness
of Terrorism

For all the attention it evokes, terrorism, in reasonable context, actually causes rather little damage, and the likelihood that any individual will become a victim in most places is microscopic. Those adept at hyperbole like to proclaim that we live in "the age of terror." However, the number of people worldwide who die as a result of international terrorism is generally a few hundred a year, tiny compared to the numbers who die in most civil wars or from automobile accidents. In fact, until 2001 far fewer Americans were killed in any grouping of years by all forms of international terrorism than were killed by lightning. And except for 2001, virtually none of these terrorist deaths occurred within the United States itself. Indeed, outside of 2001, fewer people have been killed in America by international terrorism than have drowned in toilets or have died from bee stings.

Even with the September 11 attacks included in the count, however, the number of Americans killed by international terrorism since the late 1960s (which is when the State Department began its accounting) is about the same as the number killed over the same period by lightning, or by accident-causing deer, or by severe allergic reactions to peanuts. In almost all years the total number of people worldwide who die at the hands of international terrorists is not much more than the number who drown in bathtubs in the United States.[1]

Some of this is a matter of definition. When terrorism becomes really extensive we generally no longer call it terrorism, but war or insurgency, as has happened in Iraq.[2] But Americans and others in the developed world are mainly concerned about random or sporadic acts of terrorism within their homeland, not sustained warfare. Moreover, even using an expansive definition of terrorism and including domestic terrorism in the mix, it is likely that far fewer people were killed by terrorists in the entire world over the past 100 years than died in any number of civil wars during that time.

However, those who fear terrorism essentially argue that this experience is irrelevant. Spurred by the dramatic destruction of 9/11, they insist that we have now entered a new era. Soon, they conclude, terrorists will be able to deploy "weapons of mass destruction." Moreover, the spectacular success of the 9/11 attacks is taken to suggest that international terrorists, al-Qaeda in particular, are diabolically clever and capable, and that the kind of destruction they visited on September 11, 2001, will soon come to be typical. The events of that day are taken as a harbinger. Are these two widely accepted arguments valid?

TERRORISM AND WEAPONS OF MASS DESTRUCTION

Because no weapons more complicated than box cutters were employed on September 11, it would seem that the experience ought to be taken to suggest that the scenario most to be feared is not the acquisition by terrorists of devices of mass destructiveness, but one in which terrorists are once again able, through skill, careful planning, suicidal dedication, and great luck, to massively destroy with ordinary, extant devices. Some of the anxiety about WMD, perhaps, derives from the post–September 11 anthrax scare, even though that terrorist event killed only a few people.

Not only were the 9/11 bombings remarkably low-tech, but they were something that could have happened long ago: both skyscrapers and airplanes have been around for a century now. In addition, the potential for destruction on that magnitude is hardly new: a tiny band of fanatical, well-trained, and lucky terrorists could have sunk or scuttled the *Titanic* and killed thousands.[3]

Nonetheless, terrorism analyses tend to focus on lurid worst-case scenarios, a great portion of them involving weapons of mass destruction, a concept that, especially after the cold war, has been expanded to embrace chemical and biological and sometimes radiological as well as nuclear weapons.[4] Although chemical, radiological, and most biological weapons do not belong in the same category of destructiveness as nuclear weapons, all members of the WMD list are similar in that their acquisition and deployment present enormous difficulties, especially for terrorists.

Nuclear Weapons

Nuclear weapons can indeed inflict massive destruction, and an atomic bomb in the hands of a terrorist or rogue state could kill tens of thousands of people or even, in exceptional circumstances, more. But it is also essential to note that making such a bomb is an extraordinarily difficult task. As the Gilmore Commission, a special advisory panel to the president and Congress, stresses, building a nuclear device capable of producing mass destruction presents "Herculean challenges." The process requires obtaining enough fissile material, designing a weapon "that will bring that mass together in a tiny fraction of a second, before the heat from early fission blows the material apart," and figuring out some way to deliver the thing. And the Commission emphasizes that these merely constitute "the *minimum* requirements." If each is not fully met, the result is not simply a less powerful weapon, but one that can't produce any significant nuclear yield at all or can't be delivered.[5]

Moreover, proliferation of these weapons has been remarkably slow. During the cold war there were many dire predictions about nuclear proliferation that proved to be greatly exaggerated. Among these was the nearly unanimous expectation in the 1950s and 1960s that dozens of countries would soon have nuclear weapons. For example, a report in 1958 predicted "a rapid rise" in the number of atomic powers by the mid-1960s, and a couple of years later, John Kennedy observed that there might be "ten, fifteen, twenty" countries with a nuclear capacity by 1964. In 1985 *Time* magazine devoted a cover story to the claim that "the nuclear threat is spreading" and worried that "the rate of proliferation could grow rapidly worse" thanks to what it ominously called "phantom proliferators." Yet, twenty years later, the only clear addition to the nuclear club is Pakistan. Similar alarms were issued in the early 1990s, in the aftermath of the cold war. Well over a decade ago, it was argued that Japan and Germany would, by natural impulse, soon come to yearn for nuclear weapons. The Japanese and the Germans themselves continue to seem viscerally uninterested, though problems with North Korea could alter that perspective for Japan.[6]

It is also worth noting that, although nuclear weapons have been around now for well over half a century, no state has ever given another state—even a close ally, much less a terrorist group—a nuclear weapon (or chemical, biological, or radiological one either, for that matter) that the recipient could use independently. For example, during the cold war, North Korea tried to acquire nuclear weapons from its close ally, China, and was firmly refused.[7] Donors understand that there is always the danger the weapon will be used in a manner the donor would not approve—or even, potentially, on the donor itself. There could be some danger from private profiteers, like the network established by Pakistani scientist A. Q. Khan. However, its activities were rather easily penetrated by intelligence agencies, and it was closed down abruptly after 9/11.

Warnings about the possibility that small groups, terrorists, and errant states could fabricate nuclear weapons have been repeatedly uttered at least since 1946, when A-bomb maker J. Robert Oppenheimer agreed that "three or four men" could smuggle atomic bomb units into New York and "blow up the whole city." Such assertions proliferated after the 1950s, when the "suitcase bomb" appeared to become a practical possibility. And it has now been over three decades since terrorism specialist Brian Jenkins published his warnings that the "widespread distribution of increasingly sophisticated and increasingly powerful man-portable weapons will greatly add to the terrorist's arsenal" and that "the world's increasing dependence on nuclear power may provide terrorists with weapons of mass destruction."[8] We continue to wait.

Under the stimulus of 9/11, dire warnings about nuclear terrorism have escalated. Of particular concern in this are Russia's supposedly missing suitcase bombs, even though a careful assessment has concluded that it is unlikely that any of these devices has indeed been lost and that, regardless, their effectiveness would be very low or even nonexistent because they require continual maintenance. As CIA adviser and arms inspector Charles Duelfer has stressed, the development of nuclear weapons requires thousands of knowledgeable scientists and large physical facilities.[9]

In 2004, political scientist Graham Allison opined that a dedicated terrorist group could get around the problems in time and eventually steal, produce, or procure a "crude" bomb, and he boldly declared that, unless his policy recommendations (which include a dramatic push toward war with North Korea) are carried out, "a nuclear terrorist attack on America in the decade ahead is more likely than not." It is anticipated that it might well take ten years of dedicated effort even for a state like Iran to develop a nuclear weapon, but Allison thinks that terrorists would be happy with one that is "large, cumbersome, unsafe, unreliable, unpredictable, and inefficient." In support of his prediction Allison cites the "world's most successful investor" and "legendary odds maker," Warren Buffett, as declaring a nuclear terrorist attack to be inevitable. Contacted by the *Wall Street Journal,* however, Buffett says he was worrying about any nuclear explosion, not just one set off by terrorists, and that he was talking about something that might come about over the next century, not within a ten-year period.[10]

Given the destructive capacity of nuclear weapons, it definitely makes sense to expend some policy effort to increase the difficulties for any would-be nuclear terrorists, particularly by seeking to control the world's supply of fissile material. But the difficulties for the terrorists persist, and their likelihood of acquiring the weapon any time soon remains very low—even assuming they try hard. Moreover, no terrorist group, including al-Qaeda, has shown anything resembling the technical expertise necessary to fabricate a bomb.

Allison's dire forecast is far more likely to be remembered if it proves true than if, much more probably, it goes the way of C. P. Snow's once-heralded alarmist broadside published nearly a half century ago:

> We are faced with an either-or, and we haven't much time. The *either* is acceptance of a restriction of nuclear armaments. . . . The *or* is not a risk but a certainty. It is this. There is no agreement on tests. The nuclear arms race between the United States and the U.S.S.R. not only continues but accelerates. Other countries join in. Within, at the most, six years, China and several other states have a stock of nuclear bombs. Within, at the most, ten years, some of those bombs are going off. I am saying this as responsibly as I can. *That* is the certainty.

Doomsayers have been wryly advised to predict catastrophe no later than ten years into the future but no earlier than five because that would be soon enough to terrify their rapt listeners but far enough off for people to forget if the doomsaying proves to be wrong.[11] Allison and Snow seem to have gotten the point.

Chemical Weapons

Chemical arms do have the potential, under appropriate circumstances, for panicking people; killing masses of them in open areas, however, is beyond their modest capabilities. Although they obviously can be hugely lethal when released in gas chambers, their effectiveness as weapons has been unimpressive, and their inclusion in the WMD category is highly dubious unless the concept is so diluted that bullets or machetes can also be included.[12]

Biologist Matthew Meselson calculates that it would take fully a ton of nerve gas or five tons of mustard gas to produce heavy casualties among unprotected people in an open area one kilometer square. Even for nerve gas this would take the concentrated delivery into a rather small area of about 300 heavy artillery shells or seven 500-pound bombs. This would usually require a considerable amount of time, allowing many people to evacuate the targeted area. A 1993 analysis by the Office of Technology Assessment of the U.S. Congress finds that a ton of sarin nerve gas perfectly delivered under absolutely ideal conditions over a heavily populated area against unprotected people could cause between 3,000 and 8,000 deaths. Under slightly less ideal circumstances—if there is a moderate wind or if the sun is out, for example—the death rate would be one-tenth as great. Or, as the Gilmore Commission put it later, it would take a full ton of sarin gas released under favorable weather conditions for the destructive effects to become distinctly greater than could be obtained by conventional explosives. Nuclear weapons are considered weapons of mass destruction because a single bomb can generate great devastation. By contrast, for chemical weapons to cause extensive damage, many of them must be used, just like conventional weapons.[13]

Discussions of chemical weapons often stress their ability to cause casualties, both dead and wounded. This glosses over the fact that historically most of those incapacitated by chemical weapons have not actually died. But clearly, to be classified as weapons of mass destruction they must destroy, not simply incapacitate. In World War I only some 2 or 3 percent of those gassed on the Western Front died; by contrast, wounds caused by traditional weapons were some 10 or 12 times more likely to prove fatal.[14] Troops wounded by gas also tend to return to combat more quickly than those wounded by bullets or shrapnel, and to suffer less. Against well-protected troops, gas is almost wholly ineffective except as an inconvenience. Moreover, the weapons degrade over time. In 2006, two Republican lawmakers triumphantly announced that 500 chemical weapons had been found in Iraq. These, as it turned out, dated from before the 1991 war against that country, and the weapons were now, as one expert put it, "less toxic than most things that Americans have under their kitchen sink."[15]

Although gas was used extensively in World War I, it accounted for less than 1 percent of the battle deaths. In fact, on average it took well over a ton of gas to produce a single fatality. In the conclusion to the official British history of the war, chemical weapons are relegated to a footnote, which asserts that gas "made war uncomfortable . . . to no purpose."[16]

Since that war, gas was apparently used in rather limited amounts in the 1930s by Italy in Ethiopia and by Japan in China, as well as by Egypt in the civil war in Yemen in the mid-1960s. Chemical weapons were used more significantly against substantially unprotected Iranians by Iraq in their 1980–88 war, but of the 27,000 gassed through March 1987, Iran reported that only 262 died.[17] The most notable use of chemical weapons by a terrorist group was Aum Shinrikyo's release in 1995 of sarin nerve gas into an enclosed space: a Japanese subway station. Although a more skillful effort conceivably might have done more damage, that attack inflicted thousands of casualties, but only twelve deaths.

One episode during the Iran-Iraq war is often taken to indicate the extensive destructive potential of chemical weapons: the chemical attack in 1988, apparently by Iraqi forces, on Halabja, an Iraqi town that had been the site of considerable battles between Iranians and Kurds working on their side, and the Iraqis. It is sometimes said that 5,000 people were killed by chemical munitions dropped from a single airplane during a single pass in daylight. There are a number of problems with this assessment. To begin with, attacks on the city took place over several days and involved explosive munitions as well, and there is a possible confusion over deaths caused by chemical weapons and those caused by other means. Additionally, all the reports from journalists who were taken to the town by the Iranians shortly after the attack indicate that they saw at most "hundreds" of bodies, and, although some of them report the 5,000 figure, this number is consistently identified as coming from Iranian authorities, who obviously had a great incentive to exaggerate. Moreover, the Iranians apparently claimed that an additional 5,000 were wounded by the chemical weapons, even though experience suggests that an attack killing 5,000 would have injured far more—actually *vastly* more—than that. A Human Rights Watch report on the events has an appendix in which other Iraqi chemical attacks in Kurdish areas are evaluated; in two of these attacks it is suggested that 300 or 400 might have been killed, while all the other estimates are under 100, most under twenty.[18]

An event potentially of more direct relevance involves the massive emission of deadly gas from a chemical plant in Bhopal, India, in 1984 that killed thousands in the surrounding neighborhood. Even two decades later, the incident is shrouded in controversy, but the explanation put forward for the tragedy by the chemical company, Union Carbide, could, if valid, hold cautionary lessons for contemporary considerations about terrorism. The company's line is that the event was not an accident, that there were adequate safety devices and procedures in place. Rather, it was the result of deliberate sabotage—or, one might say, terrorism—by a single disgruntled employee who removed a meter and then forced water into a large tank of deadly gas, causing it to heat up and then spew out something like forty tons of toxic gas into the atmosphere.[19] Casualties were particularly high in part because the surroundings were so heavily populated and because warning and evacuation procedures were not in existence or were poorly executed.

The incident is clearly not one in which a weapon of mass destruction was detonated—no chemical weapon carries a payload of forty tons—but rather one like 9/11, in which craft and stealth were used to transform existing objects into weapons. The lesson from this incident, of course, is not to work to prevent terrorists from obtaining weapons of mass destruction, but to make sure that procedures and processes in chemical plants are safe not only from accidental release of chemicals, but from deliberate and diabolical manipulation by knowledgeable and dedicated insiders.

Biological Weapons

Properly developed and deployed, biological weapons could indeed, if thus far only in theory, kill hundreds of thousands, perhaps even millions of people. The discussion remains theoretical because biological

20

weapons have scarcely ever been used. Belligerents have eschewed such weapons with good reason: they are extremely difficult to deploy and to control. Terrorist groups or rogue states may be able to solve such problems in the future with advances in technology and knowledge, but, notes scientist Russell Seitz, while bioterrorism may look easy on paper, "the learning curve is lethally steep in practice." The record so far is unlikely to be very encouraging. For example, Japan reportedly infected wells in Manchuria and bombed several Chinese cities with plague-infested fleas before and during World War II. These ventures (by a state, not a terrorist group) may have killed thousands of Chinese, but they apparently also caused considerable unintended casualties among Japanese troops and seem to have had little military impact.[20]

For the most destructive results, biological weapons need to be dispersed in very low-altitude aerosol clouds. Because aerosols do not appreciably settle, pathogens like anthrax (which is not easy to spread or catch and is not contagious) would probably have to be sprayed near nose level. Moreover, 90 percent of the microorganisms are likely to die during the process of aerosolization, and their effectiveness could be reduced still further by sunlight, smog, humidity, and temperature changes. Explosive methods of dispersion may destroy the organisms, and, except for anthrax spores, long-term storage of lethal organisms in bombs or warheads is difficult: even if refrigerated, most of the organisms have a limited lifetime. The effects of such weapons can take days or weeks to have full effect, during which time they can be countered with medical and civil defense measures. And their impact is very difficult to predict; in combat situations they may spread back onto the attacker. In the judgment of two careful analysts, delivering microbes and toxins over a wide area in the form most suitable for inflicting mass casualties—as an aerosol that can be inhaled—requires a delivery system whose development "would outstrip the technical capabilities of all but the most sophisticated terrorist." Even then effective dispersal could easily be disrupted by unfavorable environmental and meteorological conditions.[21]

After assessing, and stressing, the difficulties a nonstate entity would find in obtaining, handling, growing, storing, processing, and dispersing lethal pathogens effectively, biological weapons expert Milton Leitenberg compares his conclusions with glib pronouncements in the press about how biological attacks can be pulled off by anyone with "a little training and a few glass jars," or how it would be "about as difficult as producing beer." He sardonically concludes, "The less the commentator seems to know about biological warfare the easier he seems to think the task is."[22]

Radiological Weapons

Radiological weapons, or "dirty bombs," are often called the poor man's nuclear weapon, but, unlike the rich man's version, they are incapable of inflicting much immediate damage. Moreover, although a dirty bomb would be easier to assemble than a nuclear weapon, note Michael Levi and Henry Kelly of the Federation of American Scientists, the construction and deployment of one "is difficult" and would "require considerable skill." Among the problems: bombers risk exposing themselves to doses of radiation so lethal that even suicidal operatives might not live long enough to deliver and set off the device.[23]

Most analysts tend to consider radiological devices to be more nearly weapons of mass "disruption" than of mass destruction. This is because, although the sudden release of additional radiation into the environment by a nuclear device would kill few, if any, people outright (perhaps some who happen to be standing near the explosion itself), it might engender panic or mass disorientation. It could also raise radiation levels in an area into ranges officially considered unacceptable, thereby in principle necessitating expensive evacuation and decontamination procedures. But it would be almost impossible to disperse radioactive material from a dirty bomb so that victims would absorb a lethal dose before being able to leave the area.[24]

Moreover, the Environmental Protection Agency has been extremely conservative in setting its levels for unacceptable radiation. To begin with, following fairly common practice, it has extrapolated down in a linear fashion from high levels known to be harmful without any conclusive evidence that this procedure is justified. Indeed, there is considerable debate about whether raising radiation levels slightly above background levels has any health effect at all; some scientists, in fact, think it may actually be good for health. The levels conventionally deemed unacceptable are actually within the error range for determining background levels: estimates for the average background radiation routinely endured by people in the United States range from 300 to 360 millirems (mrems) per year, yet the EPA has ordained that a rise of 15 mrem above background levels is unacceptable. The only slightly less conservative Nuclear Regulatory Agency allows 25 mrem. For comparison, moving from the Gulf Coast to Denver increases radiation exposure by some 21 mrem due to increased exposure to cosmic radiation, and by an additional 63 mrem due to increased radon in the soil. Nonetheless, Denver does not seem to suffer elevated cancer rates.[25]

The EPA has deemed any enhancement of radiation to be unacceptable—that is, to be considered "contamination"—if, following this controversial extrapolation, the radiation would in principle increase an individual's chances of getting cancer by 1 in 10,000 if that individual continued to live in the affected area nonstop for 40 years. As one's chances of dying from cancer are about 20 percent already, the dirty bomb under most scenarios might then raise the rate for such a stationary individual from 20 percent to 20.01 percent, though there are controversial scenarios that suggest a rise to 21 percent or higher.[26]

The danger of small rises in radiation levels has been further questioned by an exhaustive study by eight United Nations agencies, completed some twenty years after the event, of the effects of the 1986 Chernobyl nuclear reactor meltdown in the Soviet Union. The accident, which released a huge amount of radiation into the atmosphere, resulted in the deaths of around fifty people, most of them underprotected emergency workers. Thyroid cancer rates among children rose, but almost all of the children were treated successfully, and only nine died. The UN study concludes that even in the longer term, cancer rates may rise among the affected population by less, possibly far less, than 1 percent. In addition, there was no spike in fertility problems or in birth defects. Similarly, extensive studies of the survivors of the 1945 atomic bomb attacks in Japan find that, although cancer rates are somewhat elevated, the experience has made little or no difference in mortality or in birth defect rates.[27]

The Growth of Science

Commentator Michael Ignatieff, a leading member of the terrorism industry, seems certain that in the future terrorists will be able to acquire and deploy chemical, biological, or nuclear weapons. He cheers himself up very slightly by noting with relief that, at least so far, terrorists have used only conventional weaponry which, he points out, has been available for over a hundred years. But, of course, the same could be said for chemical and biological weapons, as the basic knowledge about their destructive potential goes back many decades, even centuries in some respects. The English, for example, made some efforts to spread smallpox among American Indians in the French and Indian War.[28]

Not only has the science about chemical and biological weapons been quite sophisticated for more than a century, but that science has become massively more developed over that period. Moreover, governments (not just small terrorist groups) have spent a great deal of money over decades in an effort to make the weapons more effective. Yet, although there have been great improvements in the lethality, effectiveness, and deployment of conventional and nuclear weapons during that time, the difficulties of controlling and dispersing chemical and biological substances seem to have persisted.

Perhaps dedicated terrorists will, in time, figure it out. However, the experience in the 1990s of the Japanese cult Aum Shinrikyo suggests there are great difficulties. The group had some 300 scientists in its employ and an estimated budget of $1 billion, and it reportedly tried at least nine times over five years to set off biological weapons by spraying pathogens from trucks and wafting them from rooftops, hoping fancifully to ignite an apocalyptic war. These efforts failed to create a single fatality; in fact, nobody even noticed that the attacks had taken place. It was at that point that the group abandoned its biological efforts in frustration and instead turned to the infamous sarin chemical attack.[29]

As two analysts stress, there have been so few biological (and chemical) terrorist attacks because they would require overcoming several major technological hurdles. Among them: gaining access to specialized ingredients, acquiring equipment and know-how to produce and disperse the agents, and creating an organization that can resist infiltration or early detection by law enforcement.[30]

In the meantime, the science with respect to detecting and ably responding to such attacks is likely to grow. Although acknowledging that things could change in the future, the Gilmore Commission has concluded, "As easy as some argue that it may be for terrorists to culture anthrax spores or brew up a concoction of deadly nerve gas, the effective dissemination or dispersal of these viruses and poisons still presents serious technological hurdles that greatly inhibit their effective use."[31]

Imagining Elephants

Some spectacularly bad advice is furnished in a Turkish proverb: "If your enemy be an ant, imagine him to be an elephant." Following this approach, one would become wary about being stomped, but not about the possibility that the enemy could scurry up a tree or burrow into the sand. In fact, the process would make it impossible even to see the enemy.

Two careful reports issued in the late 1990s, one from the Gilmore Commission, the other from the General Accounting Office, warn about imagining elephants. They stressed the great difficulties a terrorist group would have in acquiring and developing devices with the capacity to cause mass casualties, and they pointedly warned against wallowing in the worst-case scenarios that were so common even then.[32] Although the 9/11 attackers did not use sophisticated weapons and although the subsequent anthrax terrorism killed only a very few people, those events have caused these sensible warnings to become much neglected.

If chemical and biological attacks are so easy and attractive to terrorists, it is impressive that none has so far been committed in Chechnya or in Israel. Although there have been plenty of terrorist attacks in the world since 2001, all (thus far, at least) have relied on conventional methods. In addition, it seems to be a general historical regularity that terrorists tend to prefer weapons that they know and understand, not new, exotic ones. Indeed, the truly notable innovation for terrorists over the past few decades has not been in qualitative improvements in ordnance at all, but rather in a more effective method for delivering it: the suicide bomber.[33] And this innovation has applied processes that are essentially sociological, not technical.

Moreover, there is little evidence that terrorists have made much, if any, progress in obtaining any kind of weapon of mass destruction, no matter how defined. However, the continual obsession about WMD has had the perverse effect of recommending at least some of them to the terrorists: as Ayman al-Zawahiri, Osama bin Laden's right-hand man, said of biological weapons, "We only became aware of them when the enemy drew our attention to them by repeatedly expressing concerns that they can be produced simply with easily available materials." Servicing this interest, a number of Pakistani scientists once apparently had wide-ranging—if, according to them, "academic"—discussions with bin Laden concerning nuclear, chemical, and biological weapons. Conceivably, these talks might eventually have led to something more extensive, but contacts were severed after, and because of, the events of 9/11.[34] In the meantime, al-Qaeda's scientific capacities seem to be very limited indeed.

SEPTEMBER 11: HARBINGER OR ABERRATION?

It should also be kept in mind that 9/11 was an extreme event. Before that day—and in the years since—no more than a few hundred have ever been killed in a single terrorist attack. The economic destruction on September 11 was also unprecedented, of course.

It once was widely assumed that this precedent-shattering event represented the wave of the future. Thus in 2004 Charles Krauthammer characterized the post-9/11 period as one in which, "contrary to every expectation and prediction, the second shoe never dropped," and Allison has noted that following 9/11, "no one" in the American national security community believed that those attacks were an "isolated occurrence." As Rudy Giuliani, New York's mayor on 9/11, reflected in 2005, "Anybody—any one of these security experts, including myself—would have told you on September 11, 2001, we're looking at dozens and dozens and multiyears of attacks like this. It hasn't been quite that bad." No, not nearly. Precisely what Giuliani's "security experts" were basing their expert opinion on is not entirely clear, but such popular, if knee-jerk, expectations, predictions, and beliefs may well continue to be confounded. As it happens, extreme events often remain exactly that: aberrations, rather than harbingers.[35]

For example, a bomb planted in a piece of checked luggage apparently by agents of Muammar Qaddafi's Libya was responsible for the explosion that caused a Pan Am jet to crash into Lockerbie, Scotland, in 1988. Since that time, tens of billions of pieces of luggage have been transported on American carriers and none has exploded to down an aircraft. (Moreover, millions of passengers who checked bags at hotels and retrieved them before heading to the airport have routinely lied to an airline agent when answering the pointlessly obligatory question about whether their luggage had at all times been in their possession.)

This doesn't mean that one should cease worrying about luggage on airlines, but it does suggest that extreme events do not necessarily assure repetition—any more than Timothy McVeigh's Oklahoma City bombing of 1995 has. Some sort of terrorist laced Tylenol capsules with cyanide in 1982, killing seven people; however, this frightening and much publicized event (which generated 125,000 stories in the print media alone and cost the manufacturer more than $1 billion) failed to inspire much in the way of imitation. The alarming release of poison gas in the Tokyo subway in 1995 by Aum Shinrikyo was once dubbed "a turning point in the history of terrorism."[36] Yet, the apocalyptic group appears to have abandoned the terrorism business, and its example has not been followed.

These observations should not be taken to suggest, of course, that *all* extreme events prove to be the last in their line. At the time, World War I, known as the Great War for two decades, was the worst war of its type. Yet an even more destructive one followed. Moreover, though Aum Shinrikyo and Qaddafi may be under control, al-Qaeda and like-minded terrorist groups are unlikely to die out any time soon. Like the communists during the cold war, they appear to be in it for the long haul: September 11, after all, marked terrorists' second attempt to destroy the World Trade Center.

Much of the current alarm is generated from the knowledge that many of today's terrorists simply want to kill, and kill more or less randomly, for revenge or as an act of what they take to be war. At one time, it was probably safe to conclude that terrorism was committed principally for specific political demands or as a form of political expression, and therefore, in the oft-cited observation of Brian Jenkins, that "terrorists want a lot of people watching and a lot of people listening, and not a lot of people dead."[37] Now many of them do seem to want a lot of people dead. In addition, the suicidal nature of many attacks, though not new, is unsettling partly because deterring the would-be perpetrator by threatening punishment becomes impossible. And, of course, terrorism itself will never go away: it has always existed and always will.

But the central question remains: Will such spectacularly destructive terrorist acts become commonplace and escalate in their destructiveness? We should certainly not assume that al-Qaeda is finished with attacks within the United States. Nonetheless, the record suggests that al-Qaeda will find it difficult to match or top the accomplishment of 9/11, and that terrorism's destructiveness, despite the creative visions of worst-case scenarists, may well fail to escalate dramatically. September 11, like the Trojan horse and Pearl Harbor, could prove to be so unique and surprising that "their very success precludes their repetition," in the words of Russell Seitz, and therefore "al-Qaeda's best shot may have been exactly that." The extreme destruction of September 11 has also raised the bar for al-Qaeda, thereby reducing the impact of less damaging attacks.[38] (On the other hand, the attention-generating terrorist attacks in Madrid in 2004 and London in 2005 suggest that terrorists can get much of the desired effect at a far lower level of damage. That might be comparatively good news: even if they try, they may be content with that.)

CHAPTER 2

Overreacting to Terrorism:
The Terrorism Industry

The chief costs of terrorism derive not from the damage inflicted by the terrorists, but what those attacked do to themselves and others in response. That is, the harm of terrorism mostly arises from the fear and from the often hasty, ill-considered, and overwrought reaction (or overreaction) it characteristically, and often calculatedly, inspires in its victims.[1]

REACTING TO SEPTEMBER 11: THE COSTS

This can be seen even in the reactions to the terrorist events of September 11, 2001. Although those attacks were by far the most destructive in history, the costs of the response have massively outstripped those inflicted by the terrorists even in this extreme case.

To begin with, the reaction to 9/11 has claimed more—far more—human lives than were lost in the terrorist attacks. Some of this derived from the fears that the terrorists inspired. Many people canceled airline trips and consequently traveled more by automobile after the event, and one study has concluded that more than 1,000 people died in automobile accidents in 2001 alone between September 11 and December 31 because of such evasive behavior.[2] If a small percentage of the hundreds of thousands of road deaths suffered after 2001 occurred to people who were driving because they feared to fly, the number of Americans who have perished in overreaction to 9/11 in automobile accidents alone could well surpass the number who were killed by the terrorists on that terrible day.

Moreover, the reaction to 9/11 included two wars that are yet ongoing—one in Afghanistan, the other in Iraq—neither of which would have been politically possible without 9/11. The number of Americans, civilian and military, who have died thus far in those ventures surpasses the number killed on September 11. Moreover, the best estimates are that the war in Iraq has resulted in the deaths of tens of thousands of Iraqis, with one analysis suggesting that 100,000 Iraqis perished during the war's first eighteen months alone.[3] This could represent more fatalities than were inflicted by all terrorism, domestic and international, during the entire twentieth century.

The mental health costs stemming from the fear and anxiety induced by the 9/11 attacks are also likely to be extensive. A notable, but probably extreme, example of how severe these can be comes from extensive studies of the health effect of the Chernobyl nuclear disaster in the Soviet Union in 1986. It has been found that the largest health consequences came not from the accident itself (fewer than fifty people died directly from radiation exposure), but from the negative and often life-expectancy-reducing impact on the mental health of people traumatized by relocation and by lingering, and greatly exaggerated, fears that they would soon die of cancer. In the end, such lifestyle afflictions as alcoholism, drug abuse, chronic anxiety, and fatalism have posed a much greater threat to health, and essentially have killed far more people, than exposure to Chernobyl's radiation. The mental health impact of 9/11 is unlikely to prove to be as extensive, but one study found that 17 percent of the American population outside of New York City was still reporting symptoms of September 11–related posttraumatic stress two months after the attacks.[4]

The economic costs of the reaction to 9/11 are also high. Although the direct economic losses imposed by the terrorists, amounting to tens of billions of dollars, were spectacular, the economic cost of the reaction runs several times that. The effects on the tourism and airline industry were monumental: indeed, three years after September 2001, domestic airline flights in the United States were still 7 percent below their pre-9/11 levels, and by the end of 2004 tourism even in distant Las Vegas had still not fully recovered. One estimate suggests that the U.S. economy lost 1.6 million jobs in 2001 alone, mostly in the tourism industry.[5]

Moreover, the cost of enhanced security dwarfs that incurred by the terrorists. The yearly budget for the Department of Homeland Security is approaching $50 billion per year, and state and local governments spend additional billions. The United States now expends fully $4 billion a year on airline passenger screenings alone, and another $4.7 billion on zapping checked baggage; the air marshal program, massively expanded after 9/11, costs over half a billion more. Safety measures carry additional consequences: one economist calculates that strictures effectively requiring people to spend an additional half-hour in airports cost the economy $15 billion per year, another puts it at $8 billion. (By comparison, total airline profits in the 1990s never exceeded $5.5 billion per year.) Longer airport waits also harm the airlines by reducing short-haul passenger traffic, and they can cost lives by encouraging people to travel more by automobile. The reaction to the anthrax letters of 2001 will cost the U.S. Post Office alone some $5 billion—that is, $1 billion for every fatality inflicted by the terrorist. Various 9/11-induced restrictions on visas have constricted visits and residencies of scientists, engineers, and businesspeople vital to the economy, restrictions that, some predict, will dampen American economic growth in a few years. Universities are deeply concerned because they depend heavily on foreign graduate students, particularly in the sciences, and student visa applications fell some 21 percent from 2001 to 2004 while the number of graduate school applications from abroad fell by 21 percent between 2004 and 2005. The Joint Economic Committee of the U.S. Congress anticipates that economic growth will be lowered because of increased spending on security. In 2006, when oil was selling for $70 a barrel, market experts estimated that $7 to $10 of that price was due to fears of another terrorist attack in the United States.[6]

Then there are the economic costs of the terrorism-induced wars in Afghanistan and Iraq. In the case of Iraq alone, these are likely to run to a monumental $1 trillion to $2 trillion.[7]

In addition, there have been great opportunity costs: the enormous sums of money being spent to deal with this presumed threat have in part been diverted from other, possibly more worthy endeavors. Some of the money doubtless would have been spent on similar ventures under earlier budgets, and much of it likely has wider benefits than simply securing the country against the rather limited threat of terrorism. But much of it has very likely been pulled away from programs that do much good—programs devoted to housing, health, and education, for example.

Thus, the country's obsessive focus on terrorism after 9/11 has resulted in severe funding distortions. For example, after 2001 the government spent extravagantly and wastefully on a perishable (and, as it happened, utterly unnecessary) anthrax vaccine while letting itself become undersupplied with influenza vaccine. In 2005, 758 scientists, including two Nobel Prize winners, raised an outcry because of what they saw as a major shift of research funds from pathogens of high public health significance to obscure organisms of high biodefense, but low public health, importance. Almost 75 percent of the appropriations for first responders went for terrorism rather than for natural disasters; and $2 billion was made available in grants to improve preparedness for terrorism but only $180 million for natural disasters, something that may have contributed to inept governmental measures to deal with the results of Hurricane Katrina in 2005. The budget for the FBI has been increased since 9/11, but not enough to pay for all the terrorism work it is now required to do. Funds have had to be shifted from its other programs, such as fighting crime: after 9/11, in fact, fully 67 percent of those working on criminal investigations were reassigned to the counterterrorism beat. A rise in the rate of violent crime in 2005 has been attributed by some police chiefs in part to the pressure on local cops to divert resources and personnel to homeland security endeavors.[8]

The costs of reaction are also extensive in other ways, many of them unmeasurable. For example, the park at City Hall in Manhattan was extensively and successfully refurbished in 2000. After September 11, 2001, major portions were chained shut in fear of terrorists, and ordinary citizens can now experience its beauties only by peering at it through a fence.

As two analysts put it, the country's priorities have become "radically torqued" toward homeland defense and fighting terrorism while other important societal needs go underaddressed. For example, one observer has suggested that if a small portion of the excessive spending on airline security had been spent instead on enforcing automobile seat belt laws, the number of lives saved would likely have been considerable. This process is especially unfortunate because, as risk analyst David Banks puts it, if resources are directed away from sensible programs and future growth to pursue "unachievable but politically popular levels of domestic security," the terrorists have won "an important victory that mortgages our future."[9]

THE TERRORISM INDUSTRY: THE PROFITS OF DOOM

Perhaps the most common reaction to terrorism is the costly stoking of fear and the often even more costly encouragement of overreaction by members of what might be called the "terrorism industry," an entity that includes not only various risk entrepreneurs and bureaucrats, but also most of the media and nearly all politicians. It is hard to think coherently when reporters, bureaucrats, politicians, and terrorism experts mostly find extreme and alarmist possibilities so much more appealing than discussions of broader context, much less of statistical reality.

Politicians

There is no reason to suspect that George W. Bush's concern about terrorism is anything but genuine. However, his presidential approval rating did receive the greatest boost for any president in history in September 2001, surpassing even that achieved by Jimmy Carter when American hostages were taken in Iran in 1979. And it would, of course, be politically unnatural for him not to notice. Indeed, his chief political adviser, Karl Rove, was already declaring in 2003 that the "war" against terrorism would be central to Bush's reelection campaign the next year. It was, and it worked. As the fear level about terrorism continued at a constant level in the next years (see Figure 1 on page 2), Rove announced in January 2006 that he was gearing up to make it a major theme in the congressional campaigns later that year.[10]

In all this, the White House may have been able to enhance things just a bit from time to time by aggressively urging the Department of Homeland Security to put the country on higher alert levels than it might have been inclined to embrace on its own. Indeed, one study documents a consistent positive relationship between government-issued terror warnings and presidential approval, and another observes that Bush's popularity rises when thoughts of death or terrorism become especially salient. In 2005, outgoing Homeland Security czar Tom Ridge attempted to "debunk the myth" that he had been responsible for repeated alerts, particularly in the 2004 election year, observing that "more often than not we were the least inclined" to do so. But, he continued, "there were times when some people were really aggressive about raising it, and we said, 'For that?' "[11]

The administration also has a terrific political incentive to stoke fear by portentously pointing to bad people who are out there and citing evidence of terrorist intrigues. Thus in 2005 President Bush touted a list of ten terrorist plots that he claimed had been uncovered even though some of these seem to have been nearly trivial and most did not even take place in the country. Then, shortly after Vice President Dick Cheney had publicly lamented that, as September 11 recedes into the past, "some in Washington are yielding to the temptation to downplay the ongoing threat to our country," the president brought up one of these plots again as if it were new news: a 2002 conspiracy in Asia to hijack a commercial airliner using a shoe bomb to blast the cockpit door away, and then to fly the plane into a tall building in Los Angeles. No one has apparently been charged, much less convicted, of any crime connected to this episode, and the "plot" appears to have been idle aspiration rather than anything remotely operational.[12] Moreover, the notions that passengers and crew would allow the takeover of a plane in the wake of 9/11 and that a shoe bomb could blow off a cockpit door without downing the plane itself (and thereby ending the possibility of using it as a weapon) went unexamined. But the president was successful in floating a bit of fear into the atmosphere, something likely to be politically beneficial to him.

The Democrats are at a decided political disadvantage on the terrorism issue. They do not want to seem to underplay the terrorist threat, and so, like the Republicans, they find it—or believe it—politically expedient to be as hysterical as possible, to exaggerate, and to inflate. For the most part, they have scurried to keep up, desperate not to be thought soft on terrorism. Those with long memories probably remember with some pain how the Republicans once tried to label them "soft on communism," perhaps with some effect in some elections. In consequence, they have stumbled all over each other to appear tough and strong while spewing out plans to expend even more of the federal budget on the terrorist threat, such as it is, than President Bush has. Thus, in the 2004 presidential campaign, Democratic candidate John Kerry repeatedly urged, "I do not fault George Bush for doing too much in the War on Terror, I believe he's done too little." In contrast to Bush, who "has no comprehensive strategy for victory in the War on Terror—only an ad hoc strategy to keep our enemies at bay," proclaimed Kerry, "if I am Commander-in-Chief, I would wage that war by putting in place a strategy to win it."[13]

The political jockeying and outbidding process on this issue could be seen in two episodes during the 2004 presidential campaign. In September, columnist Gwynne Dyer sardonically noted that Bush had "a brush with the truth" by opining that the war on terror could not be won, but that conditions could be changed to make terrorism less acceptable in some parts of the world. "This heroic attempt to grapple with reality," notes Dyer, "was a welcome departure from Bush's usual style." But his Democratic opponents quickly pounced, declaring irrelevantly, "What if President Reagan had said that it may be difficult to win the war against Communism?" Bush promptly fled to safer ground, sanctimoniously intoning in a later speech, "We meet today in a time of war for our country, a war we did not start, yet one that we will win."[14]

In October, it was Kerry's turn. In an interview in the *New York Times*, he suggested, presumably by accident, that Americans would be able "to feel safe again" when we "get back to the place we were, where terrorists are not the focus of our lives, but they're a nuisance." Like prostitution, illegal gambling, and organized crime, the idea would be to "reduce it to a level where it isn't on the rise," where "it isn't threatening people's lives every day," and where "it's not threatening the fabric of your life." Bush and Cheney quickly jumped on that one, declaring it to be proof that Kerry was "unfit to lead." Kerry, sobered, was soon back to his more usual macho mantra.[15]

Presidential candidates are not the only politicians given to hyping the threat. Senator Bill Frist, who enjoys some putative credibility on the bioterrorism front because he was a physician in an earlier life, seems to have inflated numbers about how much bad stuff is out there. The Soviet Union had stockpiled 5,000 tons annually of an anthrax strain that was resistant to sixteen antibiotics, he declared at the Harvard Medical School in 2005, when the total Soviet stockpile of anthrax happened to be 200 tons and the resistant strain they developed could defy only eight antibiotics and had never actually reached the point of being stockpiled.[16]

Other opportunities for politicians of all stripes are opened up by the popular, sudden, and massive increases in expenditures designed to enhance security against terrorism. Not surprisingly, much of this hasty spending has been rendered inefficient as pork barrel and politics-as-usual formulas have been liberally applied. Local politicians, of course, are quick to get in on the action as well. This has resulted in such imaginative spending as $180,000 to a port that receives fewer than twenty ships a year, $30,000 to buy a defibrillator for use at a high school basketball tournament, $100,000 to fund a summer jobs program in Washington, DC, $557,400 for rescue and communications equipment for a town of 1,570 in Alaska, $200,000 for a drug prevention program, $100,000 for a child pornography tipline, $202,000 to install eighty surveillance cameras in a remote Alaska town of 2,400 (that comes to one camera for every thirty residents), and $63,000 for a decontamination unit that sits gathering (hopefully uncontaminated) dust in a warehouse in rural Washington because the state does not have a team that knows how to use it. Moreover, the sense of urgency that has pervaded the political process since 9/11 has been used by adept pork-barreleers to obtain rushed approval of all sorts of expensive legislation, including a $190 billion farm bill and $2.5 billion for something enterprisingly called "highway security" that looks a lot like a project simply to build and improve roads. None too surprisingly, there has also been a great deal of waste: a congressional report in 2006, for example, points to $34 billion worth of projects that have "experienced significant overcharges, wasteful spending, or mismanagement." [17]

Perhaps not so incidentally, most national politicians happen to live in the area that seems to have benefited most from the increase in federal homeland security expenditures: Washington, DC. Although the city suffered some in the years after 9/11 by declines in tourism, these losses have been more than compensated for by the massive post-9/11 spending spree which has been disproportionately focused on the DC area, creating an artificial boom there—a "Doom Boom," some are calling it. One economist has calculated that government procurement in the area, which would have grown by $5.5 billion over four years if 9/11 hadn't happened, expanded instead by $13 billion in response to the terrorist impetus. By 2005, thanks to generous security spending, three counties in the area had become the most prosperous large counties in the country. [18]

Samuel Taylor Coleridge once observed, "In politics, what begins in fear, usually ends in folly." Although there are those who might maintain that the same result often holds even for endeavors that *don't* begin in fear, the poet's caution remains relevant.

Bureaucrats

Meanwhile, Bush's hastily assembled and massively funded Office, then Department, of Homeland Security seeks to stoke fear by officially intoning on the first page of its defining manifesto, as noted earlier, "Today's terrorists can strike at any place, at any time, and with virtually any weapon." The interactive, if somewhat paradoxical, process between government and public is crisply described by political scientist Ian Lustick with an apt dangling modifier: the government "can never make enough progress toward 'protecting America' to reassure Americans against the fears it is helping to stoke."[19]

Threat exaggeration is additionally encouraged, even impelled, because politicians and terrorism bureaucrats have an incentive to pass along vague and unconfirmed threats to protect themselves from later criticism should another attack take place. There's a technical term for this behavior: CYA. And the result, as statistician Bart Kosko points out, is a situation in which "government plays safe by overestimating the terrorist threat, while the terrorists oblige by overestimating their power."[20]

This is tidily illustrated by the FBI's "I think, therefore they are" spookiness when the purported terrorist menace is assessed. In testimony before the Senate Committee on Intelligence on February 11, 2003, FBI head Robert Mueller proclaimed that "the greatest threat is from al-Qaeda cells in the US that we have not yet identified." He rather mysteriously judged the threat from those unidentified entities to be "increasing in part because of the heightened publicity" surrounding such episodes as the sniper shootings in the Washington, DC, area in 2002 and the anthrax letter attacks of 2001, and claimed somehow to know that "al-Qaeda maintains the ability and the intent to inflict significant casualties in the US with little warning." The terrorists, he opined, would "probably continue to favor spectacular attacks," and he judged their "highest priority targets" to be "high profile government or private facilities, commercial airliners, famous landmarks, and crucial infrastructure such as energy-production facilities and transportation nodes."[21]

However, if the bad guys had *both* the ability *and* the intent in 2003 and if the threat they presented was somehow increasing, they had remained remarkably quiet by the time Director Mueller testified before the same committee two years later, on February 16, 2005. Despite that posited ability, intent, and increasing threat, despite (God knows) continued publicity about terrorism, and despite presumably severe provocation attending the subsequent U.S. invasion of Iraq, no casualties (significant or otherwise) were suffered in any attacks in the United States, and all high- (and low-) profile facilities, airliners, landmarks, and crucial (and noncrucial) infrastructure nodes (and nonnodes) remained unmolested by terrorists. Nonetheless, Director Mueller remained unflappable, calmly retreating to his comfortable neo-Cartesian mantra: "I remain very concerned about what we are not seeing," a profundity this time dutifully rendered in bold type in his published script.

He failed to mention a secret FBI report that in the meantime had wistfully noted that after more than three years of intense hunting, the agency had been unable to identify a single true al-Qaeda sleeper cell anywhere in the country—rather impressive given the 2002 intelligence estimate that there were up to 5,000 people loose in the country who were "connected" to al-Qaeda. For the Bureau's director, absence of evidence apparently is evidence of existence. Meanwhile, Mueller's counterpart at the CIA, Porter Goss, repeatedly intoned that "it *may be* only a matter of time before al-Qaeda or some other group attempts to use chemical, biological, radiological, and nuclear weapons."[22] But then again, of course, it may not.

Not to be left behind in the fear-mongering sweepstakes, analysts in the CIA who have convinced themselves that al-Qaeda already has a nuclear weapon responded to the observation that no abandoned nuclear material was found when the terrorist organization was routed in Afghanistan with the artful riposte, "We haven't found most of the al-Qaeda leadership either, and we know that they exist." We also know that Mount Rushmore exists. By the CIA's logic, that means the tooth fairy does as well. This kind of thinking is reminiscent of Groucho Marx's observation that it must be possible to be in two places at the same time because, after all, New York and Philadelphia are in two places at the same time.

Or perhaps there is an even more memorable echo:

The most real things in the world are those that neither children nor men can see. Did you ever see fairies dancing on the lawn? Of course not, but that's no proof that they are not there. Nobody can conceive or imagine all the wonders there are unseen and unseeable in the world. . . . Only faith, fancy, poetry, love, romance can push aside that curtain and view and picture the supernal beauty and glory beyond. Is it all real? Ah, Virginia, in all this world there is nothing else real and abiding.[23]

Change "fairies" and "wonders" to "terrorists" and you enter the rarefied world of our guardians at the FBI and the CIA. Dedicated al-Qaeda terrorists may be running around in the country, but thus far they have more nearly existed in the imagination.

The Media

Since 9/11 the American public has been treated to seemingly endless yammering in the media about terrorism. Politicians and bureaucrats may feel that, given the public concern on the issue, they will lose support if they appear insensitively to be downplaying the dangers of terrorism. But the media like to tout that they are devoted to presenting fair and balanced coverage of important public issues.

As has often been noted, however, the media appear to have a congenital incapacity for dealing with issues of risk and comparative probabilities—except, of course, in the sports and financial sections. If a baseball player hits three home runs in a single game, press reports will include not only notice of that achievement, but also information about the rarity of the event as well as statistics about the hitter's batting and slugging averages and about how many home runs he normally hits. I may have missed it, but I have never heard anyone in the media stress that in every year except 2001 the number of people in the entire world killed by international terrorism outside of war zones has been a few hundred.[24]

Even in their amazingly rare efforts to try to put terrorism in context—something that would seem to be absolutely central to any sensible discussion of terrorism and terrorism policy—the process never goes very far. For example, in 2001 the *Washington Post* published an article by a University of Wisconsin economist that attempted quantitatively to point out how much safer it was to travel by air than by automobile even under the heightened atmosphere of concern inspired by the September attacks.[25] He reports that the article generated a couple of media inquiries, but nothing more. A cover story by Gregg Easterbrook in the October 7, 2002 *New Republic* forcefully argued that biological and especially chemical weapons are hardly capable of creating "mass destruction," a perspective relevant not only to concerns about terrorism, but also to the drive for war against Iraq that was going on at the time the article was published. The *New York Times* asked him to fashion it into an op-ed piece, but that was the only interest the article generated in the media.

A cynical aphorism in the newspaper business holds that "if it bleeds, it leads." There is an obvious, if less pungent, corollary: if it doesn't bleed, it certainly shouldn't lead and, indeed, may well not be fit to print at all.

No less than twenty-three terror alerts were officially promulgated between 2001 and the end of 2004, and all were played as lead stories in the evening television news. In distinct contrast, only 13 percent of the subsequent decreases in alert status received top billing. The alert of May 20, 2003, was reported in hundreds of words by each of the three networks (some of them were "the level of worry is as high as it's been since September 11th" and "very imminent" and "something big is going to happen in the next two or three days"). CBS devoted forty-three words to announcing the subsequent alert reversal and twenty-five were sufficient for NBC, while ABC did not bother to mention it at all. Terrorism specialist David Rapoport was once contacted by a cable television channel about working with them on a program about terrorism and weapons of mass destruction. After several conversations, the producer happened to ask, "By the way what is your view of the problem?" Rapoport replied, "A frightening thought, but not a serious possibility now." They never called him back.[26]

Another problem concerns follow-up. It was widely reported that a band of supposed terrorists arrested in London in 2003 had been producing a poison, ricin. Contrary to initial reports, no ricin was ever actually found in their possession, but by the time that was cleared up, the press had mostly gone on to other things. In 2006, a bestselling and much discussed book revealed that al-Qaeda terrorists had developed, and had planned to use, a handy device, a "mubtakkar," for delivering poison gas: a canister with two compounds in it that would lethally interact when the seal between them is broken. "In the world of terrorist weaponry," the author proclaimed, "this was the equivalent of splitting the atom. Obtain a few widely available chemicals, and you could construct it with a trip to Home Depot." These lurid revelations were picked up by *Time* magazine when it prominently published excerpts from the book. Neither the author nor *Time* apparently bothered to check out the story with weapons experts, but one wire service reporter, United Press International's Shaun Waterman, did. They told him the device as described would likely produce very little gas and would probably destroy itself in the process of being set off. "If this is such an amazing device," queried one pointedly, "why has no one ever used it?" A Lexis-Nexis search indicates that Waterman's story, one that sought to reduce hysteria rather than exacerbate it , was not picked up by a single newspaper or magazine in the country.[27]

When a major political figure makes some sort of fear-inducing pronouncement or prediction about terrorism, it tends to get top play in the media, as, generally, it should. Although many, though not all, of these dire assertions have been subjected to later analysis in the media (and very often have proved to be based on skimpy evidence and intelligence), the follow-up reports receive much less play than the initial assertions. In addition, there have been almost no efforts, systematic or otherwise, to go back to people who have prominently made dire predictions about terrorism that proved to have been faulty (and, indeed, thus far almost *all* of them have been), to query the predicters about how they managed to be so wrong. When I asked one journalist working on a daily newspaper about this, the reply was that it was difficult to do stories that don't have a hard news component.

Finally, there are quite a few elemental aspects of the terrorism issue that have been almost entirely ignored in the media. For example, the suggestion that an American's chance of being killed by a terrorist is very, very small. Or that another hijacking attack like the ones on 9/11 is impossible because passengers and crew would forcefully interfere. Or that chemical weapons can't wreak mass destruction. Or that the number of people killed annually in the world by international terrorists in almost all years is quite low. Notions like that may be controversial, but shouldn't they at least be *discussed* in the media? Whether one ends up agreeing or disagreeing, aren't they at least *relevant* to the public policy debate?

Risk Entrepreneurs

The monied response to 9/11 has also created a vast and often well-funded coterie of risk entrepreneurs. Its members would be out of business if terrorism were to be back-burnered, and accordingly they have every competitive incentive (and they are nothing if not competitive) to conclude it to be their civic duty to keep the pot boiling. As "a rising tide lifts all boats," suggests Lustick, "an intractable fear nourishes all schemes."[28]

For example, Graham Allison, stressing the threat of nuclear terrorism, soberly relays—without the slightest effort at critical evaluation, much less skepticism—a report in an Arabic-language magazine that bin Laden's boys by 1998 had purchased no fewer than twenty nuclear warheads "from Chechen mobsters in exchange for $30 million in cash and two tons of opium." One might think they (or their Chechen suppliers) would have tried to set one of those things off by now. Meanwhile, some of those intent on spreading alarm about bioterrorism have soberly included *hoaxes* in their tabulations of "biological events."[29]

The hyping of the terrorist threat has become standard operating procedure in the publishing industry. One example, perhaps a bit extreme, is a book by Juval Aviv, who has been featured on Fox News. His 2004 book *Staying Safe* (previously published as *The Complete Terrorism Survival Guide*) includes such absorbing advice to terrorism's potential victims as these nuggets:

Stay away from crowds.

Keep in mind that a terrorist may be one of your customers.

Be wary of odd-looking neighbors.

Separate small pets from large ones.

Never take the first taxicab in line.

In a department store or other crowded public place, be careful not to get trampled.

In a multipurpose household, designate one person as the primary mail opener.

Never shake a suspect piece of mail.

Avoid long waits at U.S. border crossings.

Don't exchange currency at the airport.

Ask yourself where you stand in the hierarchy of terrorist targets.

Don't eat, drink, or smoke around mail.

Make it a standard practice to wash with antibacterial soap immediately after touching mail.

Never park in underground garages.

Avoid aisle seats on airplanes.

Spend as little time at the airport as possible.
At an airport baggage carousel, position yourself near the luggage chute.
Know the five primary means of assassination.

There have also been creative efforts by people with political agendas to fold them into the all-consuming war on terror. The gun control lobby has proclaimed, "We have a responsibility to deny weapons to terrorists and to actively prevent private citizens from providing them." Meanwhile the National Rifle Association claims to have espied an "increased momentum since September 11 for laws permitting concealed guns," and its executive director patiently explains that people would rather face the terrorist threat "with a firearm than without one." Organizations fighting AIDS in Africa have had difficulty trying to decide which is the better argument: that AIDS is a far greater killer than terrorism or that AIDS-devastated countries create breeding grounds and safe havens for terrorists. In her campaign against breast cancer, one senator creatively applied the T-word by urging people to "think of the terror a breast cancer patient feels" when she can't afford the required medication.[30]

Moreover, it turns out that many of your agile risk entrepreneurs just happen to have stuff to sell, such as data-mining software, antiradiation drugs, detention-center bed space, and cargo inspection systems. An impressive number of top-ranking Department of Homeland Security officials have already abandoned public service to serve the public by working and lobbying for such entrepreneurial firms, moves that often are associated with a considerable increase in salary—from $155,000 per year to $934,000 in one case. When the government is hastily hurling vast amounts of money at a problem, there will rather predictably be those—quite a few, in fact—who will jockey to position themselves in the receiving position.[31]

COSMIC ALARMISM: APOCALYPSE ANY DAY NOW

Members of the terrorism industry are truly virtuosic at pouring out, and poring over, worst-case scenarios—or "worst case fantasies," as security analyst Bernard Brodie once labeled them in a different context.[32]

For example, political scientist Joshua Goldstein worries about terrorists exploding nuclear weapons in the United States in a crowded area and declares this to be "not impossible" or the likelihood to be "not negligible." Meanwhile, to generate alarm about such dangers and to reshape policy to deal with them, Graham Allison opens his book by grimly (and completely irrelevantly) recycling Einstein's failed half-century-old prediction about all-out nuclear war: "Since the advent of the Nuclear Age, everything has changed except our modes of thinking and we thus drift toward unparalleled catastrophe." Both of these members of the terrorism industry want to massively increase expenditures to hedge against these "not impossible" scenarios. Allison designates the North Korean problem a "supreme priority" and is fully prepared if necessary to launch a war, potentially costing a million lives, against that country (and presumably another against Iran) to reduce the likelihood that his worst-case fantasy will materialize. (He proposes evacuating Seoul before attacking the North, however.)[33]

Of course, all sorts of things are "not impossible." A colliding meteor or comet could destroy the earth, Tony Blair or Vladimir Putin and their underlings could decide one morning to launch a few nuclear weapons at Massachusetts, George Bush could decide to bomb Hollywood, an underwater volcano could erupt to cause a civilization-ending tidal wave, Osama bin Laden could convert to Judaism, declare himself to be the Messiah, and fly in a gaggle of mafioso hit men from Rome to have himself publicly crucified.

Brodie's cautionary comment in the 1970s about the creative alarmists in the defense community holds as well for those in today's terrorism industry, inhabited as they are by "people of a wide range of skills and sometimes of considerable imagination. All sorts of notions and propositions are churned out, and often presented for consideration with the prefatory words: 'It is conceivable that . . . ' Such words establish their own truth, for the fact that someone has conceived of whatever proposition follows is enough to establish that it is conceivable. Whether it is worth a second thought, however, is another matter."[34]

What we mostly get from the terrorism industry is fearmongering, and much of it borders on hysteria. An insightful discussion seeking to put the terrorist threat into context was published by astronomers Chapman and Harris in the magazine *Skeptical Inquirer* in 2002. They suggested that terrorism deserves exceptional attention only "if we truly think that future attacks might destroy our society." But, they overconfidently continued, "who believes that?" The article triggered enormous response, much of it, to their amazement, from inquiring readers who overcame any natural skepticism to believe exactly that.[35] Those readers have a lot of company in the terrorism industry.

Some prominent commentators, like David Gergen, have argued that the United States has become "vulnerable," even "fragile," and James Carafano and Paul Rosenzweig assert that "because of the terrorists' skillful use of low-tech capabilities, their capacity for harm is essentially limitless," suggesting, apparently, that the bad guys would be *less* dangerous if they could only obtain high-tech weapons. Others, like Indiana senator Richard Lugar, are given to proclaiming that terrorists armed with weapons of mass destruction present an "existential" threat to the United States, or even, in columnist Charles Krauthammer's view, to "civilization itself." In another reach, Krauthammer has also ranked America's "war" on terrorism right up there with World War II and the Civil War.[36]

Allison, too, thinks that nuclear terrorists could "destroy civilization as we know it." Goldstein is convinced they could "destroy our society" and that a single small nuclear detonation in Manhattan would "overwhelm the nation." Not to be outdone, Harvard's Michael Ignatieff warns that "a group of only a few individuals equipped with lethal technologies" threaten "the ascendancy of the modern state."[37]

Two counterterrorism officials from the Clinton administration contend that a small nuclear detonation "would necessitate the suspension of civil liberties," halt or even reverse globalization, and "could be the defeat that precipitates America's decline," while a single explosion of any sort of weapon of mass destruction would "trigger an existential crisis for the United States and its allies." In an interview in *Cigar Aficionado*, General Tommy Franks opined that a "massive casualty-producing event somewhere in the western world" could well cause the American population "to question our own Constitution and to begin to militarize our country," in the process losing "what it cherishes most, and that is freedom and liberty." A best-selling book by a once-anonymous CIA official repeatedly assures us that our "survival" is at stake and that we are engaged in a "war to the death."[38] It has become fashionable in some alarmist circles extravagantly to denote the contest against Osama bin Laden and his sympathizers as (depending on how the cold war is classified) World War III or World War IV.

New Republic editor Peter Beinart is convinced that if any sort of weapon of mass destruction were set off in the United States, "the consequences for individual rights will be terrifying."[39] Even the thoughtful (and rare) Homeland Security skeptic Benjamin Friedman may have joined the chorus: a tactical nuclear weapon set off in Washington, he thinks, would transform the country "by fear and death into a police state." And another critic, Jeffrey Rosen, not only suggests that a dirty bomb set off in downtown Washington, DC, would "create panic entirely disproportionate to the radioactive threat," but that "constitutional strictures . . . might be tested beyond the breaking point." As noted earlier, General Richard Myers, chairman of the Joint Chiefs of Staff, has concluded that if terrorists were able to kill 10,000 Americans in an attack, they would "do away with our way of life."[40]

As the subtext (or sometimes the text) of these hysterical warnings suggests, the "existential" threat comes not from what the terrorists would do to us, but what we would do to ourselves in response. After predicting with great assurance that there would be terrorist events in connection with the 2004 elections, alarmist Ignatieff writes with equal certainty that "inexorably, terrorism, like war itself, is moving beyond the conventional to the apocalyptic," and he patiently explains how this will come about. Although Americans did graciously allow their leaders one fatal mistake in September 2001, they simply "will not forgive another one." If there are several large-scale attacks, he confidently predicts, the trust that binds the people to its leadership and to each other will crumble, and the "cowed populace" will demand that tyranny be imposed upon it, and quite possibly break itself into a collection of rampaging lynch mobs devoted to killing "former neighbors" and "onetime friends." The solution, he thinks, is to crimp civil liberties now in a desperate effort to prevent the attacks he is so confident will necessarily impel us to commit societal, cultural, economic, and political self-immolation.[41]

It seems, then, that it is not only the most feared terrorists who are suicidal. We need a reality check here. All societies are "vulnerable" to tiny bands of suicidal fanatics in the sense that it is impossible to prevent every terrorist act. But the United States is hardly vulnerable in the sense that it can be toppled by dramatic acts of terrorist destruction, even extreme ones. A nuclear explosion in the United States would be horrible, of course, and judicious efforts to further reduce the already distant likelihood of such an event are certainly justified. But in all probability the country can readily, if grimly, absorb even that kind of damage—as it "absorbs" some 40,000 deaths each year from automobile accidents—without instantly becoming a fascist state.

General Myers's prediction that the sudden deaths from terrorism of 10,000 Americans would "do away with our way of life" might be assessed in this regard. As it happens, officials estimated for a while in 2005 that there would be 10,000 deaths from Hurricane Katrina. Although this, of course, was not a terrorist act, there were no indications whatever that, though catastrophic for the hurricane victims themselves, the way of life of the rest of the nation would be notably done away with by such a disaster. It is also easy to imagine scenarios in which 10,000 would have been killed on September 11—if the planes had hit the World Trade Center later in the day, when more people were at work, for example. Indeed, early estimates at the time were much higher than 3,000.[42] Any death is tragic, but it is not at all obvious that a substantially higher loss on 9/11 would have necessarily triggered societal suicide.

In fact, as military analyst William Arkin points out forcefully, although terrorists cannot destroy America, "every time we pretend we are fighting for our survival we not only confer greater power and importance to terrorists than they deserve but we also at the same time act as their main recruiting agent by suggesting that they have the slightest potential for success." In 1999, two years before 9/11, the Gilmore Commission pressed a point it considered "self-evident," but one that nonetheless required "reiteration" because of the "rhetoric and hyperbole" surrounding the issue: although a terrorist attack with a weapon of mass destruction could be "serious and potentially catastrophic," it is "highly unlikely that it could ever completely undermine the national security, much less threaten the survival, of the United States." To hold otherwise "risks surrendering to the fear and intimidation that is precisely the terrorist's stock in trade."[43]

The fact that terrorists subsequently managed to ram airplanes into three buildings on a sunny September morning does not render this point less sound. We need to hear it again, and often.

THE ENEMY, PRETTY MUCH, IS US

Although the alarmists may exaggerate, the subtext of their message should perhaps be taken seriously: ultimately, the enemy, in fact, is us.

Thus far, at least, international terrorism is a rather rare and, appropriately considered, not generally a terribly destructive phenomenon. But there is a danger that the terrorism industry's congenital (if self-serving and profitable) hysteria could become at least somewhat self-fulfilling should extensive further terrorism be visited upon the Home of the Brave.

A key element in a policy toward terrorism, therefore, should be to control, to deal with, or at least productively to worry about the fear and overreaction that terrorism so routinely inspires and that generally constitutes its most damaging effect. Before considering such a policy, however, we should take a sharp turn backward. The next four chapters assess and evaluate an array of foreign threats that have been seized upon by the American public and leadership over the past several decades. In general, the reactions to these perceived threats, though not exactly suicidal, have often been misguided, foolish, overwrought, and economically costly, and sometimes they have been unnecessarily destructive.

PART II

HISTORICAL COMPARISONS

CHAPTER 3

Dates of Infamy:
Pearl Harbor and 9/11

The propensity to exaggerate external threats and to overreact to them scarcely began on September 11, 2001. The four chapters in this part explore the phenomenon in action in foreign policy and war issues over the past several decades. Each chapter includes suggestions about what lessons the historical experience may hold for current concerns about terrorism.

A good place to start is with Pearl Harbor. When the 9/11 terrorist assault took place, many commentators looked for parallels in American history, and the one most commonly embraced was the experience of some sixty years earlier, a surprise attack by foreigners in which about the same number of Americans were abruptly and violently sent to their deaths.

The comparison is flawed in a number of respects, of course. The strike in 1941 was carried out by a country with massive military forces and a clear, if distant, return address, and it directly triggered formal declarations of war not only by Japan and the United States but, shortly thereafter, Germany as well. However, the reactions to the attacks were similar. The shock, outrage, and fury they inspired impelled an intense desire to lash out militarily at the source of the assault. Moreover, in both cases the results of the reaction proved to be far more costly for the United States than those suffered in the attack itself. Perhaps, one might conclude, the best policy was actually arrived at. Certainly, any nation that suffers a surprise attack is likely to strike back as best it can. However, given the gravity of the decision, it seems reasonable to suggest that there should be systematic, careful thinking about how exactly to respond to all attacks, including the one on Pearl Harbor.

The spasm of rage ignited by Pearl Harbor inspired a policy of all-out war that resulted in a great number of deaths of Americans and others. Much the same could be said for the reaction to 9/11. Liberally employing hindsight, this chapter reassesses the reaction to Pearl Harbor and applies the lessons derived from, or suggested by, that experience to the reactions inspired by the costly and horrifying terrorist attack of 2001.

THE DAMAGE AT PEARL HARBOR

Postmortems of the Japanese attack on Pearl Harbor on December 7, 1941, generally describe it in dramatic, almost apocalyptic terms. The Joint Congressional Committee that investigated the event after the war labeled it "the greatest military and naval disaster in our Nation's history." Leading students of the attack use similar language, variously characterizing it as a "catastrophe," "devastating," an "overwhelming disaster" for the United States, a "debacle," "one of the worst defeats the United States suffered in its 200 years," a "crushing blow," and "our worst military disaster."[1]

The sudden loss of 2,403 military and civilian lives was tragic and horrible, of course, but in a direct military sense these dramatic characterizations are excessive: militarily, the attack on Pearl Harbor was more of an inconvenience than a catastrophe or disaster for the United States. The destruction inflicted by the Japanese was not terribly extensive, and much of it was visited upon military equipment that was old and in many cases obsolete or nearly so. Though some 20 percent of the ships at Pearl Harbor were sunk or crippled, most of the naval and other damage was soon repaired (there was a dead loss of only two viable ships), and its extent was soon made all but trivial by the capacity of America's remarkable wartime industry quickly to supply superior replacements in enormous numbers. Moreover, the attack did not significantly delay the American military response to Japanese aggression, nor did it critically change the pace of the war: the United States was unprepared to take the offensive at that time in any case, and the damage at Pearl Harbor increased this unpreparedness only marginally.[2]

REACTING TO THE ATTACK

However, the attack utterly closed off careful thought within the United States, and it propelled the country into a long, ghastly war in Asia. Could America have rolled back the Japanese empire at lower cost to all involved? Did the rollback make the world a safer place? One vicious international overlordship in Asia was demolished: Japan itself became a democracy and an ally. But the rest of its empire was replaced with a set of local tyrannies that, in many cases, especially China, were even worse.

Before Pearl Harbor, American policy toward Japanese expansion was essentially one of containment—although after the summer of 1941 American policy became more dynamic, demanding that Japan not merely stop its expansion, but withdraw from China. American tactics stressed economic pressure, a military buildup designed to threaten and deter, and assistance to anti-Japanese combatants, especially in China. There the Japanese had become painfully bogged down— although Japan's problems there were due far more to Chinese resistance than to U.S. aid, which was actually quite modest. Should Japan abandon its expansionary imperial policy, the United States stood ready, as the American ambassador put it at the time, to help Japan peacefully to gain all of the strategic, economic, financial, and social security for which it was supposedly fighting.[3] (After the war the United States had a chance to carry out this promise and did so in full measure.)

This American concern with Asia has had its critics. The observation by Warner Schilling (noted in the introduction) about the ubiquity of simplicity and spook at the summit of foreign policy was, in fact, triggered by a consideration of the process by which Japan and the United States managed to go to war with each other in 1941. Japan, he notes, launched war on the vague, unexamined hope that the United States would seek a compromise peace after being attacked, "a hope nourished in their despair at the alternatives." Meanwhile, "the American opposition to Japan rested on the dubious proposition that the loss of Southeast Asia could prove disastrous for Britain's war effort and for the commitment to maintain the territorial integrity of China—a commitment as mysterious in its logic as anything the Japanese ever conceived." At no time, he notes, did American leaders "perplex themselves with the question of just how much American blood and treasure the defense of China and Southeast Asia was worth." Similarly, historian Melvin Small observes that "the defense of China was an unquestioned axiom of American policy taken in along with mother's milk and the Monroe Doctrine. . . . One looks in vain through the official papers of the 1930s for some prominent leader to say, 'Wait a second, just why is China so essential to our security?' "[4]

Until Pearl Harbor this approach, however spooky, was comparatively inexpensive. After the attack, however, it no longer became possible even to consider the question of how much American blood and treasure the policy was worth. Americans were enraged, threatened, humiliated, and challenged by what President Franklin Roosevelt called the "unprovoked and dastardly" blow that had come without warning or a declaration of war, at a time when Japanese officials were in Washington, deceptively seeming to be working for a peaceful settlement. With the attack, virtually all remaining reservations vanished as everyone united behind a concerted effort to lash back at the treacherous Japanese. Isolationism and pacifism vanished, and just about every American instantly accepted total war.[5]

Thus, after suffering the loss of some 2,500 people at Pearl Harbor, the Americans, without thinking about it any further, reacted by launching themselves furiously and impetuously into a war spread across the Pacific Ocean in which they lost a hundred thousand more.

AN ALTERNATIVE APPROACH: CONTAINMENT AND HARASSMENT

Alternatives to all-out war went entirely unconsidered. One possibility, of course, would have been to do nothing. This option would almost certainly have been dismissed out of hand if anybody had brought it up; but it should, one would think, at least have been considered. It was entirely predictable that tens of thousands of Americans would die in any major military effort to get back at the Japanese for their sneak attack at Pearl Harbor. How many lives, a rational decision maker (or any grown-up) ought to consider, is vengeance worth?

However, there was another, less extreme, policy option, one that was at least somewhat more realistic politically and emotionally. It, too, was never considered either at the time or in the decades after, its potential advantages and disadvantages never weighed. But it may be worth considering now, at least as a hypothetical. The United States could have continued to pursue at a more aggressive level its policy of cold war rather than hot—that is, of harassment and containment, economic pressure, arming to deter and to threaten, assistance to anti-Japanese combatants, and perhaps limited warfare on the peripheries. The goal of a continued containment policy would have been more limited than the one pursued. It would have sought only to compel Japan to retreat from its empire, not, like the war, to force the country to submit to occupation. An approach like that might well eventually have impelled Japan to withdraw from its empire at far lower cost to the United States, to Japan, and to the imperialized peoples. And if it was eventually deemed to be failing, reverting to hot war would have remained an available option.

Although the strategy of containment is associated with postwar U.S. policy toward the Soviet Union, it was also basically the initial policy of the British and French in response to the German invasion of Poland in 1939. The allies did not launch direct war, but instead harassed the Germans in places like Norway. They also exerted economic pressure, built up their forces behind defensive barriers, looked for opportunities to aid resistance movements and to exploit fissures in the German empire, and sat back patiently. It was cold war, though it was called "phoney war." The crucial defect in the containment policy directed at Germany was that Germany was (obviously) capable of invading and defeating France. By contrast, Japan could not invade and defeat the United States. Furthermore, Germany did not at the time present a ripe opportunity for punishing harassment because it was not entangled in a continental war the way Japan was in China, nor could it as readily be economically strained. Thus a policy that failed against Germany had a far greater chance of success against Japan, had it been tried.

The Japanese were already vastly overextended by their intervention in China, begun in 1937. Their army there of a million and a half had made many initial gains, but it could not win: it was not strong enough to advance, and it could not force some sort of decisive battle that would end the war, nor could it properly pacify the areas it held.[6]

The resulting economic drain on Japan was considerable. Military expenditures skyrocketed from 9 percent of gross national expenditures to 38 percent, and the difference was made up by the Japanese consumer: by 1941 real consumption per capita had dropped almost 20 percent from 1937 levels. Production of almost all commodities, including steel, either fell or else rose much more slowly than the military required, and shortages of labor, especially skilled labor, developed. As historian Michael Barnhart notes, Japan went to war with the United States "on a shoestring—and a ragged one at that."[7]

In initial attacks, Japan did conquer huge areas in Southeast Asia, including some vital oil fields in the Dutch East Indies that they hoped would provide them with adequate resources to maintain their farflung ventures. However, the Chinese continued to fight, and the Japanese now found themselves in charge of an empire that was even larger and more unwieldy than before. Among the difficulties was their inability to become effective colonists. As brutal conquerors, they mainly inspired an intense hatred among the imperialized peoples, a hatred that in many cases still persists. At the time, it guaranteed resistance and hostility that exacted enormous costs for the occupier.[8]

Moreover, the advance by no means solved Japan's oil problem. In principle, there was enough oil in the newly conquered areas to supply Japan's needs, but the country did not have a tanker fleet big enough to transport all the oil it required. In addition, it took time and effort to get the new oil fields into production, and in the meantime it was necessary to draw on dwindling reserves. As a result, two prewar Japanese studies calculated that even assuming there were no major naval engagements for three full years, the Japanese would be faced with a major oil crisis, or worse, by 1944.[9]

Somewhat related was the problem of merchant shipping on which the island empire depended. Before the war 40 percent of Japan's imports were delivered on foreign ships. In its attacks Japan was able to capture some merchant ships, but it was still confronted with a 25 percent drop in shipping. It could build new ships and refit old ones, but this was a slow and agonizing process at best because its shipyards were small and inefficient and because the military was making huge demands on the industrial sector. In its conquests Japan gained the resources of Southeast Asia, but because of these shipping reductions, its own resources actually declined.[10]

Thus Imperial Japan was an especially auspicious target for a policy of containment and harassment. Even without direct U.S. military efforts, Japan's huge empire in Asia was costly and unwieldy, and in time it might have come to realize this.[11] At the time of Pearl Harbor, Japan was under the control of a fanatical, militaristic group, and there was in addition considerable war fever among many elements in the population—though no one was anxious to have a war with the United States if it could be avoided. But the grip of the romantic, imperial militarists in Japan was neither complete nor necessarily permanent. Substantial misgivings about the enervating, even disastrous expansionary policy and about the "holy war" in China were already being felt not only by some top Japanese civilians, but also by some important military leaders and by the emperor.[12] It seems entirely conceivable that these critics would have been able to moderate, and in time quietly to dismember, the frustratingly costly imperial policy. The Soviet Union at the outset of the cold war was similarly controlled by a set of dangerous, expansionary ideologues, but minds eventually changed as Soviet policies proved hopelessly unproductive and expensive.

With the benefit of hindsight, that experience suggests that the United States might well have been able productively to exacerbate Japan's dilemma of overexpansion, helping to impel it to retreat from its empire. Moreover, this might have been accomplished with far less misery and bloodshed by using containment rather than war.[13] And it seems reasonable to suggest that, given the gravity of the situation, such a policy ought at least to have been *considered* at the time, even though decision makers, of course, did not have the advantage of a half-century of hindsight.

After the war, the United States did gain a strong democratic ally in the new Japan, but it was necessary to depopulate the country by some 2 million souls to do so. Moreover, there had long been a substantial impetus toward liberalism in Japan, and in calmer times this might well have revived, as eventually it revived (after a long period of even more dedicated suppression) in Russia.

Beyond that, for the first few decades of the postwar era most of liberated East Asia was the scene of bloody civil and international war, economic and social mismanagement often of spectacular proportions, and occasionally outright genocide. A major reason the United States fought the Pacific War was to keep the heroic, persecuted, war-racked Chinese from being dominated by a vicious regime.[14] The United States did save China—but for Mao Zedong and the Chinese communists. The imperial Japanese occupiers were often cruel and murderous, but Mao surpassed them substantially in callousness, incompetence, and sheer viciousness (and even in hostility toward the United States). In the war from 1937 to 1945, the Chinese may have lost 3 million people or more.[15] But in its first three years alone, the communist regime probably executed 2 million. Then, in the four years after the start of the Great Leap Forward of 1958, the regime inflicted on the Chinese people the greatest famine in history, one that is now estimated to have taken up to 30 million lives.[16] China could hardly have been worse off in Japanese hands. Or, to put it another way, even if the containment policy proposed here had not been successful eventually in forcing Japan out of China, it is not at all clear that China would have been less fortunate under that fate than it was under the one supplied by the liberating war.

Moreover, having saved Asia from Japanese imperialism at great cost, the United States was soon back in the area centrally participating in the two bloodiest wars of the postwar era. In Korea, where it now found itself killing, rather than aiding, the Chinese, around 3 million civilian and military lives were lost. In Vietnam, some 2 million perished.[17]

The argument here deals with the Pacific War, not the European one, and it obviously relies heavily on hindsight: American decision makers could not possibly have anticipated the postwar horrors. Moreover, I am not arguing that American participation in the Pacific War was necessary for the various horrors in Asia to have taken place—they might well have happened in any case.

But, given what we now know, was the reaction to Pearl Harbor worth it? If the point of the war was to force Japan to retreat from its empire and to encourage it to return to more liberal ways, a policy of cold war (keeping the option of hot war in reserve) might have had the same result at a far lower overall cost. If the point of the war was to prevent further horrors and somehow in short order to bring peace, justice, freedom, and stability to the rest of East and Southeast Asia, the war was a substantial failure.

9/11 AND 12/7: COMPARING DATES OF INFAMY

There are a number of parallels, most of them rather cautionary, between the reactions to the traumatic attacks of December 7, 1941, and September 11, 2001. In addition, there are a few points of notable contrast between the two events.

To start with, the decision makers of 2001, like those in charge in 1941, mostly followed a process of emotion-driven reaction, or overreaction. In 1941, they instantly propelled the country into a war on a state without much consideration as to whether the costs of the ensuing war were likely to be worth it or whether there were alternative approaches that could accomplish the war's goal at lower cost. Quite possibly, of course, had the decision makers been more deliberate, they would still have adopted the same policy. And even in hindsight, a solid argument could be made holding that the policy adopted was preferable to the alternatives outlined here. However, because the decision about how to respond to Pearl Harbor was one of the most momentous in U.S. history, it seems reasonable to suggest that more care could have been taken in its creation.

After 9/11, President George W. Bush rather absurdly declared a "war" on a tactic, terrorism—a "war" that, pretty much by definition, could never logically end—and then, even more preposterously, pledged to "rid the world of evil" in a speech at the National Cathedral on September 14. With great popular support, he then proceeded to propel the country into a war in Afghanistan that happened to go remarkably well (at least at first), but at the time stood likely to result in far more American deaths than had been suffered on 9/11. With broad support from Congress, the Bush administration also instituted a massive, hasty, and often wasteful spending program to guard and defend against a domestic threat of questionable magnitude. Then, as part of its "war" on terrorism, the administration was able to propel the country into an invasion of Iraq, which developed into a debacle vastly more costly in lives and treasure than the impelling event. Except perhaps during the drive toward war with Iraq, these policies were rarely challenged, and other policies, including ones that were potentially far less costly, went substantially unevaluated. Indeed, a half decade after the event, systematic assessments of the efficacy of the "war" on terror remain rare.

The American people, notes historian Gordon Prange, reacted to Pearl Harbor "with a mind-staggering mixture of surprise, awe, mystification, grief, humiliation, and, above all, cataclysmic fury."[18] The response to the terrorist attacks of September 11, 2001, was similar. These emotions are entirely understandable, but they do not relieve decision makers of assessing and evaluating the wisdom of policy options other than lashing out in rage.

Another similarity between the two traumatic events was the country's willingness to go it alone against the threat if need be. This was not much of an issue in 1941. Japan attacked not only the United

States but also the possessions of almost all the potential American allies in the area—Britain, France, China, and the Netherlands—while posing something of a military threat to Australia and New Zealand. But no one in the United States would have thought about getting the cooperation of these countries even if they hadn't already been on board. The threat to the homeland was all that mattered.

Similarly, there was broad approval in the United States for Bush's effective declaration of war on Afghanistan after the September 11 attacks to go after terrorists based there, even though this was essentially a unilateral action. Other states were requested to help, but there would have been popular support for the effort even if no assistance was forthcoming. Indeed, except perhaps for Pakistan, the United States did substantially go it alone initially.

The two attacks had some similar political effects. Not surprisingly, they produced a pronounced rally-round-the-flag effect, sharply boosting each president's approval rating. Before Pearl Harbor, Roosevelt's approval was quite high, 72 percent, but when tapped a month after Pearl Harbor, it had risen to 84 percent.[19] The impact of September 11 on Bush's ratings was similar, except that he had farther to go. Only about 53 percent expressed approval of the job he was doing before the attacks, but this abruptly soared into the 80s, even into the 90s in some polls, after they took place—the greatest up-tick ever recorded on opinion surveys.

More interestingly, although most rally effects tend to be spike-like, the decline in presidential approval from those stratospheric highs was very gradual in each case. This was probably because each was leading the country in a continuing enterprise focused on a palpable, direct threat to American lives. Two years after December 7, when the polls last sought to tap Roosevelt's approval rating, it still stood at 66 percent. And two years after September 11, Bush's rating had declined only into the 60s, a particularly impressive achievement in light of his tepid pre–September 11 approval ratings. In consequence, each president remained difficult to touch politically for quite a while.

In both cases there was a tendency to see spooks everywhere and to quest after the enemy within. In the years before Pearl Harbor, the FBI prepared a list of "potentially dangerous" Japanese, German, and Italian residents, and shortly after Pearl Harbor more than 9,000 of these were rounded up, most of them soon to be paroled or released. But after

February 1942 this process was massively escalated, and some 120,000 individuals of Japanese descent in Western states, two-thirds of them citizens, were forced from their homes and jobs and transported to inland camps, where they were detained for three years. This came about despite the fact that FBI director J. Edgar Hoover insisted that the threat posed by these people was minimal and despite the fact that there was not then, and was never to be, a *single* prosecuted act of espionage, sabotage, or treasonable activity committed by these people. The experience demonstrated, reflected the attorney general of the time, "the power of suggestion which a mystic cliché like 'military necessity' can exercise on human beings."[20]

There was nothing so extreme in 2001, but the same sort of "mystic cliché" prevailed, and bills hastily passed by Congress in the immediate aftermath of the terrorist attacks have considerable potential for restricting civil liberties. There have been many arrests and detentions with little to show for it. There has also been a concentrated effort to restrict immigration flows that has hampered the American economy and, in particular, the functioning of its higher education system.[21]

In both cases, the public accepted   and seems to have been taken by politicians to demand—costly, dramatic, and hasty measures to deal with the perceived threat. Politicians today routinely insist that ever more money be thrown at the homeland security problem and appear to consider it politically suicidal to suggest otherwise. Similarly, politicians in 1942 assumed they were doing the people's will by incarcerating West Coast Japanese. That consummate politician, Franklin Roosevelt, fearful of upsetting West Coast voters, decided to wait until after the 1944 elections before breaking up the Japanese internment camps even though military and civilian cabinet officials had been strenuously arguing for their dismantlement for months.[22]

Also common to the two cases was irresponsible fearmongering about the supposed internal enemy by public officials. Examples for the 9/11 case have already been supplied, and they find earlier reflection in the post–Pearl Harbor period. The mayor of Los Angeles spread unsubstantiated rumors that Japanese fishermen and farmers had been waving lights along the California coast; the top Army commander for the West Coast worried about the imminent uprising of 20,000 Japanese Americans in San Francisco; the secretary of the Navy alarmingly reported that there was "a great deal of very active fifth column work" going on in Hawaii "both from the shore and from the sampans"; and a committee chaired by a Supreme Court justice promulgated unfounded charges that local Japanese had facilitated the Pearl Harbor attack.[23]

If today's FBI director is taking absence of evidence to be evidence of existence, he was far from the first official to do so. In 1942, one general found, "The very fact that no sabotage has taken place to date is a disturbing and confirming indication that the Japanese have carefully orchestrated their subversion so that when the sabotage comes it will be massive." The legendary columnist Walter Lippmann applied similarly tortured logic. Two months after Pearl Harbor, he proclaimed that, based "not on speculation but on what is known," the West Coast was "in imminent danger of a combined attack from within and without" that "might do irreparable damage." He took the fact that there had been no important sabotage on the Pacific Coast not to be a sign that there was nothing to be feared, but as indicating "that the blow is well-organized and that it is held back until it can be struck with maximum effect."[24]

There is also a parallel between the 12/7 and the 9/11 attacks in the tendency to exaggerate the enemy's capacities, to imagine an elephant instead of an ant. The precise capacity of the enemy after Pearl Harbor was unknown, but as that enemy had just carried out a spectacular deed, there was an urge to assume, or imagine, the worst. Perhaps it is happening again.

In the months after Pearl Harbor there were constant concerns, as in Lippmann's confident declaration, that Japan would attack the mainland in force, something that was wildly outside its military capacity. For example, on February 25, 1942, the U.S. Army convinced itself that Los Angeles was under Japanese air attack. It lofted 1,433 rounds of antiaircraft fire at invading planes that, as it happened, did not exist. Five people died in the melee from auto accidents or heart attacks, and there was some property damage from antiaircraft projectiles that "failed to explode in the sky but worked just fine as soon as they hit the ground," as columnist Jack Smith puts it. Throughout the war, the entire extent of Japanese bombing by airplane of the American mainland would consist of two flights by Warrant Officer Nobuo Fujita, who dropped incendiary explosives in Oregon in an attempt to set off forest fires. The missions were unsuccessful, though they did arouse some alarm on the West Coast. Japan also lofted some bomb-bearing balloons that managed to set some small fires here and there and killed a few people on a church outing in Oregon.[25]

Pearl Harbor and the early Japanese attacks were brilliant successes, but taking this to indicate that Japan had suddenly become a military giant proved to be a major error. Notes historian H. P. Willmott, thereafter Japan "managed to pick what was arguably the wrong course of action every time it was confronted with a choice." The Japanese army continually displayed a "basic lack of realism" and an unwillingness to reverse course when things were going badly; indeed, "not a single operation planned after the start of the war met with success."[26]

Post-9/11 parallels may be evident in the quest for duct tape and plastic sheeting; in polls that document persistent fears, despite years of refutation, that there will *soon* be another terrorist attack (see Figure 1 on page 2); in the fantasies of members of the terrorism industry about the "existential" threat terrorism poses; and in the spooky Osama bin Laden obsession that, in the words of Russell Seitz, "serves to inflate into satanic stature a merely evil man."[27]

In both cases political entrepreneurs sought to capitalize on the emotions of the event to push through policies that had now suddenly become politically possible. Roosevelt had been trying with little success to move the country toward war, but mainly toward the one in Europe against Germany. Although Pearl Harbor instantly solved his basic problem, there was concern for a while that the country's energies would be focused on the Pacific. Fortunately for Roosevelt's Europe-first priorities, Hitler declared war on the United States a few days after Pearl Harbor.[28]

In the case of 9/11, elements within the Bush administration who had previously yearned for the employment of force to remove Saddam Hussein from authority in Iraq almost instantly began to seek to use the terrorist attacks to support their case, even though no connection between the attacks and Saddam's regime was ever, or has ever been, shown.[29]

More generally, the dramatic, traumatic, and eventually legendary events have been liberally applied by entrepreneurs to close off thought and opposition to spending proposals that have often been massive. During the cold war, the purchase of vast numbers of missiles and other weapons was justified by the argument that to fail to do so would leave the country open to another Pearl Harbor. Today members of the terrorism industry ardently evoke memories of 9/11 to rationalize the expenditure of public monies on projects that, to a more jaded eye, might seem just a bit unnecessary.

In addition, instead of simply giving credit to the 12/7 and 9/11 attackers for considerable cleverness and for even more considerable luck, the traumatic experiences have in both cases very commonly been attributed to American intelligence inadequacies: a failure to "connect the dots," in the phrase that became something of a mantra after 9/11.[30]

Shakespeare's Hotspur proclaims, "Out of this nettle, danger, we pluck this flower, safety." (He dies soon thereafter.) After 12/7 and 9/11 a hopeless, even oxymoronic, quest for perfect intelligence eventually coalesced in schemes that sought to pluck that flower by rearranging the nettle, particularly by centralizing the intelligence bureaucracy. Thus, after World War II, the *Central* Intelligence Agency was formed, and, predictably, a half-century later the august 9/11 Commission solemnly urged, demanded, and implored that it had now become necessary to centralize the centralized, capping it all with a newly created supercentral intelligence czar.[31]

One parallel between the two cases, potentially highly relevant, is the tendency to impute undue relevance to extreme events by envisioning them as harbingers rather than as aberrations. Pearl Harbor, we now know, proved to be the latter, but at the time the former was more commonly embraced. Moreover, the experience haunted thinking for decades and was being called on to justify public policies, often extreme and highly expensive ones: because the Japanese had shown themselves to be highly risk-acceptant, clever, lucky, and desperate in 1941, we must plan, worst-case-scenario-wise, that any enemy could and would be the same.

Similar incantations are heard now applying the 9/11 experience, and agile incantors have frequently found that the image can have the desirable effect of arresting counterargument, even counterthinking. The result has been a massive and often unnecessary expansion of expenditures to protect against spooky possibilities and, in many important respects, a costly war, and potential debacle, in Iraq. By contrast, the speculation of Russell Seitz bears repeating: "9/11 could join the Trojan Horse and Pearl Harbor among stratagems so uniquely surprising that their very success precludes their repetition," and "al-Qaeda's best shot may have been exactly that."[32]

A potential comparison between the two attacks that has so far failed to develop concerns conspiracy explanations. Pearl Harbor inspired decades of popular theories variously finding deviltry in Franklin Roosevelt or other government officials. There have been efforts to blame the events of 9/11 on the U.S. government, on Jewish Americans, and on the machinations of Israeli intelligence agencies, but, in contrast to the Pearl Harbor theories, thus far these have generated little following, at least in the United States. However, they are flourishing in France, the Middle East, and elsewhere, and they will likely find increasing favor in America over time.

Another contrast concerns the demise of fear and feelings of threat. Historian John Dower has documented the savage hatreds that burgeoned during World War II between Americans and Japanese, many of which had roots in various racist incidents and policies that went back decades. In the case of the United States this was partly reflected in the Japanese internment policy. However, concerns about the Japanese threat, both domestic and foreign, could be terminated by the successful conquest of Japan, and, indeed, both the fear and the hostility dissipated quickly and almost completely at the end of the war.[33]

There is no parallel here with fears about terrorism: unlike Japan in 1945, terrorism cannot be decisively conquered and permanently eradicated. Moreover, though any nut with a bomb can put terrorism back on the central agenda, no single person could reignite the passions evoked by the Pearl Harbor attack.

A most striking difference between the two events concerns visual representations. News about the terrorist attacks of September 11, 2001, was accompanied by riveting and horrifying pictures of planes flying into buildings and of tall towers collapsing into rubble. By contrast, pictures of the Pearl Harbor attack were not published until a month or two after the event out of fear they could somehow help the enemy. However, although the American public had only verbal descriptions of what had transpired at Pearl Harbor, it is difficult to imagine how its outraged reaction could have been more intense. The comparison strongly suggests that it was the fact of 9/11 that really inspired the response, not visual depictions, however vivid, of the events.

Without thinking about it very hard, the Japanese hoped that their shocking attack on Pearl Harbor might destroy the will of the United States to fight.[34] This proved to be one of the greatest miscalculations in military history, but a thoughtful caveat by political scientist Scott Sagan ought to be kept in mind: "Anyone who has lived through the war in Vietnam cannot easily dismiss the possibility" that Americans "might have decided that the costs of continuing a war in Asia were greater than any possible gains to be made." In the event, the attack on Pearl Harbor was phenomenally successful in its shock effect, but the shock was exactly the opposite of the one the Japanese hoped for, and it turned out to be a disaster for them.[35]

As will be discussed more fully later, much the same could be said for the 9/11 attack. In many respects the venture was, like the Japanese effort in 1941, a desperate effort to shore up a declining position. But the dramatic deed did not boost effective support for al-Qaeda. Instead, strongly aided and encouraged by the Americans, most of the world, and particularly the governments thereof, turned against al-Qaeda and its look-alikes, substantially dismembering the organization.

CHAPTER 4

Cold War, Containment, and Conspiracy

Now that the cold war is over, it is possible to assess whether the fears and anxieties generated by that conflict were justified. With the benefit of hindsight, it seems clear they were not.

Throughout the cold war, the United States and sometimes its allies persistently, often vastly, and sometimes willfully exaggerated either the capacity of international communism to inflict damage in carrying out its threatening revolutionary goals, or its willingness to accept risk to do so, or both. The results of this exaggeration—or proclivity, to err on the safe side—were costly economically and emotionally. From a military standpoint (because the Soviet Union labored under similar delusions) they led to policies that, seen in retrospect, bordered on the farcical: the quest for "nuclear parity," for example, often ended up more nearly in a condition that could be called "nuclear parody." In addition, anxieties about the capacity of conspiratorial domestic communists—the "enemy within"—to do damage, much less to subvert the domestic political and economic system, proved to be based mostly on fantasy.

This is not to deny that communism, a coordinated, conspiratorial, subversive, revolutionary, and state-based international movement, did pose a threat. According to its core ideology, it was out to destroy capitalism and democracy. Moreover, it explicitly and repeatedly declared that violence—in particular, revolutionary violence—was required to accomplish this central goal. In addition, the movement was skilled at agitation, conspiracy, and subversion, as it showed in its takeover in Russia in 1917 and in Czechoslovakia in 1948, and it was willing and able to use force to maintain its control over lands it had seized that, after

World War II, included several countries in Eastern Europe. From the Western perspective the forces of international communism were aggressive and malevolent.

There has been a considerable debate about the degree to which ideology impelled Soviet policy. Over the decades major Soviet leaders repeatedly made statements like the following:

> Lenin: "The existence of the Soviet Republic side by side with the imperialist states for a long time is unthinkable. One or the other must triumph in the end. And before that end supervenes, a series of frightful collisions between the Soviet Republic and the bourgeois states will be inevitable."

> Lenin: "As soon as we are strong enough to fight the whole of capitalism, we shall at once take it by the neck."

> Stalin: "The goal is to consolidate the dictatorship of the proletariat in one country, using it as a base for the overthrow of imperialism in all countries."

> Stalin: "To eliminate the inevitability of war, it is necessary to destroy imperialism."

> Khrushchev: "Peaceful coexistence [means] intense economic, political, and ideological struggle between the proletariat and the aggressive forces of imperialism in the world arena."

> Khrushchev: "All the socialist countries and the international working-class and Communist movement recognize their duty to render the fullest moral and material assistance to the peoples fighting to free themselves from imperialist and colonial tyranny."

There is some possibility, of course, that pronouncements like these are simply theological boilerplate. Nonetheless, after they have been recited millions of times in speeches, books, leaflets, brochures, letterhead, tracts, training manuals, banners, pamphlets, proclamations, announcements, billboards, handbooks, bumper stickers, and T-shirts, one might begin to suspect that the sentiments could just possibly actually reflect true thought processes.[1]

At any rate, as they are explicitly and lethally threatening, responsible leaders of capitalist countries understandably took them seriously. The ideological threat was stressed in the quintessential and seminal declaration of U.S. policy toward international communism as published by the State Department's George Kennan in a famous article published in *Foreign Affairs* in 1947. In the first paragraphs, Kennan outlines the communist perspective. These include the notions that capitalism is nefarious and inevitably leads to the exploitation of the working class, but that it contains the "seeds of its own destruction" and will perish in a worldwide working-class revolution that must be aided by countries where such a revolutionary transfer of power has already taken place. Many people readily accepted that characterization during the cold war. For example, in his last presidential press conference, Ronald Reagan was quite clear about what he felt the cold war was about: "the expansionary policy that was instituted in the Communist revolution, that their goal must be a one-world Communist state." Similar statements were frequently made by such leading cold warriors as Winston Churchill, John Foster Dulles, John Kennedy, Lyndon Johnson, Margaret Thatcher, and George Shultz.[2]

The communist challenge registered both on the international level, where communists sought to topple noncommunist governments and sometimes threatened militarily, and on the internal level, where, it was feared, domestic communists would, in conspiratorial complicity with the international movement, seek to undermine and eventually destroy the democratic and capitalist system of the West.

CONTAINMENT

On the international level, Harry Truman's United States came up with a policy to deal with the Soviet threat, containment, which stressed that the West should do everything possible to hold the Soviet Union where it then stood, allowing it no further expansion. With that, the whole edifice might topple, because, concluded Kennan dramatically (and ultimately correctly), there was a "strong" possibility that Soviet power "bears within it the seeds of its own decay, and that the sprouting of these seeds is well advanced."[3]

The policy was strongly influenced by lessons derived from the interwar experience, and they could be summed up in the one-word slogan "Munich." Before World War II, the peace-preferring states had timorously allowed Japan, Italy, and Germany to take over peripheral areas in hopes that the acquisitions would sate the appetites for territory of those discontented countries. Instead, it was concluded, their cravings "grew with the feeding" and made them ever more daring; eventually this culminated in the very conflagration the peace-preferring states were so desperate to avoid. Appeasement, which reached its pinnacle with the 1938 agreement at Munich to give Hitler major portions of Czechoslovakia, was therefore seen to be a spectacularly counterproductive method for dealing with an aggressor. Instead, it was deemed crucial to oppose the aggressor early and everywhere, even in areas of little objective military, political, or economic importance, because if the aggressor is not confronted there, the battle will only have to be fought later under less favorable circumstances and in locales of greater significance.[4]

In applying this lesson to the Soviet Union, Western policymakers were aware that the Soviet expansionist threat was likely to be expressed primarily in what they called "indirect aggression": subversion, diplomatic and military pressure, revolution, and armed uprising, all inspired, partly funded, and heavily influenced by Moscow. The issue of direct, over-the-border, Hitlerian aggression by the Soviets, however, was more problematic. Many people, including Kennan, felt that likelihood to be exceedingly small.[5] But no one, of course, could be sure.

To say that international communism was threatening is not to say that it had the capacity—or, in the case of direct aggression, the will—to carry the threat out.[6] In retrospect and with the benefit of hindsight, it seems clear that policies designed to contain and counter the threat were based on fears that were often excessive and overwrought and that the policies themselves were unnecessarily costly and sometimes counterproductive. Moreover, shocking events were frequently taken to confirm previously alarmist warnings (whether they objectively did so or not), and then were wildly and incorrectly extrapolated, leading to costly, unnecessary, and sometimes bloody overreactions and to wasteful expenditures.

Overreacting to Indirect Aggression in Europe: Czechoslovakia

The policy of containment was formally set in motion as the United States responded to problems taken to suggest that indirect aggression was afoot in Greece and Turkey. Both countries needed help, and the United States came through with military and economic aid, accompanied by the ringing, open-ended declaration of the Truman Doctrine of

March 12, 1947, that "it must be the policy of the United States to support free peoples who are resisting attempted subjugation by armed minorities [Greece] or by outside pressures [Turkey]."

In putting forth this policy, Truman engaged in the kind of massive extrapolation that was to prove so common in the cold war. It was an early expression of what would later be called the domino theory, and it derives directly from the Munich experience. If the communists should win in Greece, predicted Truman, the effect on Turkey "would be immediate and serious," and "confusion and disorder might well spread throughout the entire Middle East." This in turn would have a "profound effect" on important countries in Europe. And then the ultimate extrapolation: "If we falter in our leadership, we may endanger the peace of the world—and we shall surely endanger the welfare of our own nation."

For various reasons, Greece and Turkey never fell to communism, but a coup by the Moscow-supported Communist Party in Czechoslovakia in 1948 suddenly brought that country into the Soviet camp, an alarming development that was readily extrapolated to conclude that the experience might be duplicated in countries like France and Italy, where there were large and well-organized communist parties.

Moreover, although the communist takeover of Czechoslovakia was entirely an exercise in indirect aggression, the experience was immediately taken to relate to the military realm, and Truman declared that "we are faced with exactly the same situation with which Britain and France were faced in 1938–39 with Hitler." Responsible American officials in Europe warned that war could come with "dramatic suddenness," and the Central Intelligence Agency concluded that war was improbable only for sixty days or so.[7]

However, fears that the coup in democratic Czechoslovakia would soon be followed by further communist takeovers in Europe proved to be unfounded. In the aftermath of World War II, communist parties in Western Europe did enjoy a fair amount of credibility and goodwill, and they were admitted to cabinets in France and Italy. But their influence soon declined considerably as suspicion of, and then coordinated opposition to, communism grew. In approaching voters and constituents, communist parties in Western democracies were constantly hobbled by their theoretical adherence to a doctrine that exalted revolutionary violence as the only method for gaining political control. Unsuccessful efforts by French and Italian communists in the late 1940s to use extralegal means like strikes and riots to improve their political position served to reinforce this wariness, as did the Czech coup of 1948. By 1950 the influence of communist parties had diminished considerably on the continent.[8]

Some of these favorable developments can perhaps be attributed to American aid and statecraft. But they were much more crucially a reaction to Stalin's brutal behavior in Eastern Europe, including his subversive takeover in Czechoslovakia and his belligerent policies over Germany. Ultimately, the threats of internal subversion and of revolution in the developed world proved to be minor.

Overreacting to Direct Aggression: Korea

In the summer of 1948 the Soviets blocked off Western land access to the German capital city of Berlin, which lay deep within their zone of occupation. Challenged, Truman concluded, "We are going to stay. Period." The area of Berlin controlled by the West was supplied by air—a remarkable humanitarian success—until the Soviets lifted the blockade a year later. The Berlin blockade was neither war nor a clear instance of direct aggression. Still, U.S. and Soviet troops seemed to be only a step or two away from shooting at each other. By 1949 the United States and eleven of its anti-Soviet allies had created the North Atlantic Treaty Organization. With NATO, containment took on its most important military component and focused on the potential for direct Soviet aggression in Europe.

Meanwhile, impelled by the Berlin blockade and even more by a successful atomic bomb test by the Soviet Union in 1949, an alarmist National Security Council report, NSC-68, was promulgated within the Truman administration, warning of a dire nuclear future and urging huge increases in defense spending. The peak period of danger was anticipated to arrive in 1954, when the Soviet Union could be expected to have amassed a sizable atomic arsenal, neutralizing the American atomic capacity. At that point, the report suggested, the USSR "might be tempted to strike swiftly and with stealth." Its principal author was the State Department's Paul Nitze, perhaps the most virtuosic, effective, and consistently mistaken fearmonger of the cold war era. He was egged on by Secretary of State Dean Acheson, who wanted a document that could "bludgeon the mass mind of 'top government' " with points that were "clearer than truth."[9]

Nonetheless, the guy actually at the top, Harry Truman, remained unbludgeoned for a while; he was unimpressed by the alarm and, in particular, unpersuaded about the economic feasibility of carrying out the defense spending recommended by the report. These perspectives, however, were abruptly cast aside when communist North Korea alarmingly attacked the South in June 1950. A direct analogy with the 1930s was readily, if glibly, applied, and all of Truman's advisers agreed that to fail to meet the challenge in Korea would be appeasement, which would lead ultimately to wider war. "I felt certain," Truman wrote, "that if South Korea was allowed to fall Communist leaders would be emboldened to override nations closer to our own shores. . . . If this was allowed to go unchallenged it would mean a third world war, just as similar incidents had brought on the second world war."[10] How, one might ask, could he, or anyone, be so *certain*?

Moreover, almost everyone simply assumed that the war was being directed from Moscow. Most Western decision makers felt it was part of a "Soviet strategic master plan," and they became concerned that it might be merely a diversionary tactic: as defense analyst Bernard Brodie recalls, many, particularly the Joint Chiefs of Staff, "were utterly convinced that the Russians were using Korea as a feint to cause us to deploy our forces there while they prepared to launch a 'general' (total) war against the United States through a major attack on Europe."[11] Utterly convinced.

Given the conditions of the times, concern was obviously justified, if not the certainty of interpretation with which it was often held. Stalin remained in full control of the Soviet system until his death in 1953, and although he had always been exceedingly wary about getting into a war with the West, his last years became "one of increasing madness and sterility," as Kennan put it.[12] Moreover, with the recent establishment of a congenial communist regime in the world's most populous nation, China, it was easy to imagine that the aging Stalin might come to yearn for an apocalyptic worldwide revolutionary upheaval, with war as its midwife, in which capitalism would finally be destroyed. Under the circumstances, to ignore the possibility of some sort of Soviet military action in Europe would have been irresponsible.

However, milder explanations—which proved to be the correct

ones—were given little or no attention, much less embraced with comparable certainty. During the Korean War, State Department counselor and Soviet specialist Charles Bohlen did argue that Korea did not indicate a willingness to risk global war. He was ignored.[13]

In fact, there was nothing in Soviet doctrine to remotely justify an assumption that they would want to risk a major war. As Bohlen stressed, according to the ideology on which the regime had been founded in 1917, world history is a vast, continuing process of progressive revolution. Steadily, in country after country, the oppressed working classes will violently revolt, destroying the oppressing capitalist classes and aligning their new regimes with other, like-minded countries. But the Soviets, however dynamic and threatening their ideology, have never subscribed to a Hitler-style theory of direct, Armageddon-risking conquest. In 1919, founding father Vladimir Lenin did write, as noted earlier, that before international capitalism could collapse, "a series of frightful collisions" between the Soviet Republic and the capitalist states was "inevitable." However, the Soviets expected that a major war between the communist and the capitalist worlds would arise only from an attack on them by the enemy. By 1935 at the latest, official proclamations had abandoned the notion that such wars were inevitable and had decided that the solidarity of the international working class and the burgeoning strength of the Soviet armed forces had made them avoidable.[14]

In general, they advocated exploiting various conflicts *among* the capitalist states, while aiding and inspiring subversive revolutionary movements and seeking to expand Soviet power and influence without directly engaging in war themselves. Moreover, Lenin's methodology contains a strong sense of cautious pragmatism: a good revolutionary moves carefully in a hostile world, striking when the prospects for success are bright and avoiding risky undertakings.[15] Aggressive, conquering Hitlerian war would foolishly risk everything; it does not fit into this scheme at all.

Brodie, one of the few defense analysts of the time seriously to think about such key issues, finally came to the Bohlenesque conclusion by 1966 that it was "difficult to discover what meaningful incentives the Russians might have for attempting to conquer Western Europe—especially incentives that are even remotely commensurate with the risks." After it was all over, a great amount of documentary evidence became available, but as Robert Jervis notes, a decade after the collapse of the USSR, "the Soviet archives have yet to reveal any serious plans for unprovoked aggression against Western Europe, not to mention a first strike against the United States."[16]

The communist venture in Korea, then, seems to have been a limited military probe at a point of perceived vulnerability in a peripheral area. Despite Western knee-jerk expressions of certainty and utter conviction, there was no evidence at the time that Stalin actually had anything broader in mind, nor has any come to light since. In fact, the attack was not Stalin's idea at all, but was broached in late 1949 by Kim Il-sung, the leader of communist North Korea. Although Stalin had some misgivings, Kim was fully certain of quick success and promised that, if prodded by his bayonet, South Korea would explode internally and quickly fall into the communist camp before the West even had much of a chance to react. What Stalin approved was a distant war of expansion by a faithful, if profoundly misguided, ally, a war that was expected to be quick, risk-free, and cheap, and he took precautionary steps to limit the war by withdrawing from North Korea not only Soviet military advisers but most Soviet equipment.[17]

The Korean War proved to be the costliest since World War II: some 2 or 3 million perished in it. It did save the people of South Korea from being taken over by one of most contemptible regimes in modern history. Moreover, it may have discouraged the communists from contemplating similar ventures elsewhere. The invasion may simply have been a somewhat tentative probe, but the Soviets never tried direct aggression again, even in a probing manner in distant corners of the globe: there were no Koreas after Korea.[18]

Meanwhile, deeply alarmed, the West massively extrapolated. It urgently armed to deter the Soviet Union from trying similar ventures elsewhere, particularly in Europe. The U.S. defense budget quadrupled, something that previously had been thought to be politically and economically infeasible. And to confront the essentially nonexistent threat of a frontal Soviet invasion of Western Europe, NATO was rapidly transformed from a paper organization (big on symbolism, small on actual military capability) into a viable, well-equipped, centrally led, multinational armed force.[19] At the same time, the United States expanded its commitment to anticommunist ventures wherever they could be found or imagined across the globe. Both responses proved to be costly and substantially unnecessary.

Overreacting to a Technical Challenge: Sputnik

The reaction in the United States to the Soviet Union's dramatic launch in 1957 of *Sputnik*, the first artificial space satellite, often bordered on the hysterical. For example, one astrophysicist predicted with certainty that the Soviets would soon be on the moon—perhaps within a week—and physicist Edward Teller declared that the United States had lost "a battle more important and greater than Pearl Harbor." A prominent political aide extravagantly opined that "the Russians have left the earth and the race for the control of the universe has started." Meanwhile, a hastily assembled, if august and authoritative committee, the President's Commission on National Goals, was soon extrapolating wildly, declaring the democratic world to be in "grave danger" from communism's "great capacity for political organization and propaganda" and from the "specious appeal of Communist doctrine." The CIA helpfully (and massively) extrapolated in 1960 that the Soviet Union's gross national product, which seemed to be surging at the time, might be triple that of the United States by the year 2000.[20] Such fears and fantasies eventually proved absurd.

Most important, *Sputnik* gave dramatic punch to the almost completely misguided message of the *Gaither Report*, which was in the works at the time. Substantially authored by the ubiquitous alarmist Paul Nitze, the *Report* asserted confidently that the United States was falling behind in the arms race and in a few years would be much inferior to the Soviet Union in intercontinental missiles: "The evidence clearly indicates an increasing threat which may become critical in 1959 or 1960." The *Report* recommended substantial spending increases in an attempt to keep up in missilery and also in conventional local war capability as it was fancied that, with the U.S. nuclear capacity neutralized or worse, the Soviet enemy would likely be tempted to spin off other Koreas, particularly in Asia and the Middle East.[21]

This calculation, which came to be known as the "missile gap," was based less on clear indications in the evidence than on some assumptions about Soviet capacities to build missiles, which may have been correct, and about Soviet intentions to do so, which were decidedly in error. The *Gaither Report* and other analyses projected that the Soviet missile strength in the early 1960s would stand at 700 (in extrapolations by the Air Force, whose budget stood to rise with high Soviet numbers) or merely at 200 (in extrapolations by the Navy, whose budget didn't). The actual figure turned out to be four, though the Air Force continued doggedly to suggest for a while that barn silos, medieval towers, a Crimean War memorial, and various mysterious-looking buildings in isolated areas were actually cleverly disguised missiles.[22]

Much of the alarm about this potential development (and actual nondevelopment) was based on the assumption that, should the Soviets achieve superiority, they would use it even if the costs and risks to them were substantial. This view, as historian David Callahan has put it, "was not a complex and thoughtful vision that mirrored geopolitical reality. Rather, it was more a mathematical model in which comparisons of military hardware constituted the starting point for almost all further analysis." In this assessment, the lessons, or supposed lessons, of Pearl Harbor loomed large for many people. For example, analyst Albert Wohlstetter's highly influential thesis that the balance of power was "delicate"—a key progenitor of the *Gaither* conclusions—rested on the assumption that the Soviet enemy could potentially come to be as clever, lucky, diabolical, and desperate as Japan was in 1941, a thesis conveniently embellished by recommendations for his wife's excellent book on Pearl Harbor. Impressed by such scary if unexamined comparisons, and mesmerized by their own exquisite, mathematized analyses of the Soviet-American arms race, many defense analysts managed to convince themselves that disaster was likely. Some declined to sign up for retirement plans, figuring they weren't likely to live that long, and others cheerily concluded that it was "perfectly conceivable . . . that the U.S. might have to evacuate two or three times every decade." Such views remained dominant even after an elaborate war/crisis simulation game set up by Harvard's Thomas Schelling failed to come up with any sort of scenario or provocation that could get a war, particularly a nuclear war, started.[23]

One of the few people, as it happened, who did not go into hysterics, programmed or otherwise, over *Sputnik*, Soviet economic progress, and the *Gaither Report* was the president of the United States, Dwight David Eisenhower. He found the concerns of the *Report* to be exaggerated. In major part, however, his reaction seems to have stemmed not so much from substance as from his hostility to the substantial defense expenditure increases it suggested or implied: he felt, incorrectly as it turned out, that either the American economy or the American people could not tolerate the bill. Yet, recalling conversations with his Soviet counterpart, Nikita Khrushchev, he also felt it improbable, correctly as it turned out, that the Soviets would gamble everything on a surprise attack. Therefore, he concluded that nuclear war was quite unlikely, apocalypse distant, and the nation's nuclear deterrent essentially adequate. In addition, he (correctly) found it implausible that the Soviets would embark on a crash program to build liquid-fuel missiles which were already in the process of being made obsolete by ones powered by solid fuel.[24]

Eisenhower had the *Gaither Report* classified, but its contents soon leaked in various ways, and they were seized on by Senator John F. Kennedy, who extrapolated apocalyptically. In an important 1958 speech he claimed that in a very few years, "the deterrent gap might shift to the Soviets so heavily . . . as to open to them a new shortcut to world domination." After becoming president in 1961, Kennedy discovered that the missile gap—so impressively, if irrelevantly, dramatized by *Sputnik*—had been a myth. Still, he moved notably to increase defense spending and to beef up conventional forces, just as the *Gaither Report* recommended, and he added a much enhanced counterinsurgency capacity to the mix. As part of this buildup, Kennedy also instituted a fallout shelter program that was partly designed to outflank potential opponents in the 1964 reelection race. The measure was substantially abandoned when it became something of a laughingstock.[25]

In an article published in the first year of the Kennedy administration, Morton Halperin characterized the response of the Eisenhower administration to the *Gaither* hysteria as "complacency" and called for "a strong, vigorous President" to overcome "bureaucratic and political opposition to the implementation of new, vitally needed programs." In this instance, complacency proved to be the far more nearly correct response to global military threats and challenges that, as it happened, didn't exist: no new programs were "vitally needed." Moreover, complacency would have saved considerable money and might even have kept the United States from wandering into the debacle of Vietnam.[26]

"Only when our arms are sufficient beyond doubt," Kennedy proclaimed in his pithy if sometimes overripe 1961 Inaugural Address, "can we be certain beyond doubt that they will never be employed." In a world of agile and creative alarmists, however, no amount of armament ever is, or perhaps could ever conceivably be, "sufficient beyond doubt."

Overreacting to Indirect Aggression in Latin America: Cuba

Radical reformer Fidel Castro fought his way into control in Cuba at the end of 1958, and he soon declared himself a reborn ideological Marxist-Leninist. He cut off ties with nearby America, rolled his country into the communist camp, and found it in his heart graciously to accept the very substantial Soviet aid that was necessary to keep his regime afloat economically. Castro also became very interested in furthering the interests of the Soviet Union and of international communism in Latin America, a third world area that had yet to be fully exploited ideologically and where revolutionary progress proved to be especially irritating to capitalist America.

The United States was alarmed that Castro's victory in Cuba and his subsequent embrace of Soviet communism would be repeated all over Latin America. In disastrous overreaction, the United States in 1961 tried and failed to eliminate Castro and to roll back communism by putting together an invasion by anti-Castro exiles at Cuba's Bay of Pigs—one of the great foreign policy fiascoes in U.S. history.

The invasion did boost Castro's star for a while, greatly enhancing American concern about the threat he seemed to present. But over time, communism and Castroism in Latin America lost their appeal. In fact, in the fifteen years after Castro's Cuban takeover, no country in Latin America, or anywhere else in the world for that matter, fell to communism, although there were alarums aplenty among Americans about places like Brazil, Venezuela, Chile, and the Dominican Republic.

Except for the last of these, where the United States sent troops to bolster friendly forces, the communists and Castroists were mostly put down (sometimes brutally) by domestic opponents. Eventually, the cold war experience of 1975–1979 would suggest that any domino toppling in the area would have been temporary, ultimately counterproductive for the communists, and historically inconsequential. Before those lessons could become apparent, however, Vietnam intervened.

Overreacting to Indirect Aggression in Asia: Vietnam

When the administration of Lyndon Johnson decided to send troops to Vietnam in 1965, there was widespread agreement with the views of

David Halberstam, a future war critic, who extravagantly argued that Vietnam was a "strategic country in a key area . . . perhaps one of only five or six nations in the world that is truly vital to U.S. interests." Or as reporter Neil Sheehan, another future critic of U.S. policy in Vietnam, spookily put it in 1964, "The fall of Southeast Asia to China or its denial to the West over the next decade because of the repercussions from an American defeat in Vietnam would amount to a strategic disaster of the first magnitude." Only the United States, he argued, could meet "the Chinese Communist challenge for hegemony in Asia."[27]

Far from closing out unpleasant alternatives in this case, the men in the White House did evaluate the various options to sending in U.S. combat troops, and they listened—none more attentively than Johnson himself—to a carefully argued proposal from Undersecretary of State George Ball for a judicious loss-cutting withdrawal, a proposal far more radical than almost anything heard at the time outside the government. They rejected Ball's proposal because they agreed with Halberstam's trendy, if absurd, assessment that Vietnam was "truly vital" to U.S. interests and because they found the same drawbacks as Halberstam to withdrawal: it might bring a bloodbath ("Those Vietnamese who committed themselves fully to the United States will suffer the most"), it would hamper American clout ("The United States' prestige will be lowered throughout the world"), and it would have a domino effect ("The pressure of Communism on the rest of Southeast Asia will intensify" and "throughout the world the enemies of the West will be encouraged to try insurgencies like the one in Vietnam").[28] Although the process of consideration was exemplary in many ways, in the end simplicity and spook prevailed.

Such spooky fears were deadly in their consequences. They implied, or sucked, the United States into a costly, spectacularly unnecessary war. It proved to be the greatest debacle in U.S. foreign policy history when, a decade later, the communists triumphed in Vietnam. Ironically, that victory was to be part of a cluster of gains that led to an existential disaster for international communism. By the 1990s, Vietnam had willingly become about as capitalistic and corrupt, and nearly as democratic, as the South Vietnamese regime the United States had attempted to save at such great cost.

Overreacting to Direct Aggression Again: Afghanistan

In the 1970s a group of august doomsayers who ominously called themselves the Committee on the Present Danger and who, none too surprisingly, included in their ranks the error-prone Paul Nitze, pushed the view that somehow the Soviet Union's military capacity was vastly and threateningly increasing. In NSC-68 and in the *Gaither Report*, Nitze had "foretold the years for maximum danger for the West in the perpetually near future," as journalist Fred Kaplan describes it, and now Nitze was at it again. The Soviets had begun an arms buildup after the humiliation of the 1962 Cuban Missile Crisis, and Nitze now ominously calculated that they might soon have "a theoretical war-winning capability." All they would have to do would be to quietly evacuate their cities and then launch enough of their missiles to knock out U.S. land-based missiles. This would theoretically leave the United States with only enough retaliatory capacity to annihilate a mere 3 or 4 percent of the Soviet population, leaving the remaining 96 or 97 percent free to dominate the world and retaliate against the United States. There were also extravagant claims from the Committee on the Present Danger and from "Team B," an overlapping group commissioned by the CIA to push the alarmist angle about Soviet intentions, that the Soviet Union was willing to accept massive casualties to acquire world domination. In fact, argued Nitze, there was a diabolical connection: "Intentions tend to grow with the capability to carry them out," a phenomenon that presumably held for the USSR, but not for the United States. Events were to demonstrate that this economically costly fear by what Brodie called "the cult of the ominous" was based on what he at the time labeled "worst case fantasies," and were much exaggerated. In fact, Team B was almost completely wrong in every respect.[29]

Initially, the hysteria and hype were resisted by the administration of Jimmy Carter, who received support from Nitze in his successful 1976 election campaign, but who declined to invite the congenital alarmist to join his administration, finding him "arrogant and inflexible" and saddled with "a doomsday approach." But when the Soviet Union invaded neighboring Afghanistan in 1979, Carter was electrified. He announced that his "opinion of what the Soviets' ultimate goals are" had undergone a "dramatic change."[30]

There were a number of potential explanations for the Soviet venture, but Carter quickly embraced what historian Raymond Garthoff has called "the *least* likely Soviet motivation—pursuit of a relentless expansionist design." Declaring that the invasion "could pose the most serious threat to world peace since World War II," Carter insisted on seeing it as an aggressive ploy relevant to the entire Middle East and South Asia. Similarly, National Security Adviser Zbigniew Brzezinski envisioned the invasion as "a strategic challenge" and fancied Afghanistan as a central element in an "arc of crisis" anchored in North Africa on one end and in India on the other—"one of those intellectual constructs that dramatizes a threat but hardly contributes to clear thinking," as political scientist Robert Johnson aptly characterizes it. Duly alarmed, Carter sternly threatened to use "any means necessary" to counter a further Soviet military move in the area, a threat basically reiterated by his replacement, Ronald Reagan, the next year.[31]

It was the first time Soviet forces had been sent directly into a country outside their empire since 1945. It also proved to be the last, and it soon became a disaster for the international communist movement.

A military coup had brought a Marxist government to Afghanistan in 1978, which the Soviet regime welcomed with aid and 7,000 advisers. However, an anticommunist rebellion soon developed when the new government vigorously instituted political, economic, and antireligious reforms. The rebellion grew stronger as the communist leaders fought among themselves, and the Soviets feared a rebel victory that would set up an intensely hostile regime in this large, neighboring state. Accordingly, they invaded Afghanistan in December 1979, murdered the ruling communist leader, installed a right-thinker of their own choosing in his place, and took over the war themselves. Thus, in the words of Robert Jervis, the invasion "was intended to salvage a faltering client, not to prepare for new adventures."[32]

The Soviets went in with a large contingent of troops, apparently planning to nip the rebellion in the bud and avoiding a long, enervating war like the one the Americans had suffered in Vietnam. Instead, they soon found themselves bogged down in exactly that sort of war. They were up against several groups that regarded it as their holy duty to fight the foreign intervention even if the war took decades. The rebels obtained sanctuary in neighboring Pakistan and were granted various forms of aid, including increasingly sophisticated weapons, from China, the United States, Saudi Arabia, and elsewhere. Their Afghan adventure also severely undercut the credibility and respect the Soviets had sought for decades to develop in the third world, particularly in Muslim areas.[33]

Duly alarmed, Carter (along with many other world leaders) withdrew from the Olympic Games scheduled to be held in Moscow in 1980, and he also essentially scuttled his Strategic Arms Limitation Treaty that had been so carefully negotiated in 1979, even though the invasion of Afghanistan was utterly irrelevant to that issue. This development had been much wished for by Nitze and the Committee on the Present Danger.

Equally irrelevantly, under Carter, and even more so under Reagan (who had been a member of the CPD), the reaction to Afghanistan also included the escalation of the defense budget to counter the supposed Soviet military threat.

Evaluating the Record of Containment

In the second half of the 1980s, under the leadership of Mikhail Gorbachev, the Soviets did mellow their foreign policy decisively, and shortly after that the whole country imploded. It is natural to conclude from this experience that the wisdom of the containment strategy and of the defense buildup has been affirmed. But while those policies *intended* a certain desirable effect, it does not follow that they *caused* it.

Actually, the policy of containment is logically flawed. If the Soviet system really was as rotten as Kennan and others more or less accurately surmised, then the best policy would not have been to contain it, but to give it enough rope: to let it expand until it reached the point of terminal overstretch. Indeed, one of Kennan's favorite quotes comes from Gibbon: "There is nothing more contrary to nature than the attempt to hold in obedience distant provinces."[34] If that is true, an expansive country will discover this lesson faster if it is allowed to gather in new distant provinces than if it is contained. That is, if the goal was to speed the Soviet Union's inevitable rendezvous with its decadent destiny, it might have been wiser—logically, at least—to let it expand to the rotting point.

In fact, what ultimately helped to bring about the mellowing of Soviet expansionism was not containment's success, but its failure. Containment's lapse began in 1975, when three countries—Cambodia,

South Vietnam, and Laos—plunged into the communist camp. Partly out of fear of repeating the Vietnam experience, the United States went into a sort of containment funk, watching from the sidelines as the Soviet Union opportunistically gathered a set of third-world countries into its imperial embrace: Angola in 1976, Mozambique and Ethiopia in 1977, South Yemen and Afghanistan in 1978, Grenada and Nicaragua in 1979. The Soviets at first were quite gleeful about these acquisitions: the "correlation of forces," they concluded, had magically and decisively shifted in their direction.[35]

However, far from whetting their appetite for more, these gains ultimately not only sated their appetite for expansion but, given the special properties of the morsels they happened to consume, the process served to give the ravenous expanders a troubling case of indigestion. By the 1980s, the Soviets' empire in Eastern Europe had already become a severe economic drain and a psychic problem (a development, however, that cannot be credited to Western policy, which had strenuously opposed the occupation from the beginning). Almost all the new acquisitions soon became economic and political basket cases, fraught with dissension, financial mismanagement, and civil warfare. Afghanistan only made the situation worse. As each member of their newly expanded empire turned toward the Soviet Union for maternal warmth and sustenance, many Soviets began to wonder about the wisdom of these ventures. Perhaps, it began to seem, they would have been better off contained.[36]

These problems were a direct result of misguided domestic and foreign policies, and they would have come about no matter what policy the West chose to pursue. Soviet domestic problems derived from decades of mismanagement, mindless brutality, and fundamental misconceptions about basic economic and social realities. Their defense dilemmas came from a conspiratorial worldview that created external enemies and then exaggerated the degree to which the enemies would use war to destroy them. And their foreign policy failures stemmed from a fundamentally flawed, and often highly romantic, conception of the imperatives of history and of the degree to which foreign peoples would find appeal in communism. After forty years of various economic and social disasters, mostly self-inflicted, the Soviets finally were able to rise above ideology and to embrace grim reality under Mikhail Gorbachev in the late 1980s.[37]

The Western policy of containment may have helped to keep some countries free from communism—particularly South Korea—but insofar as it was devised to force the Soviets to confront their inherent contradictions, the history of the cold war suggests a curious paradox. Kennan and the other early containment theorists were correct to conclude that Soviet communism was a singularly undesirable and fundamentally flawed form of government, and they were right to anticipate that it would inevitably have to mellow when it could no longer avoid confronting its inherent contradictions.[38] But Soviet communism might have reached this point somewhat earlier if its natural propensity to expand had been tolerated rather than contained.

Militarization: The Arms Race

In retrospect, one of the greatest tragedies, or perhaps absurdities, of the cold war concerns the incredible amounts of money each side felt itself compelled to expend in a frantic effort to build up arms to deter or, if worse came to worst, to fight the other. To service extravagant worst-case fears and fantasies, trillions of dollars and rubles were expended on unnecessary weaponry while millions of young men were pulled out of productive roles in the economy to serve in the bloated arms services.[39] There was a contest during the cold war, and, given the Korean experience, some deterrent military buildup was sensible. But a direct military confrontation between the two chief contestants was never really in the cards. Neither ever saw that as a remotely sensible option and both determinedly avoided it.

Major war seemed most close during the Cuban Missile Crisis of 1962. But even in this case, as two analysts who have worked with the transcripts of the American meetings have observed, even if the Soviets had held out for a deal that was substantially embarrassing to the United States, the odds that the Americans would have gone to war "were next to zero." Although there were some dicey moments, particularly in the first day or so, Khrushchev saw the horrors of potential war before him and had no intention of working closer toward that calamity. For his part, President Kennedy, haunted by the way world war had erupted in 1914, had no intention of being a central character in a repetition, and he was apparently quite willing to consider formally removing some U.S. missiles if that is what it took to get the Cuban missiles out. For their part, the Soviets never even went on a demonstration alert. It's very difficult, as war historian Evan Luard has suggested, to have a war when no one has the slightest desire to get into one.[40]

A nuclear World War III is one of those low-probability/high-consequence issues about which people tend to obsess. Or at least they used to obsess about it. They no longer do so very much, even though the weapons themselves continue to exist in large numbers. At some point, obviously, probabilities become so low that focusing, and spending massively, on seeking to prevent the great disasters one can imagine becomes exquisite self-indulgence and profoundly foolish policy. In the cold war, it now seems, both sides spent nearly a half-century wallowing in such folly. It proved to be a colossal waste.

DEALING WITH THE ENEMY WITHIN

A more credible threat presented by international communism derived not from its military potential that so alarmed people like Nitze, but rather from its judicious and determined encouragement of agitation, sabotage, conspiracy, internal subversion, espionage, and focused revolutionary violence, all with the goal of undermining and ultimately destroying both democracy and capitalism in other countries.

The communists were secretive neither about their favored methods nor about their ultimate goals; indeed, these were central to their ideological worldview. Moreover, in some places—quite strikingly in Russia in 1917, in Czechoslovakia in 1948, and in Cuba after 1959—they were variously successful in working from within to topple unfriendly regimes or to seduce friendly ones.

There was great concern during the cold war that these techniques could be applied in the United States, and, for many, the small Communist Party within the United States seemed a potential threat. However, the likelihood that domestic communists and their sympathizers could severely damage the United States proved to be much inflated. A tiny fringe group, it never garnered more than microscopic support within the United States, and its successes proved to be few, fleeting, inconsequential, and ultimately self-destructive.

The Rise of Fear: McCarthyism

Fears about the threat posed by domestic communism rose as evidence supplied by defecting American and Canadian communists in 1945 and 1946 suggested that the operatives of the Communist Party really did generally believe in the conspiratorial revolutionary ideology that filled their speeches, directives, and publications. The Moscow-oriented Communist Party in the United States had never been large, but in the first decade of the cold war it inspired a great deal of comment and concern because of its perceived links to the Soviet enemy and because of its espousal of a threateningly subversive ideology.[41]

The quest for "the enemy within" was put into high gear and became a prominent preoccupation after a few spectacular espionage cases came to light. In the late 1940s, a respected former State Department official, Alger Hiss, was accused of having earlier sent huge quantities of classified documents to the Soviets. Hiss denied this allegation under oath and was then convicted of perjury. The Hiss conviction was controversial, but other State Department officials were also accused of such dealings and confessed to them, so the possibility of spies and traitors in high office was never really at issue. In the immediate postwar period more than 200 State Department officials were fired or eased out of office because of security concerns. Then a former communist, British physicist Klaus Fuchs, admitted that he had sent atomic secrets to the Soviets during World War II—though it now appears that the Soviets did not require this or other purloined material to establish and develop their atomic bomb program. His trail soon led to the arrests of others in his spy ring and ultimately to the dramatic trial of two Americans, Julius and Ethel Rosenberg, who were convicted as atomic spies.[42]

The issue was extensively and successfully exploited by various politicians, particularly Senator Joseph McCarthy, but it reflected a genuine concern that the experience in Korea made alarmingly palpable. Because there was an international linkage among communists, and because communism now seemed to be willing to use aggressive warfare as a tool, many concluded that American communists were devoted to a system dedicated not only to the revolutionary overthrow of the U.S. government but also ultimately to a direct invasion of the U.S. homeland. It was under the impetus of the Korean War that the omnibus McCarran Act of 1950, one of the most repressive pieces of anticommunist legislation, was resoundingly passed over Truman's veto, most of it later to be declared unconstitutional. The act included a scheme put forward by Senate *liberals* to establish camps for imprisoning domestic communists in the event of national emergency. The execution of the Rosenbergs in 1953 would probably never have taken place had the Korean War not occurred.

Concern was understandable, but extrapolating extensively from the Hiss and Rosenberg cases, as it turns out, was not. One of the big fears at the time (rather as for terrorists today) was that Party members would engage in, or facilitate, acts of sabotage, particularly of defense plants. No such acts ever took place at any time. In addition, although, as the Hiss and Rosenberg cases demonstrated, the Party was linked to some acts of espionage during World War II (when the Soviet Union was an ally), it apparently engaged in none after the war.

The (Very Slow) Decline of Fear of Domestic Communists

As Figure 2 indicates, domestic communism attracted a great deal of press in the early and middle 1950s, the high point of the McCarthy era. But this interest declined thereafter, and press attention to the enemy within had pretty much vanished by the 1970s. This may reflect in part the diminution of the American Communist Party itself: estimates of its membership run to 80,000 in 1945, 54,000 in early 1950, 25,000 in 1953, 20,000 in 1955, and only 3,000 in 1958.[43] Moreover, as time went by, FBI informants probably constituted an increasing percentage of that membership.

Interestingly, however, even though press attention to the threat (if any) posed by domestic communists greatly diminished, even though the Party itself essentially ceased to exist, and even though there were no more dramatic, attention-arresting revelations like those of the Hiss and Rosenberg cases, public concern about the danger posed by domestic communism declined only gradually. In 1954, at the zenith of the McCarthy era, some 42 percent of the public held American communists to be a great or very great danger, and 2 percent held them to be no danger at all. Ten years later, this had not changed all that much: 38 percent still saw danger, and only 6 percent saw none at all. When the relevant poll question was last asked, in the mid-1970s, around 30 percent continued to envision danger, and around 10 percent saw none.

Figure 2: Domestic Communism:
the press and the public, 1940-1985

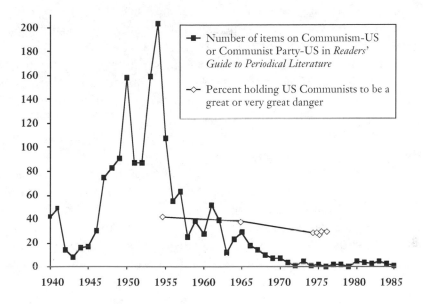

The public opinion data do track a decline of concern, but the slowness with which that decline took place is quite remarkable. Of course, the cold war did very much continue during the period surveyed, but credible (or even noncredible) suggestions that domestic communism was much of anything to worry about became almost nonexistent, as did press attention to the issue. Yet concern about this "danger" diminished only gradually.

The phenomenon suggests there is a great deal in dramatic first impressions: once a perceived threat is thoroughly implanted in the public consciousness, it can become internalized and accepted as a fact of life. Eventually, it may become a mellowed irrelevance, but unless there is a decisive eradication of the threat itself (as presumably happened in 1945 for the "threat" posed by domestic Japanese) the process can take decades.

INTERNATIONAL COMMUNISM AND INTERNATIONAL TERRORISM

The experience with international communism during the cold war resonates with, relates to, or contrasts instructively with, a number of current concerns about international terrorism.

Despite some of the contemporary alarmist rhetoric about terrorism detailed in Chapter 2, the threat posed by international communism was far more nearly "existential" than anything presented today by international terrorists—or by earlier ones either, such as the anarchists who caused such tumult and destructive overreaction in the United States early in the twentieth century.[44]

To begin with, the Soviets and their allies possessed a far greater capacity to do military damage than even the most ingenious and well-heeled terrorist groups today can dream of. Those who fear the terrorist use of nuclear weapons imagine them with perhaps a few unreliable bombs of Hiroshima size or less, whereas the Soviet Union (like contemporary Russia) had a nuclear arsenal many thousands of times larger.[45]

There are, however, key differences between international terrorism and international communism in this respect. As noted earlier, it was never communism's goal to do damage for the sake of doing damage. Indeed, it has been a central point in this chapter that direct warfare with the major capitalist states, with or without nuclear weapons, was seen by communists to be profoundly foolish and was never really in their game plan. That is, they may have had an enormous capacity to inflict damage, but they lacked the will and desire to do so. By contrast, at least some terrorist groups do seem to want to destroy for the sake of destruction, and if they were to acquire nuclear weapons, they would presumably be inclined to use them. In addition, because their atomic arsenal was clearly and unambiguously state-based, the communists were comparatively deterrable (insofar as deterrence was necessary) because their cold war opponents could credibly promise unacceptable retaliation against specific and highly valued targets in their enemy's homeland. International terrorism does not provide such convenient targets.

A more relevant comparison between international communism and international terrorism therefore derives from communism's ability to subvert and to stir up government-threatening civil violence. Indeed, in a number of states, communists had successfully applied such techniques to abolish an old order and to establish a new one of their own, one that proved in a large number of cases to be hugely destructive and deadly.[46] In this, they possessed not only a proven capacity, but the will—indeed, the duty as they saw it—to apply it, and their ultimate goal was forcefully to eradicate capitalism and democracy from the face of the earth. Today's terrorists present no comparable threat.

Instructively, there was a tendency to inflate *both* the will and the capacity of the communist enemy. This was particularly the case with respect to the Soviet military threat. The numbers were exaggerated or massively extrapolated, and, in particular, the Soviet willingness to embrace losses and to accept risks was continually, and often absurdly, overestimated. But there were exaggerations as well with respect to its subversive capacity, and this experience may be more relevant to current concerns about terrorism: although the communists possessed the will and some of the skills to overthrow Western democracy and capitalism (and, as noted, had a notable, if limited, record of success in some areas of the world), it is clear in retrospect that concerns about their capacity to do so were much inflated.

Moreover, as with terrorism, there was often a tendency to embrace a challenging episode as a harbinger and then to overreact. As it happened, Kennan was right: the communist system did carry the seeds of its own destruction. What was called for was not hasty, expensive, and often bloody response, but patience. History was clearly not on the side of the communists (including Castro), but of their prey. Nonetheless, dramatic events frequently caused decision makers to embrace doomsday warnings they had previously dismissed as overly alarmist and expensive, even though the dramatic events' relevance to those warnings was tenuous at best. Extrapolating from the Hiss and Rosenberg cases to conclude that the country's officialdom was riddled with traitors proved to be foolish and harmful. Korea was not a sure indicator that the communist challenge had turned irretrievably military (much less that domestic subversives were everywhere), but the Truman administration nonetheless quickly embraced a report essentially suggesting that it had. *Sputnik* did not mean the Soviet Union had suddenly become the wave of the future, but the reaction to it suggested that American decision makers had succumbed to such fears. The Soviet Union's ultimately pathetic and self-destructive intervention in Afghanistan had absolutely nothing to do with issues concerning the strategic arms race, but the venture was somehow taken to suggest that alarmist tracts about Soviet military superiority were sound. In a similar manner, 9/11 has played into the hands of WMD fearmongers even though the hijackers applied no weapons more lethal—or massive—than box cutters.

In addition, the experience of the cold war suggests that fears can eventually recede when they cease to garner much attention and remain unfed by dramatic disclosures for a sufficient—if perhaps sometimes rather considerable—period of time. Thus concerns about the communist enemy within did finally begin to fade after the height of the McCarthy period in the 1950s, even though the Soviets and the Chinese remained as devoted to internal subversion and revolution as they ever had been. In time, perhaps fears of terrorism will similarly begin to fade. However, the experience with lingering concerns about the dangers posed by domestic communism—internalized after dramatic first impressions—suggests it may be a long wait, perhaps one of decades.

Finally, another resonance with the post-9/11 response to terrorism in the United States (and also to the country's earlier overreaction to perils presumed to be presented by anarchists before World War I, communists in the "Red Scare" period after it, and Japanese Americans during World War II) concerns the quest for enemies within. Despite continuous dire warnings, despite the fact that there have been thousands of arrests, and despite the fact that law enforcement agencies are preoccupied with the hunt for infiltrated terrorists, no true terrorist "sleeper cells" have yet been uncovered. There has been terrorist activity in various places around the world, and there have been a few lone-wolf incidents within the country as well as the arrest of a few homegrown jihadi dreamers. These may be matters of concern. But they, thus far at least, do not indicate the existence of a brilliant, diabolical, and capable domestic enemy. It is almost enough to tempt one to apply the experience with the quest for domestic communists: perhaps there is little or nothing to find, and the quest is a very substantial waste of money and effort.[47]

CHAPTER 5

Nuclear Fears, Cold War Terrorism, and Devils du Jour

Throughout the cold war, the central focus remained on the threat presented by international communism, but there were also other anxieties that proved to be based on inflated fears and ill-founded extrapolation. One of these was concern about the imminence of thermonuclear war. A popular obsession in the first couple of decades of the cold war, it dissipated in the 1960s and 1970s even as the arms race continued or even accelerated, and then surged again for a while in the 1980s—not by notable changes in doctrine or in the weapons balance, but by rhetorical flourishes and domestic political machinations. There were also anxieties over a few unpleasant noisy dictators in third-world countries who proved to be devils du jour rather than reincarnations of Hitler. Finally, there were some episodes of international terrorism that sometimes (but, interestingly, not always) inspired obsession and deadly overreaction.[1]

NUCLEAR ANXIETIES

The terrorist attacks of September 11, 2001, have inspired a great deal of apocalyptic posturing and hand-wringing. Much of this is reminiscent of concern during the cold war that somehow a new world war was all but inevitable because nuclear weapons existed and because nuclear East and nuclear West were deeply hostile to each other. The common images were of the dangling sword of Damocles and of the death fight of two scorpions in a bottle.

Nuclear Fear during the Classic Cold War

These fears were set in motion in the aftermath of World War II and flourished at first during what might be called the classic cold war period, which ended in 1963. World War II had not brought about the annihilation of the human race or of European civilization that many in the 1930s had anticipated.[2] However, it came far closer than any previous war and certainly closer than anybody could reasonably find comfortable. The war also generated the atomic bomb, which promised destruction on a new and much heightened scale. By simple extrapolation, doomsday became a vivid nightmare.

In 1950 historian Arnold Toynbee authoritatively proclaimed, "In our recent Western history war has been following war in an ascending order of intensity; and today it is already apparent that the War of 1939–45 was not the climax of this crescendo movement." Stalin himself said he anticipated that Germany would revive fairly rapidly, after which Germany and the USSR would fight again. In 1945, Ambassador Joseph Grew, one of America's most perceptive diplomats, concluded that "a future war with the Soviet Union is as certain as anything in this world." Public opinion polls conducted in the United States in the mid-1940s characteristically found very substantial percentages opining that the next world war would occur within twenty-five years.[3]

Fears like that continued to be pronounced over the next decade and a half. In 1960, for example, strategist and futurist Herman Kahn wrote, "I have a firm belief that unless we have more serious and sober thought on various aspects of the strategic problem . . . we are not going to reach the year 2000—and maybe not even the year 1965—without a cataclysm."[4] There were also continual, if almost entirely unfulfilled, anxieties about the proliferation of nuclear weapons.

For many, the war and the bomb engendered a profound sense of despair: not only had the human race invented new and even more effective methods for devastating itself, but it also seemed utterly incapable of controlling its own destiny. World War I, for all its horror, had often seemed to carry with it the potential for an equally great postwar healing. By destroying militarism and the warring nation-state system, thought many, it might be "the war that will end war," as futurist H. G. Wells entitled a 1914 tract. Rarely in the course of human affairs has a prophecy proved to be so spectacularly in error. Despite the experience of that costly conflict, despite the revulsion with war that it inspired, and despite the deep yearnings for peace felt by practically all enlightened people at its conclusion, the human race, and particularly civilized Europe, managed to plunge into an even worse war a mere twenty years later.

In the last years before his death in 1946, Wells, ill and deeply embittered, abandoned his lifelong celebration of human progress to prophesy inevitable and inescapable doom. In his last writings he declared that "the end of everything we call life is close at hand and cannot be evaded," and that mankind was "the most foolish vermin that have ever overrun the earth." His epitaph, he told friends, should read: "God damn you all: I told you so."[5]

With some desperation, schemes were formulated at the war's end to try to invalidate such gloomy sentiments. Some Western scientists, apparently consumed with guilt over having participated in the development of a weapon that could kill with much heightened effectiveness, helped found the *Bulletin of the Atomic Scientists* in 1945. It soon sported its "doomsday clock" on the cover, suggesting that there was hope of preventing Armageddon, but only if we were quick about it. The clock has remained poised at a few minutes before midnight ever since. (Amazingly, in 2006 the *Bulletin* launched a subscription campaign boldly and unapologetically built around the slogan "Dispensing facts instead of fear for over sixty years.")

Led by the legendary Albert Einstein, many of these scientists quickly came to conclusions expressed with an evangelical certainty they would never have used in discussing the physical world. "As long as there are sovereign nations possessing great power," Einstein declared, "war is inevitable." And "Only the creation of a world government can prevent the impending self-destruction of mankind." Or, as Edward Teller, a physicist who was later to be instrumental in the development of the hydrogen bomb, put it in 1946, world government "alone can give us freedom and peace." Philosopher Bertrand Russell was equally certain. "It is entirely clear," he declared, "that there is only one way in which great wars can be permanently prevented and that is the establishment of an international government with a monopoly of serious armed force."[6] Disarmament and arms control schemes were formulated with ever increasing ingenuity and debated with ever increasing sophistication.

As it happens, peace between the major countries was maintained, but the United Nations deserves little credit for it, and disarmament and world government none at all.

Nuclear Fear Subsides: The 1960s and 1970s

In was in 1961 that C. P. Snow published his alarmist broadside proclaiming it a "certainty" that if the nuclear arms race between the United States and the USSR were to continue and accelerate, a nuclear bomb would go off "within, at the most, ten years."[7] None did. Indeed, within, at the most, three years after Snow's sobering pronouncement, anxiety about nuclear cataclysm began to subside in the aftermath of the Cuban Missile Crisis with the signing of two arms control agreements between the United States and the Soviet Union. Neither agreement reduced either side's nuclear capacity in the slightest, indeed, the two cold war contenders continued very substantially to embellish their nuclear arsenals both quantitatively and qualitatively. But the generally improved diplomatic atmosphere between the two scorpions engendered a considerable relaxation in fear that they would actually use their expensive weapons against each other.

Accordingly, whereas more than 400 articles per year on nuclear-related topics are listed in the *Readers' Guide to Periodical Literature* for 1961, 1962, and 1963, output dropped to fewer than 200 in 1964 and to about 120 in 1967. Polls reflect a similar change. Before 1963, the various polling agencies had regularly asked the public if it expected another world war within the foreseeable future. Reflecting declining interest in the issue, the agencies largely abandoned the question after 1963, and when they did manage to bring the issue up, they found the public far less concerned about war than earlier. Political scientist Rob Paarlberg has aptly called the phenomenon "forgetting about the unthinkable."[8]

In a book published in 1988, Spencer Weart characterized it as an "astonishing event" and "the only well-documented case in history when most of the world's citizens suddenly stopped paying attention to facts that continued to threaten their very survival."[9] Shortly after Weart's book was published, the "astonishing event" was to repeat itself.

Nuclear Fear Revives: The Early 1980s

First, however, anxiety about thermonuclear war became all the rage again.

In 1979, prominent realist political scientist Hans J. Morgenthau proclaimed that "the world is moving ineluctably towards a third world war—a strategic nuclear war. I do not believe that anything can be done to prevent it. The international system is simply too unstable to survive for long." In the same year, British General John Hackett published a gloomily imaginative book, *The Third World War: August 1985*. Such hair-raising utterances were still comparatively unusual at that time, but in short order the unthinkable exploded back into popular consciousness. As before, people didn't like what they found themselves thinking about. Accordingly, they launched protests, signed petitions, and organized marches. Between 1972 and 1978 the number of items on nuclear and disarmament issues in the *Readers' Guide* had averaged 71 per year; in 1981 it jumped to 318, and in 1983 it hit 665.[10]

Some of this consciousness raising, one might think, could be attributed to the vast increases in strategic nuclear arsenals that occurred after the Test Ban Treaty of 1963. Both sides built up their intercontinental ballistic missile forces until each had more than 1,000, and both also vastly increased their stock of submarine missiles. More menacingly, major improvements in missile accuracy were being made, and it had become technologically feasible to put more than one warhead on a single missile; together, these developments raised the ominous, if theoretical, possibility that one side, or both, could achieve a "first-strike capability," at least against the other's land-based missiles.[11]

But these developments don't really explain the rise of nuclear consciousness of the early 1980s. The new, vastly expanded arsenals had been in place for a decade at least, and the peculiar dilemma posed by the existence of accurate multiple-warhead missiles was neither new nor well appreciated by the protesters. Rather, it was a relatively minor weapons development—the proposed implantation by NATO of a few hundred shorter-range missiles in Europe—that triggered much of the phenomenon. Political opportunism, in both the West and the East, played its part, too.

As part of an expensive nuclear arms buildup that had begun after the Cuban Missile Crisis of 1962, Leonid Brezhnev's Soviet Union began adding sophisticated new intermediate-range (3,000 miles) triple-warhead missiles to its arsenal in Europe. The NATO countries became alarmed because they had nothing comparable, and in 1979 they scheduled the deployment of similar countervailing weapons unless the Soviets could be prevailed upon to limit their missiles.[12]

Talks on this issue were ambling on unproductively when Ronald Reagan became president of the United States in 1981. Almost instantly he began to strike a lot of people as a fire-breathing warmonger. He announced that he would substantially build up U.S. military forces (expanding the policy of his predecessor, Jimmy Carter) and would seek to develop a strategy so that the United States might manage to come out ahead, or "prevail," in a nuclear war (basically continuing a policy developed by Kennedy, elaborated by Richard Nixon, and accepted by Carter). Reagan also speculated about the possibility of having an exchange of nuclear weapons in, for example, Europe, without either the United States or the USSR becoming a target—one of those small, self-evident truths, largely enshrined in NATO doctrine, that no previous president had so foolishly and so baldly expressed in public before, having preferred the politic suggestion that any sizable Soviet attack would necessarily escalate to strategic nuclear war. At about the same time, Reagan's secretary of state, Alexander Haig, came up with the well-seasoned observation that in response to a conventional attack by the Soviets in Europe the United States might lob a nuclear bomb or two in their direction "for demonstrative purposes."[13]

A lot of Europeans were appalled, and soon they had convinced themselves that Reagan was going to drag them into a war and then watch calmly from the sidelines as the war was fought out to the last radiated European: "Euroshima," one creative pamphleteer called it.[14] By the end of Reagan's first year in office, mass demonstrations aimed at preventing the installation of the new NATO missiles were regularly staged in several European countries.

The antinuclear movement also caught on in the United States, and a 1982 *New Yorker* essay and book by Jonathan Schell, both entitled "The Fate of the Earth," served as its focal point. Schell passionately, if repetitively, argued the not entirely novel proposition that nuclear war would be terrible, and concluded ominously, "One day—and it is hard to believe that it will not be soon—we will make our choice. Either we will sink into the final coma and end it all or, as I trust and believe, we will awaken to the truth of our peril . . . and rise up to cleanse the earth of nuclear weapons." Schell was far from alone. The *Cumulative Book Index* indicates that while fewer than sixteen books on nuclear issues were published in the four-year period from 1977 to 1980, there were twenty-five in 1981, fifty-four in 1982, and eighty in 1983. In one of them, historian William McNeill asserted that unless there was global control over atomic weaponry, there would likely be "sudden and total annihilation of the human species." The Catholic bishops issued an airy pastoral letter declaring that it may be okay to threaten mass destruction but only if you didn't plan to do it. Brown University students voted 1,044 to 687 to demand that the student health service stock suicide pills for mass use in the event of a nuclear attack. As late as the mid-1980s, 20 to 37 percent of the American population told pollsters that they held the potential for nuclear war to be the most important problem facing the country.[15]

The Decline, Again, of Nuclear Fear

The protests neither changed the 1979 NATO decision nor Reagan's determination to implement it.[16] By the mid-1980s the Soviets were becoming distinctly aware that they were in deep trouble in many areas. The economic, military, and ideological excesses of the Brezhnev era were catching up with them, and soon Gorbachev led them out of the cold war.

Huge numbers of nuclear weapons continue to exist in the arsenals of East and West, but fears they will be massively slung at each other have vanished. We have neither cleansed the earth of nuclear weapons nor descended into Schell's "final coma." Apocalypse never came, though Schell himself continues to be alarmed about the possibility.[17] In short, anxieties about thermonuclear destruction have not correlated at all well with objective factors such as the size of nuclear arsenals. The United States and the USSR were far more capable of pulverizing each other with nuclear weapons in the 1970s than in the 1950s, or in the 1990s than in the 1980s. Nuclear fears have waxed and waned for other reasons.

DEVILS DU JOUR

Nuclear annihilation and cold war confrontation were not the only worries of the era. The experience with underestimating the threat posed by Adolf Hitler in the 1930s haunted perceptions in other ways as well. Robert Jervis has pointed out that "Hitlers are very rare."[18] Nonetheless, there have been, and continue to be, quite a few national leaders who have been compared to Hitler with great alarm since the conclusion of Hitler's war. As it turned out, in no case has the comparison been remotely justified. All proved to be merely devils du jour: as Shakespeare's Macbeth might put it, poor players who strutted and fretted their hour upon the world stage and then were heard no more.

Some of these were connected rather directly to the cold war. One was Yugoslavia's Josip Tito: for a few years after World War II, Yugoslavia was perhaps the most dynamically ideological and confrontational communist country in the world. This condition abruptly changed when, for various reasons, Tito and his party were summarily excommunicated from the international communist movement in 1948. In desperation, Tito sought accommodation with the West, which responded almost immediately, supplying aid year after year to this former devil. It was soon declaring that Yugoslavia was "of direct importance to the defense of the North Atlantic area" and that Yugoslavia's ability to defend itself "was important to the security of the United States." For a while Yugoslavia, in fact, was close to becoming an informal participant in NATO.[19]

North Korea's Kim Il-sung was another communist devil and remained so for the entire cold war. However, he was not usually considered to be all that much of an independent player—rather more of a puppet of Moscow and sometimes Beijing.

Cuba's Castro also enjoyed devil du jour status, particularly in the 1960s and 1970s, and was taken to be something of an independent actor especially with respect to Latin America and, later and to a somewhat lesser degree, Africa. His star faded even before the cold war did. Still, in part because of the political leverage exerted by Cuban exiles in a swing state, Florida, he continues to be shunned and routinely pilloried by the United States long after he has ceased to be even a metaphorical threat. A close colleague of Castro's, the Argentinean Che Guevara, a stateless revolutionary who might form a kind of precursor in perceived deviltry to Osama bin Laden, beguiled spotters of devils du jour for years. They harbored visions of the colorful demon popping up hither and yon—in the Dominican Republic in 1965, for example—until he was captured, ill, in the company of a tiny band of failed revolutionaries in Bolivia in 1967 and killed by the police there. Che sightings, like Elvis sightings, continue, but his aura is mostly represented now on fading T-shirts and crumbling posters. Some American officials fancied a Castro-like threat in Chile's Salvador Allende, and they were greatly relieved when he was deposed in a coup in 1973.

But several diverting devils du jour during the cold war were, for the most part, unconnected to the communist enemy, though in some cases they were seen to be leaning that way or (probably correctly) to be trying to play off one side in the cold war against the other. In part, they set the stage for the "rogue state" phenomenon (or obsession) that was to emerge after the cold war. Several of these characters deserve specific consideration.

Egypt's Nasser

Anthony Eden, Britain's prime minister in the early 1950s, had been present at, and was substantially traumatized by, Britain's appeasement of Hitler in Munich in 1938. He was strongly inclined to see a contemporary reflection in the antics of the new president of Egypt, Gamal Abdel Nasser, who in 1956 seized the Suez Canal that runs through his country but was supposed to remain under international control. Eden was outraged: "Some say that Nasser is not Hitler," he mused, but "allowing for differences in scale, I am not so sure. He has followed Hitler's pattern." Concluding from his experience that "it is important to reduce the stature of the megalomaniacal dictator at an early stage," he coordinated with the French and sent troops into the area to reestablish international control over the canal.[20] The venture proved to be a fiasco, as international and domestic pressure forced the invaders to back down and, ultimately, to turn the canal over to Nasser. Eden was swept from office, and when he penned his memoirs, he entitled them, appropriately, *Full Circle*.

The Americans had been among those who opposed the British-French venture at Suez, but they, too, soon came to see Nasser as a threat. Under what was called the Eisenhower Doctrine, the United

States even sent troops to Lebanon in 1958 to police a civil war there that seemed likely to be won by Nasserites. Nasser himself cut quite a swath through the history of the Middle East over the next decade, but then he stumbled into a very short war with Israel in 1967 in which his forces essentially collapsed and his vainglorious pretensions were substantially undercut. He died, comparatively quietly, in 1970.

Indonesia's Sukarno

Led by its mercurial president for life, Sukarno, who had a penchant for self-intoxicating rhetoric, Indonesia embarked in the 1960s on a clamorous policy of hostility—or as Sukarno dubbed it, "confrontation"—toward the West and toward its Western-oriented neighbors. Through threat and tantrum he managed to wrest the western half of New Guinea from its Dutch overseers in 1962, and in 1963, apparently as much on impulse as anything else, he launched a "Crush Malaysia" campaign that led in 1964 to a noisy, if ill-fated, guerrilla attack on his newly decolonized neighbor. To one alarmed member of Congress, Sukarno had become a "minor-league Hitler." [21]

By early 1965, Sukarno had piloted his country into an informal alliance with Mao's China, and shortly after a visit from the Chinese foreign minister, he came up with a snappy, if rather extravagant new slogan: "Crush America." Then, in what Mao called a "bold revolutionary move," Sukarno dramatically withdrew Indonesia from the United Nations and set up a rival organization. The Chinese suggested that they would join, helped Sukarno to begin building an appropriately grandiose complex to house the new organization, and, some evidence suggests, toyed with the idea of testing an atomic bomb in Indonesia and letting Sukarno take the credit for it. [22]

It was at that time that Lyndon Johnson was making his crucial decisions about sending U.S. combat troops to Vietnam. What impressed him was that South Vietnam seemed to be wedged strategically—and vulnerably—between the glowering Chinese and the clamorous Indonesians. For his part, Sukarno continued to stir the pot by explaining that the strategy for defeating imperialism was to have Communist China "strike a blow against the American troops in Vietnam from the north while Indonesia would strike from the south." In his autobiography, Johnson reprints that statement and supplies a map of Southeast

Asia with ominous black arrows projecting downward from China and North Vietnam and upward from Indonesia. He describes the phenomenon as "Communist pincers."[23]

Soon, however, devil du jour Sukarno abruptly left the world stage, and outsiders made little contribution to the exit. He proclaimed 1965 to be "the Year of Living Dangerously," and in the fall of that year the communists in Indonesia, apparently with his blessing and with Chinese encouragement, launched a clandestine effort to eliminate major anticommunist leaders in the army. The maneuver failed spectacularly: there was a violent counterreaction in which hundreds of thousands of people, including the Party's leaders, were killed. Within weeks the Party had been destroyed, Sukarno reduced to a figurehead, and the nation's foreign policy redirected toward neutrality and the West.[24]

That development, reflected Defense Secretary Robert McNamara later, substantially reduced American stakes in Vietnam.[25] But by that time, America's troops had been sent in. The country's descent into its greatest foreign policy debacle, then, was in part the result of an overreaction to a foolish and ultimately pathetic devil du jour.

Libya's Qaddafi

Colonel Muammar Qaddafi, Libya's resident dictator, achieved devil du jour status by the 1980s. A committed, if self-styled and somewhat flaky, revolutionary, he was good at spouting hostile rhetoric aimed at other Arab and African states, at the United States, and at Israel. He was also unapologetic about supporting terrorism as a method for, as he saw it, improving the world.[26]

Libya was never the most notable state sponsor of terrorism during the cold war, but it had in Qaddafi terrorism's noisiest and most colorful spokesman and, because it was isolated from the Arab world, the country could be attacked with little risk of wider political ramifications. At any rate, the Reagan administration increasingly focused its attention on that particular renegade, and, by 1986, had determined the distant, militarily feeble Libya somehow to have become a threat to America's "national security" (a conclusion giving evidence of a considerable capacity for fantasy—or paranoia) and to its "foreign policy" (perhaps true, but only because the United States let it become so). Qaddafi was fully up to the rhetorical challenge: he bellowed that "a state of war" existed between his little country and the United States, that all U.S. and NATO bases within reach were to be legitimate targets, and, shades of Osama, that "all Arab people" should attack anything American, "be it an interest, goods, ship, plane or a person."[27]

Eager to "do something" about terrorism, Reagan in 1986 bombed Libya with planes launched from Britain after terrorists linked to Libya had set off an explosion in a Berlin discotheque, killing two people, one of them American. After the bombing, in which one plane crashed and scores of people were killed (none of them Qaddafi), Reagan triumphantly proclaimed, "No one can kill Americans and brag about it. No one. We bear the people of Libya no ill will, but if their Government continues its campaign of terror against Americans, we will act again."[28]

The bombing raid, Middle East specialist Ray Takeyh points out, enhanced Qaddafi domestically and caused him to be lionized in the developing world. But it did have at least two desirable effects: other countries became more wary about cooperating with Qaddafi, and he reined in his rhetoric and ceased to "brag about it." However, he continued to *do* it: as the arch terrorism foe of Reagan's administration, George Shultz, wistfully noted later of the raid, "On the other hand, it didn't stop him." In rather short order Libyan agents had murdered an American and two Britons held hostage in another country and launched several other attacks, including an attempted bombing of a U.S. officers' club in Turkey and the attempted assassination of an American diplomat in Sudan. And then, two years later, Libya participated in the bombing of a Pan Am airliner over Lockerbie, Scotland, that killed 270, 187 of them American, and toppled the airline company into bankruptcy.[29]

Perhaps because Qaddafi wisely didn't "brag about it"—indeed, he denied any complicity in these attacks—no retaliation took place despite Reagan's ringing boast to "act again" if Libyan terrorism were to continue. Instead, despite all the previous huffing and puffing about terrorism, it proved quite possible politically to "do nothing"—that is, simply to rely on police work to go after the culprits. Three years after the Lockerbie attack investigators were lucky enough to find evidence that led to the indictment of two Libyan agents, and eventually they were found guilty of the bombing. Without that luck, however, nothing presumably would ever have been done about this terrorist act. With the indictments, the Americans were able to convince many in the international community to slap economic sanctions on Libya. Although there is considerable reason to believe Iran and Syria were also involved in the Lockerbie bombing, they remain unpunished.[30]

In time, devil du jour Qaddafi mellowed. As the cold war ended, he became isolated and his ideas came to be seen as anachronistic. By the end of the 1990s, he had rebounded and was amiably blowing with a new wind: "We cannot stand in the way of progress. . . . The fashion now is free markets and investments. . . . The world has changed radically and drastically . . . and being a revolutionary and a progressive man, I have to follow this movement." His tent was no longer host to guerrilla leaders and terrorists, but to investment consultants and Internet executives, and he began to seek to mediate crises in Africa rather than exacerbating them. Economic travail encouraged this development. The sanctions were a component in this, as was the depressed price of Libya's main export, oil, at the time.[31] But it is not at all clear they were essential to the transformation.

In the new century Qaddafi welcomed a new American president warmly, albeit with questionable prescience: "I believe that George W. Bush will be nice." He is not "malicious or imperialist" and "does not have world ambitions." In 2003, Qaddafi agreed to abandon his rather limited programs for weapons of mass destruction (mainly chemical ones), a development caused, claimed the Bush administration, by its not-so-nice invasion of Iraq in that year, but it was one that had been in the cards for years and, others argue, would have come about anyway. In fact, Qaddafi had agreed to do the same thing in 1999, but had been turned down at the time until other issues, particularly ones concerning compensation to the families of people killed on the downed Pan Am airliner, were resolved.[32]

It seems highly likely that devil du jour Qaddafi would have faded even as an imaginary threat—and a few hundred fewer people would have been killed—if his irritating rhetoric and antics had been treated with patience rather than with unnecessary, even hysterical, overreaction.

Iran's Khomeini and His Hostages

In 1979, Iran was taken over in a mostly bloodless revolution by a fundamentalist Muslim group presided over by the often opaque Ayatollah Ruhollah Khomeini. He quickly became a devil du jour when fifty-two

American diplomatic personnel were taken hostage by supporters of his unstable, ill-directed regime in November. The United States then endured over a year—444 days, by the exacting count used at the time—of official and popular angst until the hostages were returned safely after months of circuitous negotiation.

The extravagant slogan preposterously, but popularly, applied to the episode by the media, "America Held Hostage," suggests the degree to which a relatively minor incident was overblown. Commonly, the episode has been taken as one in which the United States was somehow "humiliated."[33] If so, that primarily came from the way the American people and their leaders handled the episode, not from the essence of the event itself.

When he penned his autobiography, President Jimmy Carter remained preoccupied with the crisis, characterizing it dramatically as "one of the most intricate financial and political problems ever faced by any nation." At stake, he points out, were "the lives of 52 precious human beings" as well as "almost 12 billion dollars of Iranian assets."[34] Looked at broadly, the crisis, however "intricate," seems hardly to have been worth the obsession. At the time the country was losing fifty-two lives every eleven hours on its highways, and the federal government was spending $12 billion about every week. Without being cavalier about the understandable concern for the safety of the hostages, it seems reasonable to point out that the chief foreign policy importance of the hostage taking was that the forcible detention of diplomats was being sanctioned by a *government*. Foreign relations have depended for centuries on the notion that diplomats, even in wartime, will be immune from such persecution. Had the Iranian government's policy become commonplace, the whole fabric of international relations might have broken down. But, of course, it quickly became apparent that nothing like this was going to happen. The Iranian situation was essentially unique: a bizarre, pointless, self-destructive act by a fanatical government that had only a very tentative grasp on reality, on its supporters, or on its own destiny.

Nonetheless, the issue became all-consumingly important to the leaders and the media of the most powerful nation in history, even though giving it so much attention had the perverse effect of increasing the Iranian regime's prestige among its supporters and probably helped harden the issue into a macho test of wills that became much more intractable.

An alternative approach to the problem was available, but it apparently was never considered seriously—or even, it seems, *at all*. Instead of overreacting by imitating Iran's pettiness and hysteria, the United States could have adopted an approach that might be dubbed "creative inattention." Responding to Iran with the contempt it so richly deserved, the president could have assigned some dignified citizen to head a well-staffed commission to deal patiently with the issue, ordering the group to report to him regularly. The president could then have distanced himself and his top advisers from the issue, arguing with great validity that he could not allow the daily workings of his great country to be disrupted by an act of mindless, indeed infantile fanaticism in a distant country. In retrospect, in fact, Carter's secretary of state, Cyrus Vance, has concluded that such an approach would probably have been wise. "I believe it was a mistake for us not to have played down the crisis as much as possible," he notes in his memoirs. "Obviously, we could not have kept the hostage crisis out of the nightly television news, even had we wanted to do so. But we made a mistake by contributing unwittingly to Iran's exploitation of the nation's heartfelt anxiety by letting it appear that the hostages were the only concern of the U.S. government."[35]

There are probably several reasons why a more circumspect approach was never considered at the time. It seemed reasonable to expect that the crisis, or episode, would be resolved within a few days, or at most weeks. Thus to focus the full attention of the government on it for a while may have seemed a justifiable use of resources. To a degree, then, the policymakers became trapped by their own initiatives. Out of frustration, military approaches became ever more attractive, though there was no guarantee such ventures would not take the lives of more "precious human beings" than they would save.[36]

Presumably, domestic politics were not entirely irrelevant to Carter's considerations. Before the crisis his approval ratings were at a very low ebb. The rally-round-the-flag effect caused Carter's popularity to soar some 29 percentage points—the greatest increase in presidential approval to that time, and one surpassed in polling history only by the elevation of George W. Bush after September 11, 2001. Ultimately, of course, the hostage crisis probably had the opposite effect, contributing to Carter's defeat in the 1980 election. But had he been able to negotiate the hostages' release during the campaign, or had the rescue attempt of the hostages he ordered in April 1980 been successful, he would have been much more likely to win.

It would be unfair to suggest that Carter manipulated the hostage crisis purely for his own domestic political benefit, however. Though it is difficult to imagine that he was unaware of such potential benefits, memoirs of members of his staff confirm that he soon became emotionally committed on the issue, and it seems likely he is sincere in his autobiography when he expresses how "overwhelming" his "private feelings" were on the issue, and how he sometimes felt the hostages were "like part of my own family." Such all-consuming compassion, however, while admirable in its way, may not always be desirable in a chief of state. If the "holding of the American hostages . . . cast a pall over my own life," as Carter recalls, that was because Carter let it do so, not because that reaction was somehow required by objective circumstance.[37]

The hostage episode was also a colossal media event. Cause and effect are a bit muddled in this case: perhaps the Carter people gave the event crisis priority in part because the press built it up so; perhaps the media became so obsessed with the issue in part because the administration insisted it was a crisis. But to a considerable extent both administration and press were reflecting and responding to a public sense of outrage.

The American public's deep concern about Americans held hostage resonates with earlier historical instances. For example, the only acceptable solution to the Vietnam War was one in which American prisoners of war in Hanoi were returned (in a 1971 poll 68 percent favored a withdrawal from the war, but only 11 percent favored withdrawal if it "would threaten the lives or safety" of American POWs), and to a considerable degree Japanese mistreatment of American prisoners during World War II made Hiroshima all but inevitable.[38]

But though this public reaction may be a strong one, it does not follow that leaders and press must constantly and necessarily pander to it. Yet, as the hostage episode dragged on exhaustingly, the president felt he had to let himself be seen devoting his full attention to the issue, and the media, increasingly desperate for something to report in the stalemated crisis, kept themselves busy by systematically interviewing nearly every relative, friend, acquaintance, and grade school teacher of each hostage.

The fact that an event arrests the public's attention doesn't mean all opportunities for clear thinking and leadership evaporate, however. The public's resentment and outrage were understandable, yet a dignified response to the provocation might well have been politically possible. That is, the public might have been willing to go along with a mature approach, rather than one stressing sanctimonious posturing, empty bravado, and endless hand-wringing.

Over its reign, the religious regime in Iran gradually engendered a rising tide of contempt within the country for its strictness and its corruption. This happened on its own, not as a result of U.S. policy. When the mullahs in charge allowed for a degree of limited democracy, the vote went resoundingly against their preferred candidates in presidential elections in 1997, 2001, and 2005. Nonetheless, when a candidate who was essentially antiregime was elected in 2005, America decided to obsess over whether he had been in the ranks of the hostage takers a quarter century earlier.

Economically Assertive Japan

In unintended parody of the whole concept, a somewhat improbable devil du jour was spotted in the late 1980s on the economic front: insidiously peaceful Japan. In a major best-seller of the time, historian Paul Kennedy confidently listed a set of reasons why Japan was likely to expand faster than other major powers, stressed the country's "immensely strong" industrial bedrock and its docile and diligent workforce, and predicted that, unless there were a large-scale war, an ecological disaster, or a worldwide slump as in the 1930s, Japan would become "*much* more powerful" economically.[39] Many people found this prospective development threatening, especially after the diabolical Japanese shelled out a lot of money to buy Radio City Music Hall and a major Hollywood film studio.

Figure 3 supplies some data concerning the degree to which the public became alarmed. As Gorbachev's Soviet Union was bringing the cold war to an end, Americans were becoming concerned about the new "threat" to national security perceived at the time to be presented by economically impressive, if substantially demilitarized, Japan. By the spring of 1989, the Japanese threat was seen to be nearly comparable to the one posed by the still heavily armed Soviet Union. In polls conducted in 1990 and 1991, most Americans prophesied that Japan would be the number one economic power in the next century.[40]

Those of the then-fashionable America-in-decline and FLASH! JAPAN BUYS PEARL HARBOR! schools were quickly arguing that a need had sud-

Figure 3: Threat posed by Japan and the USSR, 1986–1991

How much of a threat would you say the Soviet Union is to the United States these days: a very serious threat, a serious threat, a minor threat, or not a threat at all? Do you feel the national security of the United States is threatened because Japan has become so strong economically? If "Yes": Is the threat to U.S. national security a very serious threat, a serious threat, or only a minor threat?

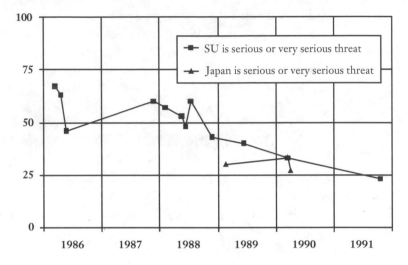

denly arisen to fear not "missile vulnerability" but "semiconductor vulnerability." "Economics," they apparently seriously warned us, "is the continuation of war by other means." For example, there were danger signals, Harvard's Samuel Huntington assured us, in the fact that Japan had become the largest provider of foreign aid and because it had shockingly endowed professorships at Harvard and MIT. One book of the time was even entitled *The Coming War with Japan*. Some analysts confidently insisted that Japan by natural impulse would soon come to yearn for nuclear weapons, even though the Japanese themselves seemed to remain viscerally uninterested in them.[41]

Such concerns soon evaporated as Japan's "threatening" economy stagnated in the 1990s. Huntington quickly decided that, as it turned out, the real problem was actually a "clash of civilizations," which didn't have much to do with economics at all. Meanwhile, Kennedy amiably moved on to warn portentously of the dangers from global warming, job-stealing robots, and—even as the rise in world population began to stagnate or even reverse—population explosions.[42]

A decade later, concerns about dire economic challenge began to focus on China and India. Neither, however, has yet made it to full devil du jour status.

TERRORISM DURING THE COLD WAR

Terrorism was not invented in 2001. Nor were the tendencies to exaggerate its capacities, to play to the galleries, and to overreact. But at times politicians have shown themselves able to refrain from giving in to such tendencies.

As analyst Jeffrey Simon points out, the administrations of John Kennedy, Lyndon Johnson, Richard Nixon, and Gerald Ford for the most part approached the issue of terrorism with a fair amount of detachment, distance, and reticence. One irritant at the time was a series of airline hijackings in which commercial airliners were diverted, mostly to Cuba; there were also several dramatic and much-televised hostage episodes, mostly in the Middle East. The presidents dealt with these challenges in an orderly manner for the most part, kept their personal distance, and did not allow them to affect U.S. foreign policy more broadly.[43]

This remarkable presidential reticence did not survive. Not only was the presidency of Jimmy Carter severely damaged in overactive efforts to deal with terrorism, but so was that of Ronald Reagan. Carter had been blindsided by terrorism—or by his inept handling of it. Reagan, by contrast, was elected during the year of the Iran hostage hysteria, and his administration came roaring into office vowing to be different from Carter's. This involved a lot of huffing and puffing about terrorism and the terrible things America would do—"swift and effective retribution" and things like that—if provoked. In particular, Reagan's normally judicious secretary of state, George Shultz, was deeply upset by the phenomenon, proclaiming in 1984 that when provoked by terrorists the United States needed desperately to blast somebody somewhere "on a moment's notice," even without adequate evidence, to avoid looking like an indecisive "Hamlet of nations."[44] (He apparently preferred the King Lear approach.)

As a consequence of all this, Reagan and his administration—

together, of course, with the media—became preoccupied with terrorism. At first they obsessed mainly on the "state-sponsored" variety, focusing on the antics of devil du jour Qaddafi in Libya. But then they became fixated on a handful of American hostages held by some terrorists in the midst of a chaotic civil war in Lebanon.

The administration's focus on Lebanon had begun in 1983, when it sent a contingent of Marines to help police the civil conflict there. At the time, Reagan extravagantly declared that "in an age of nuclear challenge and economic interdependence, such conflicts are a threat to all the people of the world, not just to the Middle East itself." Despite this overblown sales pitch, however, Reagan decided to have the Marines "redeployed to the sea" after 241 of them were killed by a suicide terrorist in October. The situation in Lebanon did not present much of a wider threat to U.S. interests, and the public was quite willing to support measures to cut losses and leave. After the fact, Americans said that, although they considered Reagan's expedition to Lebanon to have been a failure, many, with reasonable nuance, felt it still to have been "a good idea at the time."[45] Nor were there electoral costs. By the time the 1984 presidential election rolled around, voters had substantially forgotten the whole thing, and Reagan was handily reelected.

Soon, however, the Reagan administration embroiled—and boiled—itself again in Lebanon. American hostages were held by terrorists who were loyal to Iran, and the administration felt itself challenged because it liked to think it should (and could) protect Americans wherever they chance to wander on the globe. "I happen to believe," Reagan declared in a press conference at the time, "that when an American citizen, any place in the world, is unjustly denied their constitutional rights to life, liberty and the pursuit of happiness, it is the responsibility of this government to restore those rights."[46] There is nothing wrong with this position in principle. But it simply does not follow that it is the responsibility of the president and other top officials to become personally involved whenever an American is taken hostage in some distant corner of the world—any more than they become involved when one is taken hostage in New Jersey. Both crimes are the acts of minor players, and, however contemptible, these activities can and should be dealt with by the authorities at the appropriate level: low-ranking diplomatic officials in the one case, local police in the other.

There was no reason to doubt the genuineness of the presidential outrage at the criminal, or of the presidential compassion for the victim, when an American was taken hostage overseas. Furthermore, as with Carter in 1979, no politician can be expected to be completely oblivious to the political potential that attends a hostage crisis. In the process, however, Reagan anticipated post-9/11 political posturing by promulgating a set of preposterous antiwimpisms in which he vowed he would "put an end to terrorism."[47]

Most damaging, Reagan continued the policy of tying the prestige of the presidency to the hostage issue. In effect, any two-bit terrorist in any foreign land who took any American hostage could be fairly well assured of drawing the impassioned attention of the leader of the wealthiest and most powerful nation in history. The attention itself, in fact, constituted a substantial reward for terrorism.

For example, when one of the hostages, Reverend Benjamin Weir, was released in September 1985, Reagan insisted on announcing the release himself. In effect he was demonstrating that the actions of a few scruffy hostage takers were of such monumental significance that he should interrupt his schedule and take it upon himself to announce to the world what they had done for us lately. Hardly a way to discourage terrorism; rather, it's likely to make it even more fashionable, giving the perpetrators prestige and recognition far beyond their objective strength.

It could be argued, of course, that pressure from the public and from the media on this issue is so great that the president really has no realistic choice. But there seems to have been a fair amount of public sophistication on these matters. The government does have a responsibility to aid distressed Americans abroad, but the prestige and magnificence of the United States are not at stake whenever an American is kidnapped by a little band of faceless foreign fanatics. The public might be perfectly able to understand that the problem is best left to underlings while the president attends to other concerns, such as running the country. Moreover, even though Khomeini's Iran had entered the public mind as a pariah state, the discovery that the administration had been secretly trying to improve Iranian relations as insurance against the future was met with broad approval and understanding. On the other hand, when Reagan essentially reversed his own firm, or firmly announced, policy of refusing to trade goods and arms for hostages (which, it turned out, was why Weir was released), the policy was met with widespread popular disapproval for the basic, commonsense reason that such rewards would encourage further hostage taking and terrorism. The preoccupation with terrorism also was one of the elements that led to the Iran-Contra scandal that nearly brought down the Reagan presidency.

For top officials, dealing with terrorists can often be at once too hot and too unimportant to handle.

CONCLUSIONS AND COMPARISONS

A number of general observations emerge from these considerations about anxieties, even alarm, over things that never happened: nuclear weapons that never went off, devils du jour who soon descended obligingly into history's dustbin, dramatic acts of terror that proved to be at most bumps on the road.

To begin with, it is clearly tempting to reach out and embrace the worst case. If nuclear war is possible (and, needless to say, terrible), it may therefore come to seem probable, because it is tacitly and sometimes explicitly assumed, weapons cause war. In fact, a slippery slide into nuclear war can even seem inevitable unless something is done about it, and right away. When nothing, effectively, is done, anxieties logically increase.

By contrast, the best case was only rarely considered: that, in fact, nothing much actually needed to be done; that weaponry was essentially irrelevant to the situation because neither side had the slightest interest in getting into a conflict that looked remotely like World War II, much less one embellished with nuclear weapons; and therefore that the chief contestants were essentially highly unlikely to slide into major, central war no matter how menacing the arsenal each side happened to have aimed at the other. Thus, contrary to common expectation, World War III never erupted and, it seems, never even got close.

Something similar can be said for devils du jour. Those running Egypt, Indonesia, Iran, and Libya at various points during the cold war showed that their grasp on reality was less than firm and that their only sure talent was for addled self-destruction. To feed their egos and to play to their already inflated self-importance was often counterproductive, and was always unwise and undignified. Tinhorn tyrants do not become archfiends capable of acts of cosmic importance just because they huff and puff menacingly, or because a few of their followers or agents occasionally set off a bomb somewhere or kidnap a hostage. It is possible to apply pressure to these countries without lowering the

United States to their level by directly and constantly involving the president. Nevertheless, Reagan's administration, like Carter's before it, was severely shaken by misguided efforts to influence Iran (or even to find coherent Iranians to talk to) on hostage and terrorism issues. And exaggerated fears about Indonesia helped impel the Johnson administration into its Vietnam disaster in something like the process by which inflated concerns about Egypt had led Britain and France into their debacle at Suez a decade earlier.

The special fear of, and preoccupation (or obsession) with, terrorism and the antics of devils du jour that are so often embraced by presidents and other world leaders—something that has sometimes led to, or been caused by, a remarkable tendency to exaggerate the importance of such vexing rascals—may sometimes stem from an essentially petty personal animosity: big guys find their machismo besmirched when little guys seem to have gotten away with an insult. Such unjustified fears and obsessions, however derived, can also lead leaders to reject, or even ignore entirely, policy alternatives other than confrontation, particularly ones of patience that advocate treating the irritation with the contempt it deserves, while calmly waiting for it to die out of its own accord.

It is very often argued that leaders simply do not have the luxury to ignore or wait out the dramatic, colorful, and (therefore) media-attracting threats presented by terrorists and devils du jour—that, particularly in a democracy, there is a political imperative for them to "do something." But there were plenty of examples in this chapter in which leaders did not succumb to this supposed imperative and survived politically. Kennedy, Johnson, Nixon, and Ford for the most part never became fixated on terrorism at all. Reagan walked away from overcommitment in Lebanon. He and George H. W. Bush did not overreact to the Lockerbie bombing. All this without notable negative political consequences. This issue, one that is oddly not at all obvious, will be considered again later in connection with the sometimes hysterical "war" on terrorism being waged today.

It is also interesting that, like hemlines, fears and anxieties can not only rise, but also fall. This is particularly clear in the case of nuclear weapons: even though nuclear arsenals mostly continued to increase in quantity and quality, the anxieties they inspired waxed and waned. This suggests that the fears derived from concerns inspired by rhetoric and posturing, not from the objective reality of the destructive weapons themselves.

CHAPTER 6

Disorderliness
in the New World Order

In his farewell address upon leaving the presidency in January 1953, Harry Truman looked forward, and with great pleasure, to what it would be like when the communist threat, which he considered to be the "overriding issue of our time," was "overcome." It would be a "new era," he enthused, "a wonderful golden age—an age when we can use the peaceful tools that science has forged for us to do away with poverty and human misery everywhere on the earth."[1]

In 1989, the United States and its allies entered that "new era." It took a while, but the communist threat had been not merely overcome, but all but extinguished. Although the world was now free as never before to seek to do away with poverty and human misery, however, it somehow didn't really feel too much like "a wonderful golden age."

Truman's phrase is extreme, of course; it even dangerously borders on the poetic. And if it is taken to suggest a trouble-free utopia, it could casually be dismissed as an unattainable dream. Yet, though Truman may sometimes have been a bit of a dreamer, he was too realistic to expect utter perfection. Some of the difficulty in surrendering to such a characterization may be that, because of the way we tend to look at the world, we wouldn't know we were in a wonderful golden age if it came up and kissed us on the left earlobe.

A *New Yorker* cartoon published sometime in the midst of the cold war depicted some Eskimos gazing skyward at two missiles, one labeled "USSR," the other "US," hurtling past each other in opposite directions. One Eskimo remarks, "Well, I guess that's the end of the world as they know it." But when they did come to the end of the world as it was

117

then known (and without, as it happened, the launch of a single missile in hostile trajectory), the focus of alarm was fully freed to shift to other perceived threats. Golden ages, accordingly, never happen. Thus, as big problems—"overriding issues," in Truman's terms—become resolved, there is a tendency to elevate smaller ones to take their place.

This chapter assesses the alarm generated by three of these problems in the post–cold war era: complexity, ethnic warfare, and, in particular, rogue states. A fourth, international terrorism, is considered in the concluding two chapters.

COMPLEXITY

James Woolsey, head of the Central Intelligence Agency under Bill Clinton, testified darkly in 1993, "We have slain a large dragon, but we live now in a jungle filled with a bewildering variety of poisonous snakes." He helpfully enumerated these snakes: "the proliferation of weapons of mass destruction and the ballistic missiles to carry them; ethnic and national hatreds that can metastasize across large portions of the globe; the international narcotics trade; terrorism; the dangers inherent in the West's dependence on mideast oil; new economic and environmental challenges."[2]

None of these problems was new, of course, and most of them were actually of less urgent concern than they were during the cold war. But proclamations like Woolsey's helped hammer home a notion that quickly became fashionable: that international affairs had somehow become especially tumultuous, unstable, and complex. Thus, Bill Clinton proclaimed in his 1993 presidential Inaugural Address that "the new world is more free but less stable." Woolsey's predecessor at the CIA, Robert Gates, fully agreed: "The events of the last two years have led to a far more unstable, turbulent, unpredictable and violent world," or as columnist Stanley Hoffmann put it, "The problem of order has become even more complex than before."[3]

Conclusions about the comparative complexity of the world stemmed in part from a remarkably simplified recollection of what had gone on during the cold war. Woolsey recalled that the cold war threat could be characterized "precisely and succinctly" because our adversary was "a single power whose interests fundamentally threatened ours." Thomas Friedman expressed the belief that "all the policy-makers had to do was take out their compasses, point them at any regional conflict in the world, see which side Moscow was on and immediately deduce which side America should take."[4]

In fact, the communist threat was shifting, multifaceted, and extremely complicated. Most of the time there were two central sources of threat, China and the USSR, not one. Moreover, the Chinese and the Soviets, while jointly threatening the West, were often intensely at odds with each other over both strategy and tactics. It was often extremely difficult to deduce which side to take: the United States supported the Chinese group against the Soviet one in Angola, puzzled for years over which communist side Cuba's Fidel Castro was on, joined with the Soviet Union to support the formation of Israel as well as a regime in Tanzania, found that virtually all communist rebellions were confusingly associated with indigenous ones, and never really did determine whether some countries, such as Mozambique, were communist or not.

Friedman and others may suggest that the policy of containment—with its overarching theory about confronting communist expansionism—gave a clear and easily followed guideline and allowed for a great deal of consistency in U.S. foreign policy, but the actual experience of the cold war surely suggests that there was a great deal of bobbing and weaving in the application of the policy. Even as the containment policy was being formulated, the Truman administration was allowing China to fall into the communist camp. Eisenhower was unwilling to use military measures to prevent a communist victory in Indochina, but he held fast on the islands of Quemoy and Matsu off the China coast. Kennedy sought to shore up the anticommunist position in South Vietnam even as he was acquiescing in an agreement that gave the communists effective control of large portions of neighboring Laos. Containment policy may have been a useful general guide, but it clearly did not make policy easy to formulate.

Indeed, if the post–cold war world resembled a jungle filled with poisonous snakes, the cold war itself was a jungle filled with at least two dragons *and* with poisonous snakes (not to mention devils du jour), some of whom were variously, changeably, and often quite ambiguously in devious complicity with one or the other of the dragons. It seems obvious which jungle is preferable and less complicated—and it's Woolsey's post–Cold War one.

Moreover, the cold war added an especially difficult layer of complexity to U.S. relations with a whole host of countries. At one time the United States had to treat Mobutu of Zaire as a dictator who had brought his country to ruin but who was on the right side in the cold war. After the cold war it could treat him merely as a dictator who brought his country to ruin. In that very important respect, international policy became far *less* complex than it was during the cold war.

Relatedly, Hoffmann argues that the major contestants in the cold war managed to devise "a network of rules and restraints aimed at avoiding direct military collision."[5] This is true, though it is certainly worth noting that those countries still managed to get into quite a few *indirect* military collisions, some of them extremely bloody. And however "disorderly" and "complex" the post–cold war world may be, the dangers of a military collision, direct or indirect, between East and West have become so attenuated that it becomes almost absurd to suggest that "a network of rules and restraints" are necessary to avoid it—any more than one would maintain that such a network is necessary to prevent military conflict between the United States and Canada.

ETHNIC WARFARE

One of Woolsey's primary snakes was ethnic war, which had alarmingly broken out in Yugoslavia by the time he was speaking in 1993. He and many others feared it would metastasize (to use his fancy word) all over Eastern Europe, perhaps even leading to a nuclear war between Russia and Ukraine.

There was a great need for an explanation for what was going on in Yugoslavia, preferably a simple one. The fashionable travel writer and congenital doomsayer Robert Kaplan handily supplied one in a book and, probably much more important, in a front-page article in the Sunday *New York Times Book Review* in 1993. He portentously proclaimed the Balkans to be "a region of pure memory" where "each individual sensation and memory affects the grand movement of clashing peoples." These processes of history and memory had been "kept on hold" by communism for forty-five years, "thereby creating a kind of multiplier effect for violence." With the demise of that suppressing force, he argued, ancient, seething national and ethnic hatreds were allowed spontaneously to explode into nationalist violence.[6]

Some analysts were soon given to proclaiming that ethnic conflicts were "now engulfing the world," that there was "a virtual epidemic of armed civil or intranational conflict," and that the "breakdown of restraints" seen in Yugoslavia was part of "a global trend." This perspective was soon deftly elaborated by Samuel Huntington, who looked at the Yugoslav wars, declared that "conflicts among nations and ethnic groups are escalating," and creatively extrapolated it all into a cosmic (and best-selling) worldview in which he proclaimed that a "clash of civilizations" was beginning to take place. Although he acknowledged that there had been little or no ethnic violence in Yugoslavia before World War II, he still prominently designated the Bosnian war as one of those crucial clashes of civilization or fault-line wars that "rarely ends permanently" because "when one side sees the opportunity for gain, the war is renewed."[7]

Working from this perspective, leaders and publics in developed states drew the convenient conclusion that many, perhaps even all, civil wars are essentially inexplicable all-against-all conflicts, rooted in old hatreds that could hardly be ameliorated by well-meaning, but innocent and naïve, outsiders. It follows that intervention would at best be simply a short-term palliative and thus a pointless exertion. This perspective informed some of the reluctance of the first Bush administration to become involved in Bosnia and also, initially, in Somalia, and it was soon also embraced by the Clinton administration.[8] The convenient policy conclusion: the only real problem here is to contain the wars to allow them to burn themselves out, however murderously, in their own natural habitat until they inevitably erupt again, at which point containment once again would be called for.

This explanation, so convenient to those favoring passivity, was substantially flawed. Yet, as journalist Brian Hall observes, "Literary clichés do not die easily, especially when informed by superficialities." In fact, the murderous dynamic of most "ethnic" civil wars was perpetrated more by bands of thugs than by ideologues or by neighbors out to get neighbors in some sort of frenzied Hobbesian state of nature or clashing of civilizations.[9] Contrary to the fears of the alarmists of the time, they were therefore at once unlikely to spread—or metastasize—and entirely susceptible to policing by the international community, which in most cases, of course, never came.

Most such wars, particularly those in Europe, did eventually fizzle away, and did not spread.[10] And contrary to anticipations, there has been no eruption—or even an incident—of ethnic warfare in Bosnia at all since the war ended there in 1995.

In fact, by the new century, the number of wars in the world, both civil and international, had dwindled considerably, and that trend may be continuing: the number of armed conflicts inflicting more than 1,000 battle or battle-related deaths per year (a standard requirement for a conflict to be designated a "war") is now very small and may be approaching the vanishing point. People stopped worrying about it, yet they scarcely noticed because they had so many other things (particularly terrorism and America's bloody intervention in Iraq) to occupy their minds. In 2004, the United Nations Press Office released a list of the "10 stories the world should hear more about," one of which was called "the peacekeeping paradox": because so many civil wars had recently come to an end, there was a lot of peace to keep.[11] The story about the underreported story went almost entirely unreported.

ROGUE STATES

One of the continuing preoccupations of the post–cold war era, one that was often related to terrorism, concerned supposed threats emanating from a newly identified category of nations: "rogue states." This was hardly a new problem in international affairs, of course. There were plenty of such states—devils du jour—during the cold war, and some of these were in league with the big, threatening rogues: the Soviet Union and China. The post–cold war problems posed by such enfeebled, impoverished, isolated, and friendless states as Iraq and post–Soviet North Korea pale in comparison. The "rogue state" label implies that such entities are too irrational to be deterred by policies designed to deal with "normal" countries, and it therefore leads to an extreme version of what political scientists call the "security dilemma": weaponry that might be obtained by such states to deter an attack is almost automatically assumed to be designed for offensive purposes even though such use would be patently suicidal for the rogues and their regimes.

After the cold war, the United States was given to characterizing itself, with consummate self-infatuation, as "the last remaining superpower" and as "the indispensable nation. We stand tall, and we see further than other countries into the future."[12] Departing from the advice of John Quincy Adams in an 1821 Fourth of July speech in the House of Representatives, policymakers often concluded that this status requires it actively to go abroad "in search of monsters to destroy."

Panama's Noriega

One minirogue, or minimonster, was Panama's Manuel Noriega, a certifiable thug who had abrogated an election in order to continue running the place himself.[13] He never managed (or even tried, it seems) to get his hands on any weapons of mass destruction, real or imaginary, hence his diminutive status in the rogue gallery. But he did apparently play around in the drug trade, which had been escalated by the late 1980s into a matter of grave national preoccupation by various presidents, particularly after drugs had shown up as a prominent concern on public opinion surveys.[14]

In 1989 Noriega irritatingly made some defiantly hostile references to the United States in speeches, and he remained unapologetic when his goons shot and killed an American soldier in a checkpoint altercation and beat up another American serviceman and sexually threatened his wife. There were also concerns about the security of the famous Canal in Panama even though Noriega warily refrained from threatening that piece of real estate, which was due to be turned over to Panama in a decade anyway.[15]

U.S. President George H. W. Bush made many tough anti-Noriega statements during his election campaign of 1988, and he seems to have seen the dictator as "an unpleasant symbol of American impotence in the face of illegal drugs," which Bush had made a high priority issue. Bush was also bothered, it appears, by lingering concerns that he was an indecisive, hesitant wimp. Outraged at the Panamanian dictator's insolent statements and behavior, Bush ordered 24,000 American troops into action at the end of 1989. They were up against 16,000 troops in the substantially criminalized Panamanian Defense Forces, of whom 3,500 were reckoned to be capable of combat; few fought with much vigor.[16]

Noriega gave himself up and was sent to Florida, where he was tried by an American court, convicted by an American jury, and locked up in an American prison. In Panama, his thugs were stripped of authority, and a new government, not ideal but a distinct improvement by most standards, was set up. The venture seems to have had no significant impact one way or the other on the drug trade.

North Korea's Kims

The United States has consistently viewed North Korea under Kim Il-sung and then, after his death in 1994, under his successor and son, Kim Jong-il, as a continuing threat. This, even though its neighbors, especially South Korea, do not.[17]

Already the most closed and secretive society in the world, North Korea became even more isolated after the cold war, when its former patrons, Russia and China, notably decreased their support. Its economy descended into shambles, and it was having trouble even feeding its population, conditions that were exacerbated by the fact that it continued to be led by an anachronistic Communist Party dictatorship whose leaders celebrated theory and persistent self-deception over reality. In incessant fear of attack from the outside, they continued to spend 25 percent of their wealth to maintain a huge, if fuel-short, military force of more than a million underfed troops.[18]

It often seems that the chief tension-causing entity in the Korean area is the United States. Utterly obsessed by the notion that the North Koreans might obtain a nuclear arsenal, the United States has often embraced extreme, even hysterical, worst-case fantasies about what the North Koreans might do with such weapons—particularly that they might be given or sold to terrorists or (other) rogue states to use on the United States or, more likely, Israel. The United States has accordingly adopted an intensely hostile and threatening posture that only increases the North's frightened desire to build such weapons.

Some Americans even think that a war on the Korean peninsula—which, of course, would mostly kill Koreans—is preferable to letting the North pursue a nuclear weapons program. This came to a head in 1994 when a U.S. National Intelligence Estimate concluded that there was "a better than even" chance that North Korea had the makings of a small nuclear bomb. This conclusion was hotly contested by other American analysts and was later "reassessed" by intelligence agencies and found possibly to have been overstated. In addition, even if North Korea had the "makings," skeptics pointed out, it still had several key hurdles to overcome to develop a deliverable weapon.[19]

Nonetheless, the Clinton administration was apparently prepared to go to war with the miserable North Korean regime to prevent or to halt its nuclear development. Accordingly, it moved to impose deep economic sanctions to make the isolated country even poorer (insofar as that was possible), a measure that garnered no support, even from neighboring Russia, China, and Japan. It also moved to engage in a major military buildup in the area. So apocalyptic (or simply paranoid) was the North Korean regime about these two developments that some key players think it might have gone to war on a preemptive basis if the measures had been carried out. A full-scale war on the peninsula, estimated the Pentagon, could conceivably kill 1 million people, including 80,000 to 100,000 Americans, cost over $100 billion, and do economic destruction on the order of $1 trillion.[20] A considerable price, one might think, to prevent a pathetic regime from developing weapons with the potential for killing a few tens of thousands—if they were actually exploded, an act that would surely be suicidal for the regime.

In effect and perhaps by design, however, the North Korean leaders seem mainly to have been practicing extortion. No one ever paid much attention to them except when they seemed to be developing nuclear weapons, and they appear to have been exceedingly pleased when the 1994 crisis inspired a pilgrimage to their country by ex-President Jimmy Carter, the most prominent American ever to set foot on their soil. Carter quickly worked out a deal whereby North Korea would accept international inspections to guarantee that it wasn't building nuclear weapons, for which it would graciously accept a bribe from the West: aid, including some high-tech reactors that were capable of producing plenty of energy but no weapons-grade plutonium, as well as various promises about normalizing relations—promises that went substantially unfulfilled in the hope and expectation that the North Korean regime would soon collapse.[21]

In the next years, that hope sometimes seemed justified as floods and bad weather exacerbated the economic disaster that had been inflicted on North Korea by its rulers. Famines ensued, and the number of people who perished reached hundreds of thousands or more, with some careful estimates putting the number at more than 2 million. Food aid was eventually sent from the West, though in the early days of the famine there seem to have been systematic efforts in the United States to deny the famine's existence in fear that a politics-free response to a humanitarian disaster would undercut its efforts to use food aid to wring diplomatic concessions from North Korea.[22]

The same threat-exaggerating, overreactive perspective toward the North Korean rogue continued to be embraced in the new century. Richard Perle, the prominent neoconservative and Defense Department adviser for the George W. Bush administration, bluntly asserted in 2003 that the interests of South Korea and the United States are very different: the Koreans, who are obviously in the line of fire, want to avoid a military conflict, whereas the Americans think keeping North Korea nonnuclear is much more important. Meanwhile, Graham Allison, an adviser to the opposition Democrats, has maintained essentially the same view.[23]

In 2002, President G. W. Bush prominently invented an "axis of evil" and pointedly placed North Korea as well as Iraq and Iran in it. As he also suggested that the United States might very well invade one of those entities, Iraq, any day, it was reasonable for others on his little list to conclude that they needed a deterrent to keep the indispensable, tall-standing Americans at bay. With that, North Korea (and perhaps Iran as well) accelerated its nuclear weapons program.

The North Korean regime may be contemptible, but it is the people of North Korea who suffer. Regrettably, there is no way to aid the people of the North without also aiding their leaders. By contrast, a policy that intensifies the misery of an essentially innocent people out of spite for their leaders is difficult to justify morally and is probably foolish in the long run.

It is overwhelmingly apparent that history is on the side of democratic, capitalist South Korea, whereas the North is a bizarre, sometimes almost comical relic (or caricature) of a bygone and increasingly forgotten era. There is no need to take risks or act impetuously to hurry this historical process along. All that seems likely to be required in this case, as with the devils du jour of the cold war era, is judicious, watchful, and only occasionally wary patience.[24]

Iraq's Saddam Hussein

The United States supported Saddam Hussein's Iraq after it committed naked aggression against Khomeini's devil du jour Iran in the 1980s even when Saddam used chemical weapons in the endeavor. However,

126

in 1990, two years after fighting had ceased in the horrific war with Iran, Saddam launched equally naked aggression against another neighbor, Kuwait. With that, he elevated himself into full devil du jour status himself, and he remained at that level until he was forcibly deposed by an act of naked aggression thirteen years later.

The Gulf War of 1991

George H. W. Bush, still glowing from his snappy slapping down of Panama's minirogue Noriega, took umbrage at Saddam's invasion of Kuwait and saw it as a form of aggression comparable in its way to that of Adolf Hitler in the 1930s, but not comparable, of course, to his own venture into Panama a few months earlier.

Iraq's 1990 invasion of Kuwait was the only instance since World War II in which one United Nations member has tried to conquer another and to incorporate it into its own territory, and the act inspired almost total condemnation in the world. Bush led a determined international effort to impose a punishing economic blockade on Iraq, and, although it seems very unlikely that Saddam had any intention of further aggression, Bush also persuaded Saudi Arabia to accept a contingent of U.S. troops on its soil to deter Saddam from further adventures.[25]

Because it depended so heavily on oil exports, Iraq's economy was almost instantly fractured, making these sanctions far more punishing than any others ever imposed. However, Bush soon decided that the economic sanctions were not working fast enough. Moreover, if sanctions dragged on inconclusively, observed a sympathetic columnist, "Bush would lose face, popularity, and reelectability."[26] Accordingly, he substantially increased troop levels in the area to attain an "offensive military option," and he was able to sharpen the threat by getting the United Nations Security Council to authorize the use of force unless Iraq left Kuwait by January 15, 1991.

The driving force in all this seems to have been Bush himself. He became emotionally absorbed, even obsessed, by the crisis and felt he was being "tested by real fire." To some, he seemed to yearn to have a war. Bush constantly compared his problem to the situation in the 1930s, when adept policy might have prevented one of the most cataclysmic events in history, World War II.[27]

There were also fears that Saddam Hussein might acquire nuclear weapons. It is not particularly clear what Saddam would have been able to do with a nuclear bomb or two, confronted as he was by an enveloping coalition that possessed tens of thousands of those weapons. But a bomb might have helped to deter a military attack on Iraq itself.[28]

Bush's rhetoric became ever more passionate and obsessive on the issue. Saddam was worse than Hitler, Bush announced, and he projected that standing up to Iraq's aggression promised "a much more peaceful world. . . . It's that big. It's that important. Nothing like this since World War II." In launching the war in January 1991 he extravagantly announced, "We have before us the opportunity to forge for ourselves and for future generations a new world order" and "What we're doing is going to chart the future of the world for the next hundred years."[29]

Bush demanded that Saddam withdraw unconditionally and ignominiously, suffering maximum humiliation, a posture that made war very likely as public humiliation was probably Saddam's worst possible outcome. The United States could have applied a patient strategy of punitive containment, seeking an agreement while extending security guarantees to Saudi Arabia and other Gulf states and lacing Iraq in economic sanctions until it shaped up.[30] This policy, which received virtually no discussion or consideration at the time, differs from the one so ardently pursued by Bush in its rejection of war, in its suggestion that the crisis was not nearly of the overwhelming importance Bush attached to it, in its lack of a requirement even by implication for the removal of Saddam Hussein (which Bush's war failed to accomplish anyway), and in its willingness to consider making some concessions over disputed territory while tendering a no-invasion pledge—something the United States had already endorsed, at least in general terms.

The coalition could have credibly threatened to boycott Iraq again if there were violations of the agreement, as the world had shown by then that it could live quite well without Iraqi oil. And it seems extremely likely that Iraq's neighbors would have been willing to develop protective military coalitions with the United States or other strong countries. Thus, Saddam would have had no easy prey on his borders, and he would have reigned, until death or deposition, in a world of richly deserved distrust and hostility. And Kuwait would have been liberated without the deaths of thousands of people.

Although no political leader made much of a play for any sort of compromise, public opinion data suggest there was considerable potential for leadership on this issue. Most people responded that they liked the sound of compromise. That is, the public could at least as readily be led away from war as it could be led into it.[31]

In the meantime, military planners were concluding that a war against Hussein's forces could easily be won or, as Bush put it, "We're going to kick his ass out." In fact, in military terms the war was spectacularly successful. The technology, strategy, and training of the forces led by the United States proved far superior, and they easily overwhelmed the Iraqi defenders, who seemed to have little, if any, stomach for combat: Saddam Hussein promised to wage "the mother of all battles," but his troops delivered instead the mother of all bugouts.[32]

Containing and Harassing Iraq after the Gulf War, 1991–2003

Despite the terrific military success in the 1991 war and despite Iraq's pathetic showing in it, the United States continued to see the rogue as a threat. Most important, Saddam Hussein remained defiantly in control in Iraq—very much contrary to the confident assumptions by most analysts of his early demise—and his survival soured the whole enterprise. As columnist David Gergen observes, "Bush set himself up with the frequent Hitler analogy: if Saddam Hussein is Adolf Hitler, why did Bush leave him in power?"[33]

Before the war, the goal of the sanctions policy had been to pressure Iraq to leave Kuwait. During and after the war, however, the United States and the United Nations substantially escalated the requirements for sanctions to be lifted, demanding reparations and insisting that Iraq must allow various inspection teams to probe its military arsenal, particularly to make sure it had no nuclear, biological, or chemical weapons. In addition, for twelve years and at considerable cost, the United States kept up a military campaign of focused bombing to harass and intimidate the Iraqi regime and to enforce two no-fly zones. This required maintaining bases in Saudi Arabia, something that particularly exercised future devil du jour, Osama bin Laden.

These policies seemed devised to force Saddam Hussein from power. Early on, Bush announced that the economic sanctions would be continued until "Saddam Hussein is out of there," and his deputy national security adviser declared that "Iraqis will pay the price while he remains in power." In 1997, President Bill Clinton's secretary of state, Madeleine Albright, continued this policy, stating that sanctions would not be lifted even "if Iraq complies with its obligations concerning weapons of mass destruction." The British made similar statements.[34] Unlike many dictators, Saddam Hussein had no other place to go: he was reasonably safe only in office and in control in Iraq. Therefore, the rather mild-sounding notion that he should be removed from office was effectively a death sentence to him. Not surprisingly, he remained uncooperative about allowing the sanctions to have this effect, regardless of the cost to the Iraqi people—whose suffering could be beneficially used to portray Iraq as the aggrieved party.

Sanctions were particularly punishing because so much of Iraq's economy was dependent on the export of oil, because it had not recovered from its 1980–88 war against Iran, and because the effects of sanctions were enhanced by the destruction of much of its rather advanced infrastructure during the Gulf War and by the truculent, even defiant, policies of the regime. The impact appears to have been devastating: a 1999 UN report concluded that "the gravity of the humanitarian situation of the Iraqi people is indisputable and cannot be overstated": the country has experienced "a shift from relative affluence to massive poverty." Estimates are that the sanctions contributed to—were a necessary cause of—the deaths of hundreds of thousands of people in Iraq because of inadequate food and medical supplies as well as breakdowns in sewage and sanitation systems and in the electrical power systems needed to run them—systems destroyed by bombing in the Gulf War that often went unrepaired due in part to sanctions-enhanced shortages of money, equipment, and spare parts.[35]

When asked on television's *60 Minutes* whether she thought the sanctions-induced deaths of perhaps half a million Iraqi children was "worth it," Madeleine Albright, then American ambassador to the United Nations, without taking issue with the death toll estimate, replied, "I think this is a very hard choice, but the price—we think the price is worth it." Although this remarkable acknowledgment amazingly provoked no comment at the time in the United States, it quickly became famous in the Arab world.[36] In their continuing obsession with the pathetic rogue in Baghdad, then, the sanctioning countries consciously and knowingly adopted military and economic policies that necessarily resulted in the deaths of large numbers of civilians. This deadly consequence of the sanctions was one of the chief grievances against the United States proclaimed in the many broadsides promulgated by Osama bin Laden.

The Iraq War of 2003

There was wide consensus, particularly among developed countries, that Saddam Hussein's regime in Iraq was a contemptible one. Moreover, it was reasonable to expect that a conventional military invasion by a disciplined foreign army could eliminate the regime, and it seemed entirely possible that Iraq's ill-led and demoralized army, which fought almost not at all when challenged in the Gulf War of 1991, would put up little armed resistance to such an attack. Nonetheless, although public opinion in the United States remained extremely hostile to Saddam Hussein, although there were public declarations and congressional appropriations to support opposition groups, no one was really calling for a war to depose him.[37]

After the September 11, 2001, terrorist attacks in the United States, however, a war to remove Iraq's leader began to seem politically possible, and top members of the administration of President George W. Bush began to think much more seriously about launching one—rather in the way the elder Bush had deposed a lesser rogue, Noriega, in Panama a decade earlier. In 2002, after a remarkably successful military venture in Afghanistan that toppled the contemptible Taliban regime and routed international terrorists based there, Bush began determinedly to set his sights on Iraq.[38]

The Americans, with the British in tow, unlike all of Iraq's neighbors except Israel, came to imagine that Saddam presented a "grave and growing danger." Prominent fearmongers, many of whom had previously been active in exaggerating the Soviet threat, asserted that Saddam was planning to dominate the Middle East.[39] Exactly how this might have come about was never spelled out. Any notion that Israel, with a substantial nuclear arsenal and a superb and highly effective military force, could be intimidated out of existence by the actions or fulminations of this pathetic dictator lacks credibility. The process by which Saddam could come to dominate the oil-producing states in the Middle East is equally fanciful. Essentially, the argument suggests that the Saudis and other oil-rich sheikdoms in the area would soon have become so terrified of the unreliable aggressor next door that they would order the protecting and deterring U.S. forces out and then supinely give themselves over to the aggressor's dominance.

The notion that Iraq presented an international threat seems to have been based on three propositions. First, Iraq would eventually rearm

131

and would likely fabricate WMD, including maybe a small supply of atomic arms. Second, once so armed, Saddam Hussein would be incapable of preventing himself from engaging in extremely provocative acts such as ordering a military invasion against a neighbor or lobbing weaponry against nuclear-armed Israel, despite the fact that such acts were extremely likely to trigger a concerted multilateral military attack on him and his regime. And third, if Saddam were to issue such a patently suicidal order, his military would dutifully carry it out, presumably with vastly more efficiency, effectiveness, and élan than it demonstrated in the Gulf War of 1991.

The first proposition remained a matter of some dispute. At worst there was a window of several years before the regime would have been able to acquire significant arms, particularly nuclear ones. Some experts, however, seemed to think it could be much longer; others questioned whether Saddam's regime would ever be able to gather or make the required fissile material. Obviously, if effective weapons inspections had been instituted in Iraq, they would have reduced this concern greatly.

The second proposition rested on an enormous respect for what could be called Saddam's daffiness in decision making. Saddam did sometimes act on caprice, and he often appeared to be out of touch; messengers bringing him bad news rarely got the opportunity to do so twice.[40] He does seem to have been an egomaniac. However, egomania is rather standard equipment for your average third-world tyrant. Self-important street thugs like Saddam Hussein love to flail and fume in the company of sycophants, but that doesn't make them any less ridiculous. At the same time, Saddam had shown himself capable of pragmatism. When his 1980 invasion of Iran went awry, he called for retreat to the prewar status quo; it was the Iranian regime that kept the war going. After he invaded Kuwait in 1990, he quickly moved to settle residual issues left over from the Iran-Iraq War so that he had only one enemy to deal with.[41]

Above all, he seems to have been entirely nonsuicidal and was primarily devoted to preserving his regime and his own personal existence. Much of his obstruction of arms inspectors seems to have arisen from his fear that intelligence agents among them could fatally triangulate his whereabouts—a suspicion that press reports suggest was not exaggerated.[42] Even if Saddam did acquire nuclear arms, it seems most likely that he would use them as all others have since 1945: to deter an invasion rather than to trigger one. Even he was likely to realize that any aggressive military act in the region was almost certain to provoke a concerted, truly multilateral counterstrike that would topple his regime and remove him from existence.

The third proposition was rarely considered in discussions of the war, but it is important. One can't maintain that Iraq's military forces can easily be walked over—something of a premise for the war makers of 2003, and one that proved to be accurate—and also that this same demoralized and incompetent military presented a coherent international threat. Even if Saddam did order some sort of patently suicidal adventure, his military might very well disobey, or simply neglect to carry out, the command. His initial orders in the 1991 Gulf War, after all, were to stand and fight the Americans to the last man. When push came to shove, his forces treated that absurd order with due contempt. Moreover, the regime appeared to enjoy very little support, and Saddam Hussein so feared a coup by his own army that he supplied his troops with little or no ammunition and would not allow the army to bring heavy weapons anywhere near Baghdad. In addition, the regime really controlled only a shard of the country. The Kurds had established a semi-independent entity in the north, and the antipathy toward its rule was so great in the Shiite south that government and party officials often considered it hostile territory.[43]

There were also arguments connecting Iraq to terrorism. Most were based on arm waving, particularly those brandishing the fear that Saddam might palm off weapons of mass destruction to shadowy terrorists to deliver for him. Far more likely, he would selfishly keep them himself to help deter an attack on Iraq. Moreover, international terrorism was hardly likely to be deflated if Iraq's regime were to be defeated. Indeed, it was a reasonable prediction—and it was predicted—that an attack on Iraq would likely supply terrorists with new recruits, inspire them to even more effort, and provide them with inviting new targets in the foreign military and civilian forces that would occupy a defeated, chaotic Iraq.[44]

A humanitarian argument could be made for a war against Iraq: to liberate its people from a vicious tyranny and from the debilitating and destructive effects of the sanctions the United States and Britain apparently were congenitally incapable of really relaxing while Saddam Hussein remained in power. However, calls for war did not stress this argument. Indeed, as commentator Francis Fukuyama has put it, a request for hundreds of billions of dollars and thousands of American lives to bring democracy to Iraq would "have been laughed out of court." Instead, those driving for war raised alarms about vague, imagined international threats that, however improbably, could conceivably emanate from Saddam's miserable, pathetic regime.[45]

Although they tried hard, the Americans were never able to get a resolution of support from any international body. The leaders of most countries, including those bordering Iraq, never seemed to see that country as nearly as much of a threat as did the distant United States and its only notable ally on the issue, Tony Blair's government in the United Kingdom. Whether or not they found the evidence that Iraq possessed or was developing weapons of mass destruction convincing, they felt the militarily feeble Saddam could readily be deterred and contained. Many American analysts agreed.[46]

Determined nonetheless to see it out, Bush shrugged off international disapproval and sent the U.S. military into action. As expected, the Iraqi military crumbled pathetically, incoherently, and predictably under the onslaught and seems to have lacked any semblance of a coherent strategy of resistance.[47]

Standing tall and peering confidently into the future, the Bush administration had anticipated that the Iraqis would greet their benevolent conquerors by dancing happily in the streets and then somehow quickly coordinate themselves into a coherent, and duly appreciative, government. Many in Iraq were glad to see Saddam's tyranny ended, but the invaders often found the population resentful and humiliated rather than gleeful or grateful. Moreover, bringing order to the situation was vastly complicated by the fact that the government-toppling invasion had effectively created a failed state, a condition that greatly facilitated widespread and massive criminality, looting, and eventually militia warfare. In addition, some people, including some foreign terrorists drawn opportunistically to the area, were dedicated to sabotaging the victors' peace and to killing the policing forces. Although military planners for the Gulf War of 1991 had planned for and worried about the possibility that they might be drawn into urban irregular warfare in Kuwait City, those planning the 2003 version rather amazingly never really considered that contingency. Moreover, shunned by the Bush administration, the international community was not eager to join in the monumental reconstruction effort. The inability of the conquerors to find any evidence of those banned and greatly feared weapons of mass destruction, much less links to international terrorism, only enhanced this reluctance.[48]

The American war on Iraq was based on a massive extrapolation from an unrelated, if dramatic, event and on a systematic, extravagant, and fanciful exaggeration of a threat that was of very questionable magnitude. The result was a bloody and costly foreign policy debacle.

CONCLUSION: COMPLEXITY, ROGUES, TERRORISM, AND THE CATASTROPHE QUOTA

Several conclusions about international threat perception emerge from this assessment of international anxieties in the post–cold war world. All of them relate, in one way or another, to perceptions about terrorism after 9/11.

First, there seems to exist something that might be called a catastrophe quota: when big problems go away, smaller ones become magnified in importance to compensate. Accordingly, things never get better. Once the defining horror of the post–World War II era—the prospect of global destruction through thermonuclear war—faded, comparatively minor ones were deftly elevated to fill the gap: civil or ethnic war in distant places, problems presented by little countries with noisy, if pathetic, dictators, and the ever-present "complexity."[49] None of these was remotely new, anymore than terrorism is after 9/11, but they often seemed that way because they had previously been obscured by more monumental preoccupations.

Second, when unfamiliar problems come to arrest the public and political consciousness, there is a demand for easily graspable, if often simplistic and spooky, explanations that can set the mind at rest. Thus, the wars in Yugoslavia became exercises in "ancient ethnic hatreds," even though Serbs and Croats, for example, had virtually never fought each other before the distinctly nonancient event known as World War II. The Kims of North Korea and Saddam Hussein of Iraq (a former semially) were typecast as irrational devils (or rogues) who were out to get the mighty, if distant, United States, therefore representing an international threat that was sometimes seen to be on the scale of the one once presented by the well-remembered and truly devilish Adolf Hitler. Much of the post-9/11 (and some of the pre-9/11) rhetoric and public wisdom about terrorism and about the diabolical demons of al-Qaeda has inspired similar comforting, if knee-jerk and misdirecting, explanations.

Third, the dramatic—that is to say, attention-arresting—appeal of singular devils in the world remains. In this, we seem to be repeating past experience with Egypt's Nasser, Indonesia's Sukarno, Cuba's Castro, Libya's Qaddafi, Iran's Khomeini, and others. In all cases, the threat these devils du jour actually posed to American and global interests proved to be very substantially exaggerated. Nasser and Sukarno are now footnotes, Castro a joke, and Qaddafi a mellowed irrelevance, while Khomeini's Iran became just about the only place in the Middle East where Americans were regularly treated with popular admiration and respect, at least until around 2003. (Significantly, Iran was also just about the only place in the area where the United States had been unable to meddle for over twenty years; it is possible there is a lesson here.) This experience notwithstanding, the preoccupation in the post–cold war era with the antics of colorful tyrants in minor countries, and in particular the imaginings about the international, even global, threat they supposedly pose, very much continues. First it was Iraq's Saddam, now it is Iran's Ahmadinejad.

Fourth, top leaders of major countries can become so emotionally obsessed and personally infected by even minor challenges that they can become absurdly preoccupied by them, neglect sensible policy alternatives, and flail about without much in the way of careful analysis. The generally even-tempered Jimmy Carter obsessed over hostages in Iran. The normally cautious and judicious George H. W. Bush became massively preoccupied by the irritating tinpot dictator, Noriega, and even more so by the rogue Saddam in Iraq, against whom he launched a war that might have been unnecessary while determinedly (and emotionally) ruling out other potential solutions to the problem and extravagantly, even absurdly, promising that a "new world order" would emerge from his exertions in one pocket of the Middle East. Ten years later, his son, who entered the presidency proposing that a sensible foreign policy should be "modest," reacted to the challenge presented by the diabolical work of nineteen clever suicide terrorists by instantly shucking aside any semblance of modesty and preposterously proclaiming that he was now taking upon himself the distinctly unhumble responsibility to "rid the world of evil."[50] He and others also allowed themselves to imagine that a "grave and gathering threat" was presented by the pathetic dictator who had so obsessed his father. Accordingly, he launched a destructive war against that devil/rogue while systematically refusing to consider the potential long-range quagmire-like, even self-destructive, consequences of his actions.

Finally, the post–cold war experience provides another example of the way a dramatic event, in this case 9/11, can be seized upon by policy-makers to force through a preexisting agenda—removing Saddam, in this instance—that has little or no relevance to the event itself.

PART III

APPROACHING TERROR AND TERRORISM

CHAPTER 7

An Alternative Terrorism Policy:
Absorbing, Policing, Reducing Fear, Avoiding Overreaction

The previous chapters surveyed the history of the past several decades to explore, with the benefit of hindsight, a series of threats that have proven to be much inflated. Reactions to these threats were often costly, sometimes extremely so, in financial resources and in human life, and simply doing nothing, or next to nothing, would have been wiser policy in many—probably most—cases. At the time, of course, there was sometimes no way to know for sure whether the fears these threats inspired were exaggerated, and there was a tendency to embrace worst-case-scenario thinking and to ignore more moderate, but equally plausible, perspectives.

That anxieties were commonly and often massively exaggerated in the past does not prove that today's concerns about international terrorism are similarly inflated. Nonetheless, the experience with threats that once were embraced as severe, even "existential," should at least give one pause.

In reasonable comparison, the effects of terrorism have generally not been, and probably will not become, massive. Nonetheless, terrorism will not disappear. It may be true that the average American is extremely safe: the chances of being hurt by terrorism are microscopic. Yet, this does not mean that *nobody* will ever be killed by terrorists; although the average lottery ticket holder is also very safe from winning, this does not mean that no one will do so. Somewhere in the world terrorist bombs will occasionally go off, some of them, perhaps, in America. What should be done about this?

141

Concern over terrorism is justified, but alarm, hysteria, and panic are not. Nor is massive extrapolation, obsession with worst-case scenarios, or policy overreaction. Indeed, they play into the terrorists' hands. In the foreign policy threats discussed in previous chapters, the creation of panic, hysteria, and overreaction was only a byproduct. For terrorists it is a central objective.

Frantz Fanon, the revolutionary, reportedly held that "the aim of terrorism is to terrify." The inspiration of consequent overreaction seems central to bin Laden's strategy. As he brayed in the 2004 message noted at this book's outset, it is "easy for us to provoke and bait. . . . All that we have to do is to send two mujahidin . . . to raise a piece of cloth on which is written al-Qaeda in order to make the generals race there to cause America to suffer human, economic, and political losses."[1] His policy, in fact, depends on, and is designed to provoke, overreaction by the target.

This means that the reduction of fear, anxiety, and overreaction is in fact actually quite central to dealing with terrorism. That is, it may make sense to heighten security and policing measures and perhaps to ask people to maintain awareness—as with crime, to report suspicious behavior to authorities. But it is important that this be done without inducing unnecessary fears. Alarmism can be harmful, particularly economically, and it can help to create the damaging consequences the terrorists seek but are unable to perpetrate on their own. Indeed, because the creation of insecurity, fear, anxiety, hysteria, and overreaction is central for terrorists, they can be defeated simply by not becoming terrified and by resisting the temptation to overreact.

EXPLORING A POLICY ALTERNATIVE

Terrorism generally becomes a high-consequence phenomenon not because of its direct effects, but because it manages to scare people and, partly as a result, to inspire unwise policies. Most to be feared is not terrorism itself, but fear itself, and the central focus should be on dealing with the costly and often unnecessary fear and with the costly and often unwise overreaction terrorism so regularly inspires. As Benjamin Friedman aptly notes, "One way to disarm terrorists is to convince regular Americans to stop worrying about them."[2] That, of course, is much easier said than done.

In due humility—and perhaps futility—the final chapters advance, evaluate, and explore a set of policy considerations for dealing with terrorism. This chapter proposes the policy, and the next one evaluates where we are now (pretty safe, actually).

Calvin Coolidge once overcame his natural taciturnity to reflect, "If you see ten problems coming down the road at you, chances are nine of them will go into the ditch before they ever get to you."[3] The sentiment is a most sensible one and deserves consideration: if you go out to meet a problem before it arrives you will be ahead of the game once in a while, but most of the time you will be exerting effort and expending resources to deal with problems that, but for your intervention, would have been taken care of by others or have gone away by themselves.

Many of the threats in recent decades that caused so much anguish, and often costly and destructive overreaction, in time died out substantially of their own weight without much assistance. Devil du jour after devil du jour eventually faded quietly from view: none became, as was so often feared when they thrust themselves upon the international scene, "a new Hitler." That process substantially held even for the Big One: the cold war threat presented by international communism.

So perhaps there should be at least two cheers for complacency. As they put it in New York, maybe sometimes it is wise simply to fuhgeddaboudit. Complacency can, of course, charm one into a false sense of security. But on average, this may well be better than the alternative: a false sense of insecurity that can lead people to become too cautious to live, and can cause them to spend unwisely and to lash out foolishly and self-destructively at threats they have exaggerated—or even at ones that may not, in fact, actually exist, like the one supposedly posed by domestic Japanese during World War II.

Seeking to control terrorists and terrorism can certainly be part of the policy, but if we already are rather safe, efforts to make us even safer are likely to be, at a minimum, inefficient. In the end, if we really want to deflate terrorism's impact we will need particularly to control ourselves.

Current policy puts primary focus on preventing terrorism from happening and on protecting potential terrorist targets, a hopelessly ambitious approach that has led to wasteful expenditures, an often bizarre quest to identify potential targets, endless hand-wringing and political posturing, and opportunistic looting of the treasury by elements of the terrorism industry. By distinct contrast, the policy I propose stresses three issues. First, the country can readily absorb just about anything the terrorists can dish out, and policy should mostly focus on some limited preventive and protective measures, particularly those that might make the development of nuclear weapons more difficult, and on policing endeavors, particularly ones coordinated with governments overseas, where such measures have shown some success. Second, to minimize the damage terrorism can do, there should be efforts to reduce or limit the erratic and foolish fears it characteristically inspires, insofar as this is possible. And third, policymakers should seek to control their political instincts to overreact when provoked by acts of terrorism—something that, contrary to conventional thought, may be, however unnatural, entirely possible politically.

PROTECTING, PREVENTING, POLICING, AND ABSORBING

As RAND's Bruce Hoffman notes, "Unfortunately, terrorism is just another fact of modern life. It's something we have to live with." Although terrorism has sometimes been just another fact of not-so-modern life as well, Hoffman's basic perspective is certainly sound. Terrorism, like crime, can be committed by any single person or small group that is willing to make the effort and take the risks, and there is no way to make everything completely safe from terrorists any more than every store can be protected against shoplifting or every street can be made permanently free of muggers. One cannot "put an end" to terrorism any more than one can completely stop arson or drunk driving or political backbiting. Gains can be statistical and meaningful, but "victory" is impossible.[4]

In Shakespeare's *Midsummer Night's Dream*, Theseus defines the lunatic as one who "sees more devils than vast hell can hold." That often seems to be the spirit under which Homeland Security bureaucrats (none of them to my knowledge a certifiable lunatic) labor. After 9/11 they set out at congressional urging to tally up a list of potential targets in the United States. By 2003, they had enumerated 33,000, to the apparent dismay of Homeland Security czar Tom Ridge. Dismay was premature: within a year, the list had been expanded to 80,000. Although the list has remained secret (we wouldn't want to put ideas into the head of your average diabolical terrorist, after all), there have been a number of leaks indicating that miniature golf courses are included, as well as Weeki Wachee Springs, that roadside waterpark in Florida.[5]

"Homeland security cannot be had on the cheap," proclaims Senator Joseph Lieberman. The problem is that it cannot be had on the expensive either. It is possible to make any individual target, such as the Washington Monument, more secure from terrorism. But, unless funds are infinite, society can't defend against every possibility. To be blunt (and obvious), it is simply not possible to protect every bus, every shop, every factory, every tunnel, every bridge, every road, every mall, every place of assembly, every mile of railroad track. Some relevant statistics: in the United States there are 87,000 food-processing plants, 500 urban transportation systems, 80,000 dams, 66,000 chemical plants, 590,000 highway bridges, 5,000 airports, 12,800 power plants, 2 million miles of pipeline, and 2 billion miles of cable, not to mention some 13,000 McDonald's (at this writing). Meanwhile, the Post Office handles nearly 200 billion pieces of mail each year. Nor is it possible to secure every border or have perfect, or for that matter, semiperfect, port security—a particular vulnerability, among billions, that has attracted the focused attention of many in the terrorism industry, if not so far of any actual terrorists. The United States can import over a billion dollars' worth of shoes in a single month: is each shoe box to be inspected? [6]

Moreover, if one tempting target becomes less vulnerable, your inventive terrorist could simply move on to others. Thus, if the Washington Monument has become a difficult target after years of expensive renovation, the agile terrorist might be led to cast an eye about for other notable tall, pointy objects—the Seattle Space Needle, for example. A displacement effect might even increase casualties: the destruction of the Washington Monument might be more embarrassing than that of the Space Needle, but it would probably cost fewer lives.

To simplify things, it might seem to make more sense to come up with a list of things that *aren't* prospective targets. A tree in the middle of a forest might seem a likely prospect for this list. But what about forest fires? Five skilled terrorists, each armed with a match, could set off five of those simultaneously. They would be aided in their efforts by the Park Service's propensity prominently to publicize which forests at any given moment are the driest and most tinderbox-like. Maybe in our determined quest to inconvenience terrorists we'd need to classify that information, hoping that campfire builders as well as smoking backpackers and motorists (but not your wandering malevolent terrorist) would have enough sense to be able to tell whether they are venturing through forested areas that are dry or not.

Because international terrorists active in the United States—thus far at least—have eschewed trees to concentrate on major cities, many think it reasonable to suggest that protective efforts should disproportionately focus on major cities. Thoughtful and presumably well-paid planners had by 2003 come up with a terrorist hit list of seven: New York, Washington, Chicago, San Francisco, Seattle, Houston, and Los Angeles. This exercise in metropolitan chauvinism, however, proved to be notably unpopular in places like Columbus, Ohio—not to mention Oklahoma City, kept off the list presumably because, although it has suffered more deaths from terrorism than all but two of the cities on the list, it had been the target merely of a domestic terrorist. Accordingly, the list was quickly expanded to thirty and, by 2005, to seventy-three (including Oklahoma City).[7] It is not at all clear how one can even *begin* to "protect" large (or even not-so-large) cities against random acts of terror that can be carried out by a single individual with a bomb in a backpack.

Moreover, it is entirely possible that international terrorists might one day come to realize that there is more payoff in hitting more ordinary and typical targets because that would scare more people. Of particular appeal to terrorists, perhaps, would be towns that tend to be synonymous with ordinary America, in part because they have peculiar or amusing names, like Peoria, Illinois, Sheboygan, Wisconsin, Pocatello, Idaho, Azusa, California, or Xenia, Ohio. After all, if a bomb goes off in one of those, it can go off anywhere.

Actually, although the big-city premise holds thus far for the United States, terrorists overseas even since 9/11 have often targeted tourist areas that are *not* in major cities, particularly hotels, in the case of Egypt, and a nightclub, as in the case of Bali.

Massive efforts to screen communications are also likely to prove to be wasteful exercises. Some people have characterized the process as trying to find a needle in a haystack by adding more hay. The effort principally leads to the cumulation of monumental amounts of data, and it creates an impossible number of false positives. Not only does this effort cost a large amount of money (no one yet seems to have tallied up how much), but it has not led to the detection of many—or maybe even of any—real terrorists in the United States. Moreover, notes security expert Bruce Schneier, gathering massive surveillance banks of such data not only constitutes an invasion of privacy, but the databases themselves become hugely attractive targets for criminals and identity thieves.[8]

Analyst Véronique de Rugy sensibly stresses that "among other vulnerable targets the United States has thousands of miles of borders, thousands of bridges, sports stadiums and shopping malls, hundreds of skyscrapers and power plants." She concludes from this that improving homeland security is a "challenging" task. It seems to me that it is more nearly a hopeless one. Not to mention expensive and disruptive. The Pentagon has extrapolated extravagantly from 9/11 to conclude that "it is unsafe to have employees in urban office buildings" and is in the process of moving tens of thousands of people in its more obscure agencies out of the area with little consideration about how they will manage to get to work on highways that are already congested.[9]

Why not abandon, or at least substantially reduce, the quixotic policy of seeking to make everything (or even a lot of stuff) safe, and use the money saved to repair any terrorist damage and to compensate any victims? A useful comparison might be made with the concern in 1999 about the millennium bug, codenamed Y2K, that was expected to wreak havoc with computer systems when the clock turned over to a new century. The response to this fear was to put into action a huge number of hasty and (therefore) costly preventive schemes to stave off disaster. A more rational approach might have been simply to focus preventive efforts on only a few especially dangerous concerns—nuclear weapons and the power grid, perhaps—and then to wait for the event to take place, fixing problems as they arose. Given the modest impact of the problem, it seems likely that, although this approach would have led to some spotty inconveniences very early in the new century, a fix-it-after-it-breaks approach would have been far less costly than the often panicky preventive one actually adopted.

We already absorb a great deal of tragedy and unpleasantness and still manage to survive. We live with a considerable quantity of crime, and the United States regularly loses 40,000 lives each year in automobile accidents. Moreover, countries have endured massive, sudden catastrophes without collapsing. In 1990 and then again in 2003, Iran suffered earthquakes that nearly instantly killed some 35,000 in each case. A tsunami that hit Indonesia in 2004 killed several times that many. But the countries have clearly survived these disasters; they constitute major tragedies, of course, but they hardly proved to be "existential" ones.

In approaching a sensible terrorism policy, three key issues set out by risk analyst Howard Kunreuther require, but rarely get, the careful discussion they deserve:

How much should we be willing to pay for a small reduction in probabilities that are already extremely low?

How much should we be willing to pay for actions that are primarily reassuring but do little to change the actual risk?

How can certain measures, such as strengthening the public health system, which provide much broader protection than terrorism, get the attention they deserve?[10]

My policy approach arises from an appreciation of the rarity and the likely limited destructiveness of terrorist attacks, and it stresses the country's ability to absorb just about any damage terrorists are apt to be able to inflict. It can still allow for some role for protection, prevention, and policing, however. The likelihood that terrorists will be able to explode nuclear weapons seems very low, but because such an explosion could be very consequential, it makes sense to devote some systematic effort to reduce that likelihood even further—particularly by working internationally to keep tabs on, and responsible control over, fissile material.

Former Congressman Christopher Cox argues that "a dollar spent on preventing the next terror attack is vastly superior to spending on cleaning up the mess after we fail to do job one, which is preventing terrorism." That holds only when prevention is feasible. Work along this line is certainly justifiable where credible leads develop, as in the case of the disrupted London bombing plot of 2006. This has so far been most effective with international cooperation.[11] In general, then, terrorism would be handled essentially as a criminal matter.

REDUCING FEAR

Because the main cost of terrorism generally derives from the anguish and overreaction of the terrorized, policies should seek to reduce the fear and anxiety that are so often unjustified and costly and to do so as inexpensively as possible. This is at least as important as attempting objectively to reduce the rather limited dangers terrorism is likely actually to pose.

In reaction to the 2001 anthrax attacks, the Post Office continues to spend billions on anthrax defense. The budgets for the Department of Homeland Security and Transportation Security Administration routinely escalate annually, with little focus on the process of fear reduction. But the lesson from the anthrax attack is not so much that damage was inflicted but, as Bruce Hoffman argues, that "five persons dying in mysterious circumstances is quite effective at unnerving an entire nation." To the degree that is true, policies for limiting terrorist damage should focus on such unwarranted reactions. As risk analyst Cass Sunstein puts it, "The reduction of even baseless fear is a social good."[12]

Actually, however, in some respects the fear of terrorism may not shift ordinary physical behavior all that much. Thus, real estate prices in the 9/11 target areas, Manhattan and Washington, DC, continue to climb. Similarly, a Columbia University study noted (with alarm) that two years after 9/11 only 23 percent of Americans and 14 percent of New Yorkers confessed to making even minimal efforts to prepare for disaster, such as stocking a couple of days' worth of food and water (no data on duct tape), buying a flashlight and a battery-powered radio, or arranging for a meeting place for family members. By 2004, Americans were being scolded by the Red Cross president and CEO for being "asleep at the switch when it comes to their own safety." So, in an important sense, the public does not seem to be constantly on edge about the threat of terrorism, any more than it was during the McCarthy era about the threat of communism, when people mostly mentioned mundane and personal issues when asked what concerned them most, or during years of heightened cold war "crisis" when scarcely anyone bothered to build, or even think very seriously about, the fallout shelters the Kennedy administration was urging on them.[13]

Moreover, the potential for panic is probably not a major problem either. There is extensive evidence that by far the most common reaction to disaster is not self-destructive panic, but resourcefulness, civility, and mutual aid.[14]

The main concern, then, is not hysteria or panic, except perhaps in exceptional, and very localized, circumstances. Instead, terrorism-induced fears can be debilitating in two ways.

First, they can cause people routinely to adopt skittish, overly risk-averse behavior, at least for a while, and this can much magnify the impact of the terrorist attack, particularly economically. The evasive and wary reactions of many residents of the Washington, DC, area to the scary antics of a sniper team in 2002 illustrate this tidily.

The problem is not that people are trampling each other in a rush to vacate New York or Washington, then, but that they may widely adopt other forms of defensive behavior, the cumulative costs of which can be considerable. The reaction to 9/11 led to a great many deaths as people abandoned safe airplanes for dangerous automobiles. It also had a negative economic impact, particularly in the airline and tourism industries, that lasted for years—a highly significant issue economically because travel and tourism has become the largest industry in the world. There is at present a great and understandable concern about what would happen if terrorists are able to shoot down an American airliner or two, perhaps with shoulder-fired missiles. Obviously, this would be a tragedy in the first instance, but the ensuing public reaction to it, many fear, could be extremely costly economically—even perhaps come close to destroying the industry—and it could indirectly result in the unnecessary deaths of thousands.[15]

Second, fears about terrorism tend to create a political atmosphere that makes it at least appear to be politically unwise, or even politically impossible, to adopt temperate, measured policies. "Fearful people," notes a county official in mid-America, "demand more laws and harsher penalties, regardless of the effectiveness or ineffectiveness of such efforts." Or, in Cass Sunstein's words, "When strong emotions are involved," as in a terrorist attack, "even if the likelihood of an attack is extremely low, people will be willing to pay a great deal to avoid it." Indeed, one study conducted a decade before 9/11 appears to have found that people would be willing to pay more for flight insurance against terrorism than for flight insurance against all causes including terrorism.[16] Name the beast, and wallets open. A fearful atmosphere inspires politicians to outbid each other to show their purity (and to gain votes), a process that becomes self-reinforcing as, to justify their wasteful and ill-considered policies and expenditures, they find it expedient to stoke the fears that set the policies in motion in the first place.

I argue later that, although there may be a willingness on the part of people to pay, and although this has certainly inspired foolish and wasteful policies, the phenomenon does not necessarily specifically *require* those policies. The reaction to Pearl Harbor did not specifically make the incarceration of Japanese citizens necessary; the McCarthy scare did not specifically require the setting up of concentration camps; concern about Soviet military capacity did not specifically require a fallout shelter program. By contrast, a restrained policy approach even to such a dramatic provocation as terrorism may be entirely possible politically.

Putting Risks in Context

One element in a policy that seeks to deal with the main costs of terrorism is to seek to put risks in context rather than, as at present, to exacerbate the fear. Where risks may be underappreciated—as in the cases of smoking, obesity, alcoholism, and automobile driving—it could make sense to stoke fear: people should be *more* afraid, less complacent, and less in denial about these dangers than they are at present. However, where the real risks for any given individual are far smaller—as with terrorism, shark attacks, and airplane flying—fear becomes the problem, and accordingly it makes policy sense to attempt to reduce it.

Thus there should be an effort by politicians, bureaucrats, officials, and the media to inform the public reasonably and realistically about the terrorist context instead of playing into the hands of terrorists by effectively seeking to terrify the public. That is, instead of inducing hysteria, which seems to be one of the terrorism industry's central goals, officials and the media should responsibly assess probabilities rather than simply stressing extreme possibilities so much and so exclusively. What is needed, as one statistician suggests, is some sort of convincing, coherent, informed, and nuanced answer to a central question: "How worried should I be?" In Kunreuther's words, "More attention needs to be devoted to giving people perspective on the remote likelihood of the terrible consequences they imagine." That would seem to be at least as important as boosting the sale of duct tape, issuing repeated and costly color-coded alerts based on vague and unspecific intelligence, and warning people to beware of Greeks, or just about anybody, bearing almanacs.[17]

What we need are more pronouncements like, or more or less like, the one in a book by Senator John McCain: "Get on the damn elevator! Fly on the damn plane! Calculate the odds of being harmed by a terrorist! It's still about as likely as being swept out to sea by a tidal wave. Watch the terrorist alert and go outside again when it falls below yellow. Suck it up, for crying out loud. You're almost certainly going to be okay. And in the unlikely event you're not, do you really want to spend your last days cowering behind plastic sheets and duct tape? That's not a life worth living, is it?" The inclusion in that list of the counsel to go outside when the alert level falls below yellow is, to say the least, odd. The ever-watchful and ever-cautious Department of Homeland Security seems unlikely *ever* to lower the threat level below yellow, and therefore McCain's admonition seems effectively to contradict the spirit in the rest of the passage by encouraging everyone to cower inside for the rest of their lives.[18]

Declarations like McCain's (with or without the unfortunate yellow alert curiosity) are exceedingly rare, almost nonexistent. Moreover, although the existence of this one presumably demonstrates that even politicians can issue them without necessarily suffering negative political repercussions, we get plenty of alarmism from the terrorism industry and almost nothing—*nothing*—about realistic risks and probabilities.

Thus, for those who understandably worry about the economic reaction to the shooting down of an airliner by terrorists, it would seem to be reasonable to publicize a few relevant facts, such as how many airliners, exactly, would have to crash before flying becomes as dangerous as driving the same distance in an automobile? In an article in *American Scientist*, Michael Sivak and Michael Flannagan have determined there would have to be one set of September 11 crashes a month for the risks to balance out. More generally, they calculate that an American's chance of being killed in one nonstop airline flight is about 1 in 13 million (even including the September 11 crashes in the mix), whereas to reach that same level of risk when driving on America's safest roads, rural interstate highways, one would have to travel a mere 11.2 miles.[19] Knowledge of such data may or may not calm fears, but the information should at least be widely known.

There ought to be at least *some* public discussion of the almost completely unaddressed, but seemingly obvious, observation that, in the words of another risk analyst, David Banks, "It seems impossible that the United States will ever again experience takeovers of commercial flights that are then turned into weapons—no pilot will relinquish control, and passengers will fight." The scheme worked in 2001 because the hijackers had the element of surprise working for them: previous airline hijackings had mostly been fairly harmless as hijackers generally landed the planes somewhere and released the passengers. In fact, just a few months earlier, in March 2001, three Muslim terrorists, in this case Chechens, had commandeered a Russian airplane with 174 aboard and had it flown to Saudi Arabia, where they were then overcome by local security forces. Three people, including one of the hijackers, were killed in the episode, but all the others survived. The passengers and crew on the fourth plane on September 11 had fragmentary knowledge about what the earlier hijackings that day had led to, and they prevented the plane from reaching its target. This is likely to hold even more for any later attempted hijackings; that is, terrorists might be able to blow up a plane, but they would not be able to commandeer it. Nonetheless, continues Banks, "enormous resources are being invested to prevent this remote contingency." There is a distinction, he argues, "between realistic reactions to plausible threats and hyperbolic overreaction to improbable contingencies."[20]

To help put terrorist risks in broadest context, it might even be helpful from time to time to examine a well-traveled cliché that became even more popular after 9/11, the one holding that "the world is a dangerous place." It would be useful to supply some context.[21] During the course of the bloody twentieth century, somewhere between 1 and 2 percent of the world's population died violent deaths in wars and through the systematic use of mass killing by governments. This rate of violent death may seem high, but something of a benchmark might be established by comparing death rates from automobile accidents: an American's chance of dying in an automobile accident over a lifetime is, as it happens, about the same. Also relevant might be the fact that the most murderous societies in all of history have had yearly homicide rates of around 100 in 100,000—that is, ones in which an individual has (only?) about 1 chance in 1,000 per year of being murdered; while the vast majority of societies, of course, have far lower rates. Indeed, what is remarkable about almost all societies is how few in number are the police forces required to maintain acceptable order. The world, this all might be taken to suggest, is actually not a terribly dangerous place: war, terrorism, and crime may not be all that difficult to pull off, but they don't occur very often. The most reliable restraints on violent behavior likely stem from the fact that the key goal for most—indeed, almost all—people is to live in peace and security, and they do this in part by adopting a live-and-let-live philosophy and by sharpening their skills from a very early age for determining whom to trust and befriend.

The Difficulties of Risk Communication

In the end, however, it is not clear how one can deal with the public's often irrational, or at least erratic, fears about remote dangers. It is easy, even comforting, to blame the terrorism industry—politicians, bureaucrats, risk entrepreneurs, and the media—for the distorted and context-free condition under which terrorism is so often discussed, and to want to agree wholeheartedly with H. L. Mencken's crack, "The whole aim of practical politics is to keep the populace alarmed (and hence clamorous to be led to safety) by menacing it with an endless series of hobgoblins." [22]

In many respects, however, the alarm is not so much aroused by the politicians and other "opinion leaders" as by their auditors. Edward R. Murrow's comment about McCarthy applies more broadly: "He didn't create this situation of fear, he merely exploited it." Hysteria and alarmism often sell. That is, although there may be truth in the cynical newspaper adage "If it bleeds, it leads," this comes about not so much (or at any rate not entirely) because journalists are fascinated by blood, but because they suspect, quite possibly correctly, that their readers are.

The record with respect to fear about crime, for example, suggests that efforts to deal responsibly with the risks of terrorism will prove difficult. Fear of crime rose notably in the mid-1990s even as statistics were showing it to be in pronounced decline. When David Dinkins, running for reelection as mayor of New York, pointed to such numbers, he was accused by a *New York Times* columnist of hiding behind "trivializing statistics." [23]

Some people say they prefer dangerous forms of transportation like the private passenger automobile (the necessary cause of over 3 million American deaths during the twentieth century) to safe ones like commercial airliners because they feel they have more "control." [24] But they seem to feel no fear on buses and trains (which actually are a bit more dangerous than airplanes) even without having that sense of control and even though derailing a train or crashing a bus is likely to be much easier than downing an airliner. People also tend to be more alarmed by dramatic fatalities, which the September 11 crashes certainly provided, than by ones that cumulate statistically. Thus in the United States the 3,000 deaths of September 11 inspire far more grief and fear than the 150,000 deaths from auto accidents that have taken place there since then.

In some respects, fear of terror may be something like playing the lottery, except in reverse. The chances of winning the lottery or of dying from terrorism may be microscopic, but for monumental events that are, or seem, random, one can irrelevantly conclude that one's chances are just as good, or bad, as those of anyone else. As Sunstein notes,

"Those who operate gambling casinos and lotteries . . . play on people's emotions in the particular sense that they conjure up palpable pictures of victory and easy living, thus encouraging people to neglect the question of probability. With respect to risks, insurance companies, extreme environmental groups, and terrorists do exactly the same."[25]

The communication of risk, then, is no easy task. In summarizing some of the literature on this issue, risk analyst Paul Slovic points out a number of regularities. People tend greatly to overestimate the chances of dramatic or sensational causes of death. Realistically informing people about risks sometimes only makes them more frightened. Strong beliefs in this area are very difficult to modify. A new sort of calamity tends to be taken as a harbinger of future mishaps. A disaster tends to increase fears not only about that kind of danger but of all kinds. People, even professionals, are susceptible to the way risks are expressed—far less likely, for example, to choose radiation therapy if told the chances of death are 32 percent than if told that the chances of survival are 68 percent. Studies have also shown that when presented with two estimations of risk from reasonably authoritative sources, people choose to embrace the alarmist opinion regardless of its source.[26]

Sunstein focuses on what he calls "probability neglect" and relates it directly to the experience with terrorism. "When their emotions are intensely engaged," he finds, "people's attention is focused on the bad outcome itself, and they are inattentive to the fact that it is unlikely to occur." Under such conditions, he argues, "attempts to reduce fear by emphasizing the low likelihood of another terrorist attack [are] unlikely to be successful."[27]

Although they could responsibly point to all sorts of studies that prove the point, airline companies do not routinely stress how safe flying is, especially when compared to driving. The reason for this, I strongly suspect, is that the airlines have come to conclude that telling people how safe flying is will only increase their fear of flying. Concern about safety rises when people discuss a low-probability risk even when what they mostly hear are apparently trustworthy assurances that the danger is infinitesimal.[28]

Risk, then, tends to be more nearly socially constructed than objectively calculated. And sometimes it gets constructed differently in societies that otherwise are quite similar. For example, Romanians seem to be more accepting of a wide variety of risks than the neighboring, and somewhat more prosperous, Bulgarians. Americans worry about nuclear power but not about genetically modified food, whereas the French worry about genetically modified food but not about nuclear power (and the Germans appear to worry about both). But one study finds that the French acceptance of nuclear power arises not from the fact that they think it is less dangerous, but because they see greater value in it than do Americans and because they trust their scientists, industry, and government more.[29]

Also puzzling in this regard are the dogs that don't bark. Despite a huge number of books and movies depicting the danger of asteroids, comets, and other space objects colliding with the earth, no one seems to have gotten terribly hysterical over this distinct, dramatic, and profoundly dreadful possibility. Moreover, despite the efforts and machinations of legions of agitators, Americans seem to be comparatively unmoved by threats supposedly presented by global warming and genetically modified food. Moreover, fears can rise and fall over time. They did so in the case of thermonuclear war. Something similar happened with nuclear energy: once embraced as a very positive development in the United States, it was later reduced almost to pariah status.[30]

There is an additional problem. There is a wariness about trying to refute doomsayers because there is more reputational danger in underplaying risks than in exaggerating them. People routinely ridicule futurist H. G. Wells's prediction that the conflict beginning in 1914 would be "the war that will end war," but not his equally confident declaration at the end of the Second World War that "the end of everything we call life is close at hand." Disproved doomsayers can always claim that caution induced by their warnings prevented the predicted calamity from occurring. (Call it the Y2K effect.) Disproved Pollyannas have no such convenient refuge.[31]

Reducing fear in emotion-laden situations such as terrorism is very difficult. In fact, suggests Sunstein, the best response may be to "alter the public's focus." That is, "perhaps the most effective way of reducing fear of a low-probability risk is simply to discuss something else and to let time do the rest." He also finds potential promise in efforts to stress "the affirmative social values associated with running the risk," lauding "President Bush's effort, in the wake of the terrorist attacks of 9/11, not to emphasize that the statistical risks were low, but to treat flying as a kind of patriotic act, one that would prevent terrorists from obtaining victory."[32] (As Bush has proved to be 9/11's most accomplished fearmonger and has been the individual to have most benefited politically from that effort, the lauding in this case may be just a bit misplaced.)

For all the gloomy difficulties, however, risk assessment and communication should at least be part of the policy discussion over terrorism, something that may well prove to be a far smaller danger than is popularly portrayed. By contrast, the constant unnuanced stoking of fear by politicians, bureaucrats, experts, and the media, however well received by the public, is on balance costly, enervating, potentially counterproductive, and unjustified by the facts.

Policies Focusing on Fear

An unorthodox but potentially beneficial approach would be systematically to determine which policy measures actually do reduce fear and then to put the least expensive of these into effect. If a measure actually increases safety, that would be all to the good. But because the dangers terrorists present appear to be rather limited (barring some very massive technological breakthroughs on their part), the actual effect on safety would be a secondary consideration.

Exploring Security Theater

One possibility would be to explore the potential benefits of what security expert Schneier derides as "security theater" and Richard Posner calls "cheap, showy gestures." [33]

Experience with crime fears may hold useful lessons here. During the late 1990s, New Yorkers did eventually come to feel safer from crime, but this was probably less because crime rates actually declined than because of atmospherics. Graffiti, panhandlers, aggressive windshield washers, and the homeless were banished or hidden from view, and New Yorkers apparently became more comfortable. [34]

Accordingly, it may have made sense in the months after the September 11 attacks to have armed reservists parading menacingly around in airports. It is highly doubtful that they prevented any terrorist attacks, and pulling them from productive jobs hardly helped the economy. Still, if this exercise in security theater made people feel significantly safer, it may have been worth it. Similarly, maybe (but only maybe) it helped to have police making random checks of backpacks at New York subway stations after bombs exploded in tube stations in distant London in the summer of 2005. The installation of security cameras at Weeki Wachee Springs in Florida is unlikely to have much effect on the likelihood of terrorism there (or anywhere else), but conceivably they would make people more comfortable when they checked out the mermaids. Whether such exercises in security theater would be worth the expense is a matter for empirical assessment.

For example, in a thoughtful analysis Véronique de Rugy notes that the Transportation Security Administration claims to have "intercepted seven million prohibited items at airport checkpoints, including just over 600 firearms." She notes that this means "0.008 percent of items intercepted are actually firearms and that 99.992 percent of intercepted items are tweezers and breath fresheners." She asks, "Is that really supposed to make us feel more secure?" She apparently thinks this monumental exercise in tweezer confiscation has not done so, and she may very well be right. But it is something that ought to be studied. People are presumably not actually safer when other passengers have been relieved of their tweezers, but perhaps they feel they are, and, if so, the absurd exercise in security theater may be, on balance, a useful expenditure. She is also concerned that over 90 percent of the TSA budget is devoted to air transport. But many people fear flying, whereas few seem to experience much angst when boarding trains, cars, taxis, and buses—even after terrorist bombs exploded on trains and buses in Madrid in 2004 and in London in 2005. Accordingly, to the degree that fear is the problem, focusing terrorism funds almost entirely on reducing the fear of flying is sensible policy even if flying is actually safer than getting there by almost any other means of transportation.[35]

Similarly, columnist Anne Applebaum derides "passengers who continue to believe that engaging in ritualistic shoe-removal gives them mysterious, magical protection against terrorism." But if they really believe that (and I question whether many do), the ritual would make policy sense if, without it, many fewer will fly. Applebaum also claims that "we want every passenger to have the chance to recite that I-packed-these-bags-myself mantra to a uniformed official before boarding an airplane" because "magic words, it seems, are what make Americans feel really safe."[36] As that peculiar mantra has been abandoned without any apparent effect on flyers' fears, Applebaum seems to have overstated the case. But if there really are magic words that will make us feel safe, it should be a primary quest of those in charge to find out what they are and to bellow them endlessly from the highest lamppost.

More generally, policymakers should constantly be on the lookout for cheap, even costless measures that could reduce fear. For example, when concerns about shark attacks soared in the summer of 2001, a Florida commission sternly forbade the feeding of sharks.[37] Whether this measure, or "magic words," actually did reduce fears is a matter for empirical investigation, but if it did, its value certainly outweighed its cost.

To the degree that people are less fearful when they have a sense of control, policies should seek to advance that rather vaporous quality whether it actually makes them safer or not. For example, if some people believe they gain control when they purchase duct tape and plastic sheeting at the instigation of convincing and authoritative imprecations from the all-knowing Department of Homeland Security, that office has done a service—not because it has reduced danger but because it has reduced anxiety.

Some studies suggest that people deeply angered by the 9/11 attacks also tended to be less fearful.[38] It is not clear how one stokes anger rather than fear, nor is it clear that doing so would necessarily be a good idea. But further research on this issue would be of value.

Instead of maintaining that terrorists might strike anywhere at any time, thereby stoking the fear of random violence, it might make sense to suggest that only certain (relatively small) areas are primarily at risk. If the benefit from the reduction of fear in the excluded areas is greater than the cost of fear enhancement in the designated ones, the measure would presumably be, on balance, sound public policy.

That security theater can be a serious issue is suggested by a preliminary study conducted at the University of Florida. Visible security measures such as armed guards, high walls, and barbed wire made people feel less vulnerable to crime. However, when these same devices are instituted in the context of dealing with the threat of terrorism, their effect is to make people feel tense, suspicious, and fearful; in other words, they generate exactly the effect terrorists hope to induce themselves.[39] This, surely, is something that needs further study.

Reducing Costs

Studies should be made of safety measures currently in effect with an eye toward reducing costs. For example, one might suspect that airline passengers are not made to feel any safer because they are forced to remove their shoes as they pass through inspection, or because they are required to show their boarding passes twice rather than once to uniformed authority figures, or because cars picking them up are not allowed to loiter at curbside even when such traffic is light. Maybe we could even get rid of those ritualistic announcements about oxygen masks poised to plunge into our laps from above. Experimental studies could easily be set up in airports to test whether these suspicions are valid.

Some (very limited) progress along this line has already been made. After the Lockerbie bombing of 1988, airlines were mindlessly required, as Applebaum notes, to ask every passenger if a stranger had given them something to carry in their luggage and if their luggage had been with them at all times. After more than a decade in which this procedure apparently produced nothing whatever, it was quietly dropped, and the flying public does not seem to have become notably distressed—or even to have noticed. Similarly, in late 2005 airline restrictions were relaxed to allow passengers to carry scissors up to four inches long and tools, such as screwdrivers, up to seven. The media had a field day with this, delightedly showing pictures of now acceptable scissors shot from as lethal an angle as they could manage. Despite all the negative publicity, however, the TSA heroically went ahead with the relaxation on schedule, and apparently without any impact on passenger traffic.

Following up on the scissors triumph, the TSA might consider substantially abandoning the air marshals program. It is primarily designed to deal with a problem that doesn't seem, actually, to exist: as discussed earlier, airline hijackings are probably impossible in the post-9/11 era because passengers and crew will no longer cooperate. Moreover, the program, which costs hundreds of millions of dollars per year, doesn't even provide useful security theater for timorous flyers: although there are now thousands of marshals (from fewer than fifty before 9/11), the program is not well-known and these bored, seat-occupying entities with high attrition rates travel incognito.[40] Their chief, or at any rate most publicized, achievement thus far seems to have been to kill an apparently deranged and menacing, but innocent and unarmed, passenger during a Florida airport altercation in 2005.

Remembering False Alarms

It might even be useful to plumb the "cry wolf" phenomenon for possibilities. The boy who repeatedly and alarmingly proclaims to his village that he has seen a wolf among the sheep ends up relaxing fear because people become less concerned about wolves when his alarms repeatedly prove false. If there are in fact no threatening wolves out there, or if the villagers generally are more concerned about wolf attacks than is objectively justified, he is providing a community service by reducing anxiety.

However, for this to work, there are four special issues. First, because the people in charge are aware of the cry-wolf problem, it is important that they not give in to the temptation to refrain from issuing warnings after they have repeatedly been proved mistaken: they must keep it up. Second, the warnings must be specific enough to be falsifiable; according to one version, Aesop's boy cries "Wolf! Wolf! The wolf is chasing the sheep!," a claim the villagers are able quickly to falsify. He does not issue such unfalsifiable outcries as "I have intercepted some chatter recently suggesting that a wolf might chase the sheep at some time in the indefinite future, or, then again, maybe not." Third, it would be important to factor in the expense of the alert itself; for example, raising the alert level from yellow to orange costs the Los Angeles Airport alone $100,000 per day in extra security outlays.[41] And fourth, it is crucial to the process that the community remembers the false alarms. In the real world, doomsday scenarists are rarely held to account because few listeners keep track of the extravagant predictions when they fail to materialize.

Taking the last point more generally, a useful public service would be to cumulate a record of the many false warnings that have been issued by the terrorism industry and routinely and repeatedly to publicize them. Although each warning has tended to elevate short-term concern, the cumulative impact of the series of false alarms could be, if people are jogged into remembering them, beneficially to create a numbing effect and to reduce anxiety. As it is now, not only are failed predicters of doomsday rarely held to account, but they have proved remarkably agile at creative nuance and extrapolation after failure.

It should be remembered that in 2004 the terrorism industry repeatedly insisted that some Big Terrorist Event was likely in connection with (a) the Athens Olympics, (b) the 4th of July celebrations, (c) the Democratic Party convention in Boston, (d) the Republican convention in New York, (e) the election campaign, and/or (f) election day in November. For example, there was the sobering pronouncement that was issued from a meeting in late 2003 "of more than 200 senior business and government executives, many of whom are specialists in security and terrorism related issues":

> Almost three-quarters of them said it was likely the United States would see a major terrorist strike before the end of 2004. A similar number predicted that the assault would be greater than those of 9/11 and might well involve weapons of mass destruction. . . . These are serious people, not prone to hysteria or panic—military officers, policymakers, scientists, researchers and others who have studied such issues for a long time. They know that in country after country, elections have held an irresistible lure for terrorists.

Many other "serious people" uttered a similar mantra over the next several months. In May 2004, for example, the widely published pundit Michael Ignatieff confidently assured us, "We can confidently expect that terrorists will attempt to tamper with our election in November."[42]

Then, at the end of that month, it got really official. With FBI Director Robert Mueller in tow, Attorney General John Ashcroft delivered a set of punchy points to the press:

> Credible intelligence from multiple sources indicates that al-Qaeda plans to attempt an attack on the United States in the next few months.
>
> This disturbing intelligence indicates al-Qaeda's specific intention to hit the United States hard.
>
> Beyond this intelligence, al-Qaeda's own public statements suggest that it's almost ready to attack the United States. Just after New Year's, al-Qaeda announced openly that preparations for an attack on the United States were 70 percent complete.
>
> After the March 11th attack in Madrid, Spain, an al-Qaeda spokesman announced that 90 percent of the arrangements for an attack in the United States were complete.

Within days intelligence insiders were noting to the press that the 70 and 90 percent figures were issued by a largely discredited group with a web site that had claimed credit for power blackouts and for just about everything else except, noted one, the 2004 "cicada invasion of Washington"—something that, unlike Ashcroft's terrorist events, actually happened that year.[43]

In July, it was Homeland Security czar Tom Ridge's turn: "Credible reporting now indicates that Al Qaeda is moving forward with its plans to carry out a large-scale attack in the United States in an effort to disrupt our democratic process." The next month he followed this up with another warning based mainly on intelligence that was three or four years old. Rating the reports on which these warnings were at least partly based on a scale of 1 to 100, one senior American counterterrorism official said, "I'd give it about a two." Meanwhile, European and Middle East officials indicated they'd seen not a single piece of solid intelligence to back up the warnings.[44]

When nothing happened during the summer (a defrocked priest wearing kilts did show up to disrupt the marathon in Athens briefly, but this, I think, does not count), the fearmonger focus deftly turned to the fall election itself. "It's practically an article of faith among counterterrorism officials that al-Qaeda will try to hit the U.S. homeland in the run-up to the presidential election," *Newsweek* informed us in a mid-October cover story. It went on to quote a supremely confident senior law enforcement official: al-Qaeda "wants to strike a blow against everything we hold dear. What better way than to attack democracy itself? It's coming."[45]

After the election passed uneventfully into history, the argument was floated that a taped encyclical issued by bin Laden in late October somehow demonstrated that he was too weak to attack before the election and also that he was marshalling his resources such that the several months *after* the election had now become especially dangerous. Others issued a special alarm for inauguration day, January 2005, ominously identified as "the single most vulnerable moment for our constitutional system." A notable terrorist attack during that time would have generated hundreds of thousands of news items and a veritable paroxysm of breast-beating by the terrorism industry. The absence of an attack, needless to say, went scarcely noticed. In the meantime, Richard Clarke, counterterrorism coordinator from the Clinton administration, issued a cheery scenario that appeared in the *Atlantic* as a cover story in early 2005 in which he anticipated shootings at casinos, campgrounds, theme parks, and malls in 2005, bombings in subways and railroads in 2006, missile attacks on airliners in 2007, and devastating cyberattacks in 2008.[46]

A systematic and very public tabulation of such doomsaying might prove to be a notable contribution to fear reduction. Someone should try.

Another possibility stems from studies indicating that trust in the source of the information can be important.[47] The Department of Homeland Security and President Bush tend to enjoy considerable trust on this issue, and they have been, as repeatedly noted, mostly inclined to stoke fears of terrorism. Efforts to undermine their credibility, therefore, could potentially have the effect of reducing fear.

Reassessing Safety Standards

Any problems caused by radiological (and chemical and perhaps biological) weapons are likely to stem far more from the fear and overly evasive behavior they may induce than from the direct harm the weapons themselves may inflict. Therefore, in these cases, the potential for fear and perhaps panic should be very much a primary concern. In fact, "dirty" bombs simply raise radiation levels somewhat above normal background levels in a small area, and a common recommendation from nuclear scientists and engineers is that those exposed should calmly walk away. This bit of advice has not been advanced prominently (or even, perhaps, at all) by those in charge. Effectively, therefore, they encourage panic, and the danger is, as one nuclear engineer puts it, "If you keep telling them you expect them to panic, they will oblige you. And that's what we're doing." By contrast, urge other specialists, the public should be "psychologically immunized" against a radiological attack through an extensive public education campaign stressing that such attacks rarely pose immediate threats to life. Risk analyst Baruch Fischoff, noting how rare real panic actually is, puts the issue most bluntly: "planning for panic" is at best "wasting resources on a future that is unlikely to happen," and at worst it "may be doing our enemies' work for them—while people are amazing under pressure, it cannot help to have predictions of panic drummed into them by supposed experts."[48]

It would be useful as part of this process to reconsider the standards about what is harmful in some cases. A "dirty" bomb might raise radiation 25 percent over background levels in an area and therefore into a range the Environmental Protection Agency officially considers undesirable, but there ought to be some discussion about whether that really constitutes "contamination" or indeed much of a danger at all given the somewhat arbitrary and exceedingly cautious levels declared to be acceptable by the EPA. In fact, some analysts advocate raising the permissible levels by a factor of ten.[49] If trusted government officials can truthfully say that the contamination does not reach levels considered unsafe, undesirable negative psychological and economic reactions might be beneficially reduced and might far outweigh any risks involved.

The risk communication literature suggests that this would be a difficult sell—perhaps even a counterproductive one—and the CYA literature suggests that it is hugely unlikely to be seriously undertaken. However, there are indications that the Department of Homeland Security is beginning to reevaluate cleanup standards, which currently require radiation to be reduced to 15 percent of the amount of radiation that is emitted by building materials in the U.S. Capitol and therefore absorbed by people working there. Overly strict rules, says one of the guideline examiners, only aids and abets the terrorists.[50] It remains to be seen whether the aiding and abetting will continue.

AVOIDING POLICY OVERREACTION

A common reaction to terrorism is to become overly protective and to overspend on defenses, and also to lash out impetuously at the perceived threat without much in the way of careful analysis. It is a key running conclusion of this book that such policy overreaction can be expensive and counterproductive and that it is exceedingly important for officials to keep this in mind.

Many examples of policy overreaction in the history of terror and counterterror can be detailed. The costly results of Reagan's response to terrorist attacks concerning Libya were discussed in Chapter 5. More recently, when two American embassies in Africa were bombed in 1998, killing more than 200 (including a few Americans), President Bill Clinton, apparently working on information that was at best incomplete, retaliated by bombing a pharmaceutical factory in Sudan suspected of producing chemical weapons. The loss of the factory may have led to the deaths of tens of thousands of Sudanese over time because vital medications were no longer available and replacements were slow to arrive. Also bombed were some of Osama bin Laden's terrorist training camps in Afghanistan, which, according to at least some reports, caused the Afghan government, the Taliban, to renege on pledges to extradite the troublesome and egoistic bin Laden to Saudi Arabia. The attacks also made him into an international celebrity, essentially created his al-Qaeda organization by turning it into a magnet for funds and recruits, and converted the Taliban from reluctant hosts to allies and partners. In the following year, responding to several vicious acts of terrorism apparently perpetrated by Chechens, the Russian government reinstituted a war against the breakaway republic that has resulted in far more destruction of Russian (and, of course, Chechen) lives and property than the terrorists ever brought about.[51]

It is a key policy recommendation, accordingly, that policymakers should seek to avoid or control their instinctual tendency to respond to terrorism with the foolish and counterproductive policy reactions terrorism so often inspires. Most important, of course, public and private members of the terrorism industry would need to try to restrain and contain any instinct to destroy their own societies in response should they ever be provoked to the extreme by terrorists.

Exploiting Adversity

One caveat should be registered. Sometimes what appears to be a massive overreaction is actually a conscious policy decision opportunistically seized on to exploit the emotions of the event to carry out a policy desired for other reasons. Thus, the North Korean attack of 1950 and the *Sputnik* launch of 1957 were productively exploited by those who wanted to further militarize the cold war.

Terrorist attacks have often been used in like manner. Perhaps the most spectacular instance is Austria-Hungary's massive overreaction in 1914 to the assassination of a political figure in Sarajevo by a fanatical Serb. Itching to have it out with Serbia, Austria leaped at the opportunity and issued a huge list of demands, most of which the Serb government met, and then launched military action. Unfortunately for the Austrians, the Serbs, and everybody else on the continent, this brash, opportunistic action soon escalated into one of the most horrendous wars in history.

Something comparable might hold for the U.S. war on Iraq in 2003. Quite a few people in the administration had been yearning for such a war for years, and they clearly seized the opportunity provided by the trauma of 9/11 to push their agenda. Similarly, in the aftermath of some attacks by Chechen terrorists on a school in 2004, Russian President Vladimir Putin instituted some "reforms" that enhanced his control over the country's political process.[52]

In such cases, the terrorist act is used as an excuse for, or is seized on to carry out, a policy that has been desired for other reasons. To say that World War I or the Iraq War were "caused" by terrorism, or even by overreaction to terrorism, really stretches the distinction. The terrorist acts do not "trigger" such ventures, but rather facilitate them by shifting the emotional or political situation, potentially making a policy desired for other reasons possible but no more necessary than it was before the terrorist act.

In addition, regimes have often allowed their participation in peace talks to be critically affected by terrorists. By stating that they will not negotiate as long as terrorist attacks continue, both the Israeli government and the British government (over Northern Ireland) effectively permitted individual terrorists to set their agendas. However, if those governments actually didn't want to negotiate anyway, the terrorist acts simply supplied a convenient excuse, as they did for the Austrians in 1914.

Managing Rhetoric

That consideration aside, dramatic acts of terrorism very often have negative reverberations because they stimulate or service the politician's natural desire and propensity to play to the galleries, to wallow in the art of the rhetorical flourish. Some of that can be seen in instances discussed earlier: Carter with his hostages in Iran, Reagan with his in Lebanon. If an act of fulmination proves to be a productive exercise in security theater by somehow reducing fears, it could be a desirable, and certainly inexpensive, palliative: cheap talk, indeed. And if it serves as a substitute for unwise action, that would be all to the good. However, more commonly and more dangerously, stormy rhetoric can commit, or self-entrap, the country in expensive, foolish, or even counterproductive policies and actions—precisely what happened to Carter and Reagan.

There are, in this regard, special problems with the rhetorical metaphor "war on terror," so popular among politicians and others in the terrorism industry. If it really meant "a war on fear," it might be sensible, following the argument presented here. But actually, of course, it really means, rather preposterously, a war on a tactic, "terrorism," not on "terror."

In general, the efforts against terrorism should be considered more like a campaign against crime than like a war, however much the war imagery may get the juices flowing.[53] Wars end, but because they are carried out by isolated individuals or by tiny groups at times of their own choosing, terrorism and crime never do. Moreover, one cannot "conquer" terrorism or "bring it to an end." Like crime, one can at best seek to reduce its frequency and destructiveness in the hope that people will come to feel reasonably—but never perfectly—safe from it. Of course, military measures may sometimes be useful in the campaign, as they may have been in Afghanistan. But to frame the challenge presented by some terrorist as a "war" risks the danger of raising unreasonable expectations.

The war imagery also suggests that people should be asked to make sacrifices. This popular conclusion is at least partly fanciful. Few Americans except those directly involved in the wars in Korea or Vietnam really made much of a sacrifice, and, although there were shortages and inconveniences on the homefront during World War II, consumer spending by the Greatest Generation generally surged.[54] A goal of terrorism presumably is to hamper the economy, and therefore the best response to it, hardly much of a sacrifice, would be to go out and buy a refrigerator or to take an airplane to a vacation resort. The war imagery suggests that people should be cutting back; but cutting back actually helps the terrorists.

The Political Feasibility of Restraint

It is often argued that a policy of restraint toward terrorism as advocated here is simply not possible politically. That is, there is a political imperative for public officials to "do something" (which usually means overreact) when a dramatic terrorist event takes place: "You just can't not do anything."

However, refraining from overreacting after a terrorist attack is not necessarily politically unacceptable, nor does it necessarily mean "do nothing." In this case, judicious efforts to control nuclear material are certainly wise, and there should be continued support for international policing to further dismantle terrorist networks and to infiltrate terrorist organizations as much as possible.

At the same time, history supplies plenty of instances when reactions to dramatic terrorist events were restrained and officials did not suffer politically or otherwise. Consider, for example, the two cases of terrorism that killed the most Americans before September 2001. Ronald Reagan's response to the first of these, the bombing in Lebanon in 1983 that killed 241 American Marines, was to make a few speeches and eventually to pull the troops out. The venture seems to have had no negative impact on his reelection a few months later. The other was the December 1988 bombing of the Pan Am airliner over Lockerbie, Scotland, that resulted in the deaths of 187 Americans. Perhaps in part because this tragic event took place after the presidential election in that year, the official response, beyond seeking to obtain compensation for the victims, was simply to apply meticulous police work in an effort to tag the culprits, a process that bore fruit only three years later and then only because of an unlikely bit of luck. That cautious, deliberate response proved to be entirely acceptable politically.

Similarly, after an unacceptable loss of American lives in Somalia in 1993, Bill Clinton responded by withdrawing the troops, without noticeable negative effect on his 1996 reelection bid. Although Clinton reacted with (apparently counterproductive) military retaliations after two U.S. embassies were bombed in Africa in 1998, his administration did not have a notable response to terrorist attacks on American targets in Saudi Arabia (Khobar Towers) in 1996 or to the bombing of the USS *Cole* off the coast of Yemen in 2000, and these nonresponses never caused him notable political pain. The anthrax attacks of 2001 did lead to some extravagant expenditures by the Post Office and other agencies, but it is not at all clear these were required politically. George W. Bush's most notable and visible public response to those attacks was the same as Clinton's had been to the terrorist attacks against the World Trade Center in 1993 and in Oklahoma City in 1995 and the same as the one applied in Spain when terrorists bombed trains there in 2004: the dedicated application of police work to try to apprehend the perpetrators. This approach proved politically acceptable even though the culprit in the anthrax case (unlike the other ones) has yet to be found.

An alternative low-key approach to the Iran hostage situation was proposed and examined in chapter 6. It is difficult to imagine how such a policy could have worked worse politically for Carter than the one he unwisely embraced at the time. Most interestingly, there have been a large number of instances in which Americans have been held hostage during the war in Iraq. Unlike the hostage issues that ultimately held the Carter and Reagan administrations themselves hostage, the Bush administration has mostly ignored, or at least downplayed, the problem, and this has proved to be politically acceptable.

The demands for retaliation may be especially problematic in the case of suicide terrorists as the direct perpetrators of the terrorist act are already dead. Nonetheless, the attacks against Americans in Lebanon, Saudi Arabia, and against the *Cole* were all suicidal, yet no direct retaliatory action was taken.

Thus, despite short-term demands for some sort of action, experience suggests that politicians can often successfully ride out this demand after the obligatory (and inexpensive) security-theater expressions of outrage are prominently issued.[55]

Extreme cases like Pearl Harbor and 9/11 would put this proposition to the greatest test, but it seems likely that even here a communicative leader could have pursued more patient and more gradual policies. In the case of Pearl Harbor, the alternative policy suggested and examined in chapter 3—dealing with the challenge in the Pacific by relying mostly on patient, if aggressive, containment, military buildup, and harassment rather than on direct military confrontation—might have been accepted in time. There was no overwhelming public demand to get it over quickly, particularly if American casualties could be minimized by a more patient strategy.

Similarly, as will be discussed more fully in the next chapter, a policy that could probably have been sold to the public after 9/11 might have emphasized coordinating with other countries (almost all of them, including the crucial one, Pakistan, very eager to cooperate after the shock), putting pressure on the Afghan regime, and applying policing and intelligence methods to shore up defenses and to go after al-Qaeda and its leadership. The war in Afghanistan was widely supported, and its remarkable success makes second-guessing difficult. But there was no guarantee at the time that the costs to the United States would be so low, and that specific venture was not clearly required from a political standpoint, whereas lesser measures could have been accepted, particularly if they showed some tangible results. And, of course, whatever the resonances of 9/11, there was no political imperative to launch a costly ground war against Iraq. In fact, public support for going to war against Iraq did not rise when the Bush administration pushed for it in the runup to the war.[56]

CHAPTER 8

Terrorism and Terror

What is the most likely future of the terrorism saga? To assess where we stand, and to suggest where we may be headed, it helps to distinguish between terrorism and terror.

Although it could possibly be derailed by America's foolishly overreactive (or perhaps merely foolishly opportunistic) war in Iraq or by a hugely counterproductive attack on Iran, the campaign against international terrorism seems to be in fairly good shape. This is not due particularly to the efforts of the Department of Homeland Security, or to amber warnings, or to the accumulation of large quantities of duct tape. Rather, it stems principally from the mind-concentrating effects of 9/11 itself and from the subsequent increased international policing cooperation impelled by that event, as well as, later, from counterproductive acts of destruction in a variety of countries by the terrorists. There is a good chance, as well, that al-Qaeda is anything but the omniscient and omnicompetent adversary so often envisioned.

The gloomy news, by contrast, is more real than potential: terror continues to boom even as terrorism struggles. The sometimes self-destructive propensities to exaggerate threat, to obsess on worst-case fantasies, to fear both unwisely and too well, to engage in massive extrapolation, and consequently to overreact and overspend are alive and kicking and will likely always be with us.

In short, the "war" on *terrorism*—on the occasional explosion by al-Qaeda and by other individuals and small bands of dedicated fanatics around the world—seems to be going rather well overall (at least outside Iraq, Afghanistan, and the Palestine area). However, the "war" on *terror*—on stemming and mitigating the fears and overreactions terrorism so commonly inspires in people, in the media, and in officials—

seems to be going nowhere, and not only because it is being almost entirely unwaged.

TERRORISM

For the present at least, insofar as international terrorism—particularly al-Qaeda—is a problem, it seems likely that things are improving. Let us examine our enemy.

Al-Qaeda's Capacity

To begin with, al-Qaeda's capacity to do damage and its ubiquity may, as with so many other perceived international threats, have been exaggerated. If hindsight suggests that the anxieties generated about Imperial Japan, international and domestic communism, and glowering devil du jour and rogue states were much inflated, perhaps the same can be said for al-Qaeda.

It is important to consider capacity as well as intent. Al-Qaeda's intent is murderous, but how capable is it? The American Communist Party included a dedicated band of conspirators in league with foreign enemies who were devoted to using subversion and violence to topple democracy and capitalism; if successful, they would presumably have established a murderous tyranny. The intent was there, but not, as it turned out, the capacity. In the present instance, one should not assume that because some terrorists may wish to do great harm, they will necessarily be able to do so.

In 1996 Osama bin Laden issued a religiously oriented proclamation that is usually taken to be a personal declaration of war on America—though actually the document seems to restrict bin Laden's wrath to the Americans stationed in Saudi Arabia and is entitled, "Declaration of War against the Americans Occupying the Land of the Two Holy Places." In 1998, he broadened his horizons, urging Muslims, as Libya's resident blowhard, Qaddafi, had a decade earlier, to attack American interests and kill Americans wherever they could find them. Writing in *The Skeptical Inquirer* a year after 9/11, Clark Chapman and Alan Harris quite reasonably expressed incredulity that, however the documents are interpreted, anyone would take seriously a declaration of war promulgated by a single individual. Under the emotional impetus of the 9/11 attacks, a considerable portion of the readership even of that magazine apparently did so judging from the letters the article inspired.[1]

By contrast, Middle East specialist Gilles Kepel's extensive assessment of the radical Islamic movement finds this reaction to be singularly unjustified. Although a fringe element, radical Islamists did expand in influence, particularly in Iran, Sudan, and Afghanistan in the 1980s and early 1990s, and they fought viciously to do so in Algeria. But the pattern since has been mostly one of retreat or utter collapse in all those places (in Iran, they have in effect been overwhelmingly voted out of office at least twice). Moreover, their acts of spectacular terrorist violence, he concludes, have utterly failed to spur the masses into upheaval as hoped. In this view, the attacks on the United States in 2001 were a symbol of the movement's desperation, isolation, fragmentation, and decline, not of its strength.[2]

Another Middle East specialist, Fawaz Gerges, parses the issue further. He agrees that mainstream Islamists—the vast majority within the Islamist political movement—have given up on the use of force and that the remaining jihadis who are still willing to apply violence constitute a tiny minority. But he goes on to note that the vast majority even of this small group primarily focus on various "infidel" Muslim regimes and on Israel and consider those among them who carry out violence against the "far enemy"—mainly Europe and the United States—to be irresponsible and reckless adventurers who endanger the survival of the whole movement. As *Washington Post* columnist Richard Cohen puts it vividly, to hold that terrorists think that by controlling one country, they will be able to create a radical Islamic empire from Spain to Indonesia, as Vice President Cheney believes, "is to give credence to the fantasies of Islamic nut cases."[3]

Chief among these nut cases is, of course, Osama bin Laden. The 1998 bombings by the United States of Sudan and Afghanistan in response to al-Qaeda's attacks on American embassies in Africa and the failure of these efforts to kill him did elevate his star for a while, Gerges notes. But in 1999 and 2000 Gerges interviewed a wide variety of former jihadis, Islamists, activists, and civil society leaders and found general agreement that al-Qaeda did not have much of a future. Few even took it, or bin Laden, seriously, though by obsessing on him, the Americans risked turning him into a star and a hero.[4]

The 9/11 attacks demonstrated, of course, that al-Qaeda—or at least nineteen of its members—still possessed some fight, though the level of damage inflicted apparently surprised its planners. Fears of and anxieties about the omniscient terrorist, so reminiscent of those inspired by images of the twenty-foot-tall Japanese after Pearl Harbor or the twenty-foot-tall communist at various points in the cold war (particularly after *Sputnik*), have made a stateless recluse, Osama bin Laden, into the devil du jour par excellence. The image of Osama bin Laden "sharing a tent with a mountain goat and a well-thumbed Koran" may go too far. After all, he is still out there communicating and inspiring and maybe even commanding in one way or another.[5] But that image may be closer to the mark than any vision of a dark devil marshalling powerful armies.

Explaining the Absence of Post-9/11 Terrorism in the United States

If it is so easy to pull off, and if al-Qaeda and like-minded terrorists are so omnicompetent, why hasn't there been an attack within the United States since 9/11? Why don't they snipe at people in shopping centers, collapse tunnels, poison food, cut electrical lines, derail trains, set forest fires, blow up oil pipelines, cause massive traffic jams?[6]

One easy, convenient, and attractive explanation for the absence of international terrorist attacks in the United States since 9/11 is to argue that the protective measures so hastily and expensively erected after that tragic event somehow prevented a repetition. This explanation, not surprisingly, has become increasingly popular with the Bush administration, and by 2006 Vice President Cheney was proclaiming that the country had been "successfully defended" by "a lot of good work by some very able and capable people."[7]

Yet, Israel, with a far more extensive antiterrorism apparatus in place, has experienced a considerable amount of terrorism since 2001. And although it is true, of course, that the number of international terrorist incidents in the United States in the several years after 9/11 has been zero, that was the same number registered in the several years before the attacks, at a time when antiterrorist policing exertions were much lower. Moreover, as it only takes one or two guys with a gun or explosive to terrorize vast numbers of people, as was found with the sniper attacks around Washington, DC, in 2002, governmental measures would have to be nearly perfect, something that its monumental imperfection in dealing with Hurricane Katrina in 2005 suggests is remarkably unlikely.

The field intelligence groups set up in the FBI after 9/11 to coordinate information had yet to obtain, more than four years later, the capacity to e-mail analysts at other agencies or even to access the Internet. Multibillion-dollar computer upgrades at the National Security Agency were in shambles.[8]

Immigration procedures have been substantially tightened (at considerable cost to the tighteners) and suspicious border guards have stopped or turned away a few probable bad apples. Immigration control can have some effect (though not, obviously, against homegrown terrorists). Indeed, the planners of the 9/11 attacks apparently had wanted to have more men on the planes, but some jihadists selected for the mission were unable to gain entry into the United States for various reasons. But those planners, assuming Middle Eastern males would be unable legally to enter the country after the attack, had already put into motion schemes to rely thereafter on non-Arabs with passports from Europe and Southeast Asia. More than 300 *million* people are admitted legally into the United States every year, and, despite the planners' wary anticipations, quite a few of them are Middle Eastern males.[9] The idea that border security by the agencies who also gave us the Katrina response has been so elegantly effective that not even a handful of crafty terrorists could have filtered through boggles the imagination.

Moreover, visitors and immigrants have continued to flood into the country illegally; the number of such crossings overland and through tunnels is often said to tally upwards of 1,200 per day, or more than 400,000 a year. Along with them have come generous quantities of forbidden substances that the government's "war on drugs" has been unable in decades of strenuous and well-funded effort adequately to intercept or interdict—or even, mostly, detect. (As some have put it, if you want to get a weapon of mass destruction into the United States, embed it in a bale of marijuana.) Every year a number of people from Islamic countries, perhaps hundreds of them, are apprehended among the illegal flow from Mexico.[10] And many trespassers are never caught, of course.

If terrorists haven't filtered into the country in potentially damaging numbers, this can't be because of U.S. border security. It must be because they aren't trying very hard or because they are far less dedicated, diabolical, and competent than the common image would suggest.

Also popular are assertions that, although the invasion of Afghanistan

in 2001 embarrassingly never managed to capture or kill the top terrorism gurus it was gunning for, the venture still served a purpose by
severely disrupting al-Qaeda and its operations and "training camps."
But the terrorist attacks in Madrid in 2004 were carried out by a tiny
group of men who had no connection to al-Qaeda whatever, except perhaps atmospherically or inspirationally, and none had ever been to
Afghanistan, much less to any of its training camps. In fact, only one of
them had anything that could be called "training" (or for that matter
"experience") and that was in the civil war in Algeria. Nonetheless,
perhaps working from information about bomb making available over
the Internet, and without any outside funding, they were able to pull off
a coordinated nonsuicidal attack with thirteen fabricated remote-
controlled bombs, ten of which went off on schedule, killing 191 and
injuring more than 1,800. Nor, apparently, did the London bombers of
2005 require Afghan training. Such experiences suggest, note analysts
Daniel Benjamin and Steven Simon, that for a terrorist attack, "all that
is necessary are the most portable, least detectable tools of the terrorist
trade: ideas." [11]

It is also sometimes suggested that the terrorists have become so busy
killing Americans and others in Iraq, that they simply didn't have time,
recruits, or energy to pull off similar deeds in the United States. Because
terrorists with al-Qaeda sympathies or sensibilities did manage during
the war in Iraq to carry out destructive attacks in Madrid, London, Bali,
Istanbul, Saudi Arabia, Egypt, Tunisia, Jordan, and elsewhere, the claim
is ludicrous. Indeed, a study by London's respected International
Institute for Strategic Studies concludes that the al-Qaeda types who
may have ventured into Iraq represent only a "minute fraction" of its
followers. [12]

Perhaps, some suggest, terrorists are unable to mount attacks because
the Muslim community in the United States, unlike many countries in
Europe, has been well integrated into society. But the same could be said
for Britain, which experienced a significant terrorist attack in 2005.
And European countries with poorly integrated Muslim communities,
such as Germany, France, and Norway, have yet to experience Muslim
terrorism. Indeed, if terrorists are smart, they will *avoid* the local Muslim community because that is the lamppost under which policing
agencies are most intensely searching for their lost keys. Moreover,
the experience both in Spain and with 9/11 suggests that tiny terrorist

conspiracies hardly need a wider support network to nourish their schemes; those involved in the 9/11 attacks, in fact, were mostly ordered to stay away from mosques and American Muslims.[13]

Another popular argument is that al-Qaeda is very patient and is craftily biding its time, and therefore, as Hamlet put it, "If it be not to come, it will be now; if it be not now, yet it will come." Certainly it can take time to plan and carry out a big attack. Yet 9/11 took only some two years to prepare. And since that tragic event, there have been plenty of attacks in Iraq by al-Qaeda friends, allies, sympathizers, and wannabes, and, to say the least, they have not let years elapse between deadly explosions. The carefully coordinated, very destructive, and politically productive terrorist attacks in Madrid in 2004 were inspired, planned from scratch, and then executed within six months; in fact, the bombs were set off less than two months after the conspirators purchased their first supplies of dynamite (paying in hashish).[14] Similarly, Timothy McVeigh's devastating bombing in Oklahoma City in 1995 took less than a year to put together.

Given the extreme provocation of America's invasion of Iraq in 2003, one would think that the Bad Guys might have shifted their timetable into higher gear. Furthermore, if they are so patient, why do they continually claim that another attack is just around the corner? It was in May 2003 that al-Qaeda's second in command, Ayman al-Zawahiri, promised attacks in Saudi Arabia, Kuwait, Qatar, Bahrain, Egypt, Yemen, and Jordan, and shortly thereafter Osama himself cited Italy, Japan, Australia, and the United States as targets.[15] Three years later, bombs had gone off in Saudi Arabia, Egypt, Yemen, and Jordan (as well as in some unlisted countries), but not in the other explicitly threatened countries, which were all outside the Middle East and mostly non-Muslim. Every attack is tragic, but their sparseness could be taken to suggest that it is not only the American terrorism industry that is given to extravagant huffing and puffing.

Exploring the Hypothesis That Dare Not Speak Its Name

One might tentatively be led, then, into considering a rather radical explanation: perhaps terrorists scarcely exist in the United States. That is, could it be that the threat from within has been exaggerated? As the threat posed by domestic Japanese during World War II and the one presented by domestic communists after it proved to be substantially, even massively, inflated, are we at it yet again? Is it possible that the haystack is nearly free of needles?

In 2001 the 9/11 hijackers received no aid from U.S.-based al-Qaeda operatives for the simple reason that no such operatives appear to have existed. And it is not at all clear that that condition has changed. That is, despite the conventional (or congenital) alarmism that permeates FBI Director Robert Mueller's testimony before Senate committees, there is precious little to suggest that there is anything out there for his organization to uncover, at least within the United States. Although there were official U.S. intelligence estimates in 2002 that there were as many as 5,000 al-Qaeda terrorists and supporters in the country, by 2005, as noted earlier, the FBI had been unable to find a single true terrorist cell anywhere in the United States after years of obsessive questing.[16]

Moreover, the Bureau's extensive and well-funded counterterrorist accomplishments seem to be remarkably limited. For example, as enumerated by its director's testimony in 2005, its accomplishments in the previous year appear to have consisted of the following: (1) They picked up evidence that bad guys had conducted surveillance of financial targets and forthwith called an expensive orange alert; the surveillance, however, had actually been done years earlier.[17] Moreover, if it was somehow relevant to 2004, the alert presumably ought still to be going on because any year after 2004 was just as much not the year of the surveillance as 2004 was. (2) The British picked up some bad guys, and the FBI dutifully set up a "task force" to see if there was a "U.S. nexus" to these guys. If any was found, Mueller failed to mention it. (3) After receiving information "suggesting" an attack was being planned "possibly timed to coincide with the presidential election," they set up another "task force" consisting of "thousands of FBI personnel." Over the course of six months, this multitude of spooks found no evidence not only of a plot but even of whether "an operation was indeed being planned." On the positive side, however, Mueller somehow managed to be "certain" that it was the "FBI's tremendous response to the threat" (not "suggested threat" or "imagined threat") that "played an integral role in disrupting any operational plans that may have been underway," assuming, of course, any existed, for which, as noted, they had only "suggestions." (4) They made three arrests: a "spiritual leader" in Virginia who may actually have been worth arresting, a man in Minneapolis who admitted to doing some sniping in Afghanistan and Chechnya in the 1990s (it is apparently illegal in the United States to have sniped overseas in an earlier century), and a third on money laundering charges "connected" to a "possible" plot to kill a Pakistani diplomat.

Similar sorts of zeros and near-zeros have been chalked up in other ways. Thousands of people in the United States have had their overseas communications tapped under a controversial warrantless surveillance program that the Bush administration claims is legal. Of these, fewer than ten U.S. citizens or residents per year have aroused enough suspicion to impel the agencies spying on them to seek warrants to carry out surveillance of their domestic communications as well, and none of this activity, it appears, has led to an indictment on any charges whatever. Meanwhile, 80,000 Arab and Muslim immigrants have been subjected to fingerprinting and registration, another 8,000 have been called in for FBI interviews, and more than 5,000 foreign nationals have been imprisoned in initiatives designed to prevent terrorism. This activity has not resulted in a single conviction for a terrorist crime. Then there are the yearly issuance, without judicial review, of 30,000 "national security letters" in which businesses and institutions are forced to disclose information about their customers and are forbidden from telling anyone they have done so, a process that has generated "thousands of leads" that, when pursued, led nowhere. Nor, it seems, has much come from the costly requirement that banks report to Homeland Security information about everyone who suddenly pays off an unusually hefty chunk of their credit card balance.[18]

In fact, only a handful of people picked up on terrorism charges have been convicted at all, and almost all of these convictions were for other infractions, particularly immigration violations.[19] Some, perhaps most, of those picked up or convicted have clearly been mental cases, or simply flaunting jihadist bravado—rattling on about taking down the Brooklyn Bridge with a blowtorch, blowing up the Sears Tower if only they could get to Chicago, beheading the Canadian prime minister, or flooding lower Manhattan by somehow doing something terrible to one of those tunnels over there.

It seems unlikely that the administration is modestly declining to disclose the arrest of significant bad guys. Indeed, to show it is on the job, its clear proclivity is to announce any positive developments with great official fanfare. And sometimes exaggeration. In 2002, Bush trumpeted that the newly captured Abu Zubaydah was "one of the top operatives plotting and planning death and destruction in the United States," when the guy was actually not only a low-level flunky, but a certifiable nut. "I said he was important," the president later noted to his CIA director. "You're not going to let me lose face on this, are you?" "No sir, Mr. President," was the reply. Captured injured, Zubaydah was carefully and meticulously nursed back to health to permit his captors productively to torture him. He proved to have little knowledge of much of anything, though under duress he did helpfully suggest that al-Qaeda's ambitious target list included shopping malls, banks, supermarkets, water systems, nuclear plants, apartment buildings, the Statue of Liberty, and the increasingly famous Brooklyn Bridge.[20]

The irreverent might conclude from this experience that (a) the terrorists are amazingly clever, (b) the FBI is doing a pretty terrible job, or (c) we are questing after beasts that scarcely exist.

In 2005, a Department of Homeland Security report remarkably went against comfortable orthodoxy by questioning whether al-Qaeda could still pull off attacks on the scale of those of September 11, 2001.[21] Because those attacks required only a small number of perpetrators and minimal funding and weaponry, and because they relied only on stealth, careful planning, suicidal determination, and a great deal of luck, it is not clear how any such incapacity could be physical. But the 9/11 attacks, like those on Pearl Harbor, did require that quite a few stars be in correct alignment. In particular, the passengers on the planes had to be caught unaware.

None of this is to argue that continued attacks have become impossible, of course. A capacity for destructive bombings, such as the one in Oklahoma City, clearly remains; the materials used to concoct the explosive are still readily available.[22] It certainly continues to be easy to carry a backpack bomb into a bus, train, or subway car. And there have been a number of terrorist attacks around the world, albeit none remotely as destructive as those of 9/11. (In fact, outside of Iraq and Afghanistan, fewer people have been killed since 2001 by al-Qaeda and al-Qaeda types across the globe than have drowned in bathtubs in the United States.) Further events outside battle zones like Iraq are likely to continue to be rare, and they will hardly stop a country in its tracks, any more than those in Madrid or London did.

The Counterproductive Impact of 9/11

If al-Qaeda, or al-Qaeda types, do not seem to be in the United States trying hard to redo 9/11, one reason may be that that dramatic act of destruction has itself proved to be substantially counterproductive from their standpoint. In particular, it massively heightened concerns about terrorism around the world. And, no matter how much they might disagree on other issues (most notably on America's war on Iraq), there is a compelling incentive for states—including Arab and Muslim ones—to cooperate to deal with any international terrorist threat emanating from groups and individuals connected to, or sympathetic with, al-Qaeda. Because methodical, persistent international policing of individuals and small groups is most needed, the process seems to be on the right track.

Most important in all this was the almost immediate move, after 9/11, of the Pakistan government from support of the Taliban regime in neighboring Afghanistan to dedicated opposition. Contacts between Pakistani scientists and al-Qaeda were abruptly broken off after 9/11.[23] Pakistan was also highly cooperative in dealing with the London bombings of 2005 and the London airline plot of 2006. All told, the Pakistani government has captured well over 600 real or putative al-Qaeda and turned over more than half of them to the United States.

More generally, there has been a worldwide cooperative effort to deal with the terrorist problem. The FBI may not have been able to uncover much of anything within the United States since 9/11, but quite a few real or apparent terrorists overseas have been rounded, or rolled, up with the aid and encouragement of the Americans. This may further suggest that the absence of results in the United States has less to do with terrorist cleverness or investigative incompetence and more to do with the fact that few, if any, international terrorists exist within the country's borders.

Given what seems to be the rather limited capacity of al-Qaeda and similar entities, these cooperative international policing efforts may not have prevented a large number of attacks, but more than 3,000 "suspects" have been arrested around the world, and doubtless at least some of these were dangerous. Although these multilateral efforts, particularly by such Muslim states as Sudan, Syria, Libya, and even Iran, may not have received sufficient publicity, these countries have a vital interest because they feel directly threatened by the militant network, and their diligent and aggressive efforts have led to important breakthroughs against al-Qaeda. In sum, bin Laden and his gang seem mainly to have succeeded in uniting the world, including its huge Muslim portion, against their violent global jihad.[24]

Although some Arabs and Muslims took a certain pleasure in the suffering inflicted on 9/11—*schadenfreude* in German, *shamateh* in Arabic—the key result among jihadis and religious nationalists was a vehement rejection of al-Qaeda's strategy and methods. Moreover, even former jihadist associates came to view it as a loser and were reluctant to gamble on it.[25]

In addition, continuing, and perhaps accelerating, a long-range trend, state sponsorship of terrorism (at least against countries other than Israel) seems to be distinctly on the wane after 9/11, a phenomenon noted even by the Department of Homeland Security in a 2005 report.[26]

The Counterproductive Impact of Other al-Qaeda Terrorism

The post-9/11 willingness of governments around the world to take on international terrorists has been much reinforced and amplified by subsequent, if sporadic, terrorist activity in such places as Pakistan, Saudi Arabia, Turkey, Indonesia, Egypt, Spain, Britain, Morocco, and Jordan. The phenomenon is hardly new. In 1997, terrorists attacked a Luxor temple in Egypt, killing sixty-eight foreigners and Egyptians. It triggered a very substantial revulsion against the perpetrators that critically set back their cause.[27]

The terrorist bombing in Bali in 2002 galvanized the Indonesian government into action. Extensive arrests and convictions—including of leaders who had previously enjoyed some degree of local fame and political popularity—seem to have severely degraded the capacity of the chief terrorist group, Jemaah Islamiyah (although its spiritual leader, Abu Bashir, has since been released). When terrorists attacked Saudis in Saudi Arabia in 2003, that country, very much for self-interested reasons, became considerably more serious about dealing with internal terrorism, including a clampdown on radical clerics and preachers—though the United States still complains about the number of Saudi nationals who infiltrate into Iraq to fight, often suicidally, the U.S. occupation there. Some rather inept terrorist bombings in Casablanca in 2003 inspired a similar determined crackdown by Moroccan authorities.[28]

Al-Qaeda-linked suicide terrorists killed sixty in simultaneous explosions in three hotels in Jordan in 2005. The most destructive of the bombs was set off in the midst of a group of Jordanians and Palestinians at a wedding party. It would be difficult to imagine a target likely to be more stupid from the perspective of the terrorists. Not surprisingly, the main result of the attacks was to outrage Jordanians and other Arabs against the perpetrators. Massive protests were held in Jordan, and in polls, the percentage claiming that violence against civilian targets to defend Islam is *never* justified jumped from 11 to 43, while the percentage expressing a lot of confidence in Osama bin Laden to "do the right thing" plunged from 25 to less than 1.[29]

For reasonably clear reasons of self-interest, then, Muslim states (including Syria) have increasingly sought to police the radical Islamic movement. As it continues to alienate the moderates by attacking targets in mainstream Islamic countries, it is likely that Kepel's verdict will continue to hold: "Their political project," he writes, "now has a track record showing that it banks on the future, but is mired in the past."[30]

The War in Afghanistan

Because of the surge in international antiterrorism cooperation impelled by 9/11 and by subsequent al-Qaeda or al-Qaeda-like terrorist attacks in other countries, it is not entirely clear that the U.S. war in Afghanistan was really that much of a requirement in the campaign against international terrorism. Insofar as al-Qaeda is a movement, it scarcely needed or needs "bases" or "training camps," and therefore the disruption of these may not be all that much of a setback. Obviously, as noted earlier, terrorists did not require a base in some far-off country in order to pull off destructive acts in Madrid in 2004 and in London in 2005.

The invasion of the country did oust the contemptible Taliban regime, and at rather low cost. That is a notable achievement by most standards. Still, especially with the post-9/11 conversion of Pakistan, its chief—and nearly only—international friend and sponsor, the feeble regime in Afghanistan would have been very much susceptible to pressure, perhaps even to the point of turning Osama bin Laden and his top associates over to international justice, which is more than the invasion accomplished.[31] (It may not have had the capacity to do so by 2001; if so, this would suggest that, far from being a state sponsor of terrorism, it was the terrorists who were sponsoring the state.)

The war's direct impact on international terrorism may thus have been limited at best. An International Institute for Strategic Studies report suggests that the attack may have "offensively hobbled" al-Qaeda, at least for a while, but may also have "defensively benefited" the organization by forcing it "to disperse and become even more decentralised, 'virtual' and invisible."[32]

Afghanistan is undoubtedly under better management as a result of the invasion. But a major dilemma remains. There is no really effective countrywide governmental control, and by far the most lucrative export commodity is opium, for which traffic boomed after the defeat of the Taliban. The United States and other developed countries have solemnly declared this commodity to be evil, and, as they seem to be incapable of keeping their own citizens from wishing to purchase it, they are exerting enormous, even devastating pressure on the shaky new government of the impoverished Afghan state to stamp out the country's most important, if untaxed, moneymaker, ruining, or potentially ruining, the livelihood of a huge number of its citizens. The desperate hope is that by massively hampering Afghanistan's recovery, there will be so little opium for people in rich countries to purchase that they will curb their evil desires and turn to other, more socially acceptable substances. The money the shaky new Afghan government could make by taxing a legal opium trade might well generate a larger, and far more reliable, income stream than the country is likely to receive in aid from its international backers. In fact, the U.S. government, preoccupied with other matters, forgot to include Afghan aid in its initial budget proposals a year after the war. With friends like that, the new government scarcely needs enemies. The stakes, we are to believe, are very, very high in all this. The U.S. State Department has solemnly and imaginatively proclaimed the Afghan drug trade to be "an enormous threat to world stability."[33]

Whatever the value of the invasion, a key point is stressed by Gerges. When Soviet troops invaded Afghanistan in 1979, there were calls for jihad from almost everywhere in Arab and Muslim lands, and tens of thousands of Muslim men flooded to the country to fight in the resistance. By stark contrast, when the Americans invaded in 2001 bent on toppling an Islamic regime, there was a "deafening silence" from these same corners and mosques, and only a trickle of jihadis went to fight. This was yet another counterproductive consequence of those directing the 9/11 attack. The hope was that the dramatic confrontation with the United States would galvanize and unify, but instead, other jihadists publicly blamed al-Qaeda for their post-9/11 problems and held the attacks to be shortsighted and hugely miscalculated.[34]

The War in Iraq

There is a danger in all this, however, that the heedless (even reckless), internationally opposed, and unnecessary war in Iraq will prove to be counterproductive—perhaps even disastrously so—in the campaign against international terrorism and particularly against al-Qaeda.

Although there were very few cries of outrage in the Muslim world when the United States attacked Afghanistan, even moderate and pro-Western Muslims condemned its invasion of Iraq, and they urged Muslims throughout the world to make violent jihad against it. Thus, the war radicalized a large segment of the Arab and Muslim population, furnishing al-Qaeda and other militants with a new opening into a large pool of outraged Muslims around the world.[35]

After the U.S. invasion of Afghanistan, Abu Musah al-Zarqawi, an especially bitter and violent jihadist who sympathized with al-Qaeda's ideology and agenda, moved with thirty supporters from Afghanistan to Iraq. Pursued by Saddam Hussein's security services, this tiny band had difficulty linking up with antiregime elements, a problem, of course, that was soon conveniently removed by the Americans whose war and subsequent disorder and chaos played perfectly into Zarqawi's hands. Soon he was the leader of a small army of dedicated and brutal terrorists numbering perhaps in the thousands, recruited or self-recruited from within and abroad. In late 2004, Zarqawi linked himself up with al-Qaeda (although bin Laden harbored considerable misgivings about Zarqawi's violently anti-Shiite sentiments), and this connection seems to have helped further in attracting recruits and in generating financial and logistical support for Zarqawi's followers, something that apparently continued after Zarqawi's death in 2006. The insurgents have been further benefited by the tendency of the Americans to credit them with a far larger portion of the violence in Iraq than they probably committed, a process that also helped to burnish Zarqawi's image in much of the Muslim world as a resistance hero.[36]

Thus, the ill-considered American venture in Iraq has inspired recruits from around the world into embracing the al-Qaeda movement, and the insurgency in Iraq seems to have developed into something of a terrorist breeding and training experience within the country as well as an exhilarating inspiration to those elsewhere.[37] Polls suggest that the percentage of Jordanians with a favorable opinion of the United States plunged after the invasion of Iraq from 27 to 1. This surely suggests that the recruitment of terrorists would be easier there—though their focus is more likely to be on Israel than on the United States.

Moreover, no matter how it comes out, the war in Iraq will probably prove encouraging to international terrorists because they will take even an orderly American retreat from the country as a great victory— even greater than the one against the Soviet Union in Afghanistan.[38]

People like Osama bin Laden believe that America invaded Iraq as part of its plan to control the oil in the Middle East and to dominate the world, a perspective, polls suggest, that enjoys huge popularity in Muslim countries as well as in such non-Muslim ones as France and Germany.[39] But the United States does not intend to do that (at least not in the direct sense bin Laden and others doubtless consider to be its goal), nor does it seek to destroy Islam, as many others around the world also bitterly assert. Thus, just about any kind of U.S. withdrawal will be seen by such people as a victory for the harassing terrorist insurgents, who, they will believe, are due primary credit for forcing the United States to leave without accomplishing what they take to be its key objectives.

Therefore, Osama bin Laden's theory that the Americans can be defeated, or at least productively inconvenienced, by inflicting comparatively small but continuously draining casualties on them will achieve apparent confirmation, and a venture designed and sold in part as a blow against international terrorists will end up emboldening and energizing them. A comparison might be made with Israel's orderly, even overdue, withdrawal from Lebanon in 2000 that insurgents there took to be a great triumph for their terrorist tactics; most important, so did like-minded Palestinians who later escalated their efforts to use terrorism to destroy Israel itself. Similarly, the Israeli withdrawal from the Gaza Strip in 2005 was sometimes hailed by the Palestinian terrorist group

Hamas as a triumph for its tactics, and it may have helped the group in its election victory in the following year.

Consequences of a Perceived Terrorist Victory in Iraq

It is not clear what a terrorist "victory" in Iraq, whether real or imagined, would lead to. Victory for the insurgents against the Soviets in Afghanistan in 1989 did not lead to a massive export of terrorism to other countries or areas, though a considerable number of roaming freelance jihadists were spun off. Often unable to return home for security reasons, some of them variously showed up to help their coreligionists in ongoing conflicts in such places as Bosnia, Chechnya, the Philippines, Kashmir, Eritrea, Somalia, Burma, and Tajikistan. Something like that may happen after the Americans leave Iraq—whether in orderly fashion or in substantial disarray. Both the CIA and the Saudis have voiced concern that the training and experience violent jihadis have received in Iraq will prove even more effective and exportable than that of the Afghan enterprise because it includes a much greater element of urban conflict.[40]

The post-Afghanistan experience suggests that any violence inspired by the Iraq War is likely to be fairly limited in scope and less likely to be visited upon the United States and Europe than on Arab countries considered to be led by infidels as well as on Western interests in those countries. Such violence would be facilitated if there were to be ongoing armed civil conflicts to join, like the one in Algeria in the 1990s perhaps. In the present instance, Chechnya may provide some opportunities.

However, it may be difficult to sort out any precise effect from the Iraq War. The Iraq enterprise may, like the one against the Soviets in Afghanistan, provide a degree of training for terrorists, but, as noted earlier, the experience with the Madrid bombings suggests that such training is scarcely needed for those dedicated to the cause; that is, some instances of post-Iraq terrorism might happen anyway. Some violent jihadists may be drawn to the conflict against Israel, a cause that continues to inspire activists and to fuel rage.[41] As that conflict is already well developed, however, the added impact of outsiders may not be terribly noticeable. Some people maintain that in fabricating the Iraq War, at least some of the designers were centrally trying to help make the Middle East safe for Israel.[42] To the degree that may be true, the venture will likely prove to be substantially counterproductive. Of course, if even a small portion of any roaming post-Iraq jihadists decide violently to focus on the United States—something that certainly remains a worrisome possibility—the invasion of Iraq will have proved counterproductive for America's "global war on terrorism" as well.

The Effects of an Iraq Syndrome

An additional result of the Iraq debacle for the United States, however, might be to encourage it to back away some from the Middle East. It would thus present less of an irritant to Islamic militants.

After Vietnam, there was a strong desire, usually called the Vietnam Syndrome, not to commit to such a venture again, and something similar happened after Korea. In fact, there never were other Koreas or Vietnams for the United States during the cold war. Due to fears of "another Vietnam," the administration was kept by Congress even from comparatively modest anticommunist ventures in Africa and, to a lesser extent, in Latin America (though there was bipartisan support for aiding the anti-Soviet insurgency in Afghanistan, a venture, however, that of course did not involve sending U.S. troops).

No matter how the war there comes out, an "Iraq Syndrome" seems likely. If the venture there is deemed to have been too costly, any desire for a repeat performance will be, to say the least, attenuated. A poll in relatively war-approving Alabama in 2005 asked whether the United States should be prepared to send troops back to establish order if full-scale civil war erupted in Iraq after a U.S. withdrawal. Only a third of the respondents favored doing so.[43]

Among the casualties of the Iraq Syndrome for American policy could be the Bush Doctrine, empire, unilateralism, preemption (actually, preventive war), last-remaining-superpowerdom, and indispensable-nationhood. Indeed, these once fashionable (and sometimes self-infatuated) concepts are already picking up a patina of quaintness. There will probably be notable increases in skepticism over the notion that the United States should take unilateral military action to correct situations or regimes it considers reprehensible but that present no very direct and very immediate threat to it. As part of this, there will also be very substantial suspicions about any administration claims that such entities do present a threat. Just as the Democrats (and quite a few Republicans) strongly opposed other potential Vietnams after the American debacle there, they are likely severely to question any other Iraqs proposed by the administration unless there is severe, unambiguous provocation.

Also declining in force will be the notions that the United States can and should apply its military supremacy to straighten out lesser peoples, even if a result of this policy becomes the establishment of something of an American "empire"; that the United States should and can forcibly bring democracy to nations not now so blessed; that it has the duty to bring order to the Middle East; that it should embrace a mission to rid the world of evil; that international cooperation is of only very limited value; and that Europeans and other well-meaning foreigners are naïve and decadent wimps. The country may also become more inclined to seek international cooperation, sometimes possibly even showing perceptible signs of humility.

The chief beneficiaries of the Iraq War are likely to be the rogue (or devil du jour) states of Iran and North Korea. In part because of the U.S. military and financial overextension in Iraq (and Afghanistan), the likelihood of any coherent application of military action or even of focused military threat against these two unpleasant entities has substantially diminished, as it has against what at one time seemed to be the next targets: Syria especially, as well as Libya, Saudi Arabia, Egypt, and Lebanon (not to mention France and the State Department).[44] The Iraq Syndrome suggests that any intelligence that such states have become threatening will be deeply questioned, that moves to apply military force to them will be met with widespread dismay and opposition, and that any additional persecution by such regimes of their own people will be effectively tolerated and ignored. Accordingly, all those entities have the greatest incentive to make the American experience in Iraq as miserable as possible. Some of these may also come to consider that deterring an invasion by the world's last remaining superpower can be accomplished simply by prominently and credibly training a band of a few thousand willing to fight and die in dedicated irregular warfare against foreign occupiers.

Evidence of the Iraq Syndrome emerged within two years of the invasion. When North Korea abruptly declared in February 2005 that it now actually possessed nuclear weapons, the announcement was officially characterized as "unfortunate" and as "rhetoric we've heard before."[45] In addition, Iran became notably defiant, and its elected president actually had the temerity later that year to suggest that he did not consider the United States to be the least bit indispensable. These two countries, along with Iraq, were prominently designated as "axis of evil" states in Bush's State of the Union Address in January 2002. In the 2006 rendition, however, North Korea was mentioned only in passing and its nuclear weapons program not at all, while Bush suggested that any problems with Iran would have to be dealt with by "the world."

Most important for present purposes, the Iraq Syndrome might increasingly lead to the conclusion in the United States that American interests in the Middle East are actually rather limited. Quite a bit of oil comes from the Middle East, of course, but discussions of the U.S. interest on that score tend to ignore simple economics. Those in control of an oil-producing state will still have to export the oil unless they are willing to bankrupt their own societies. There is in addition an attachment to Israel, but that country seems fully capable of taking care of itself. In time, perhaps, mediation efforts between Israel and the Palestinians can become productive again. But for now at least, the conflict is so deep that there is little any outsider (even an "indispensable" one) can do about it.

Conceivably, this could develop into something of a backing away from the area, adopting a strategy of "offshore balancing," as it is sometimes fancily called.[46] A policy readjustment like that might in turn reduce the importance of the United States itself as a terrorist target.

An Attack on Iran

Potentially more counterproductive for the "war" on terrorism than the results of the invasion of Iraq could be a unilateral U.S. military attack against Iran's growing nuclear capacity. In response to a preventive attack, Iran is likely to put its political divisions behind it at least temporarily and to seek out methods to retaliate, probably with very wide support within the Muslim world.

Among these could be efforts to more fully aid and to more directly participate in anti-American insurgencies in both Afghanistan and, with much assistance from local Shiites, Iraq. In addition, concerted efforts, probably in complicity with such allied and skilled terrorist groups as Lebanon's Hezbollah, could be made to inflict damage on Israel and on Americans and American interests worldwide—including potentially in the United States itself.

TERROR

If the process of dealing with terrorism is—on balance and thus far—in fairly good shape, there seems to have been little progress in dealing with terror. The fears and anxieties inflamed and exacerbated by the attacks of 9/11 may be with us for a long time.

The threats and dangers confronted in World War II could be fully eliminated by conquering the offending countries and deposing their regimes. By contrast, international terrorism is a tactic carried out by individuals or by very small groups that are usually more or less stateless. Terrorism is therefore much more like crime than like war. Like crime, terrorism has always existed and always will, and the best hope is to reduce its frequency and consequences sufficiently that people come to feel generally, though never completely, safe from it.

Like crime, terrorism cannot be "crushed." However, its incidence and impact can sometimes be reduced, and some of its perpetrators can be put out of business. This is likely to come about through patient, diligent, and persistent international police work rather than through costly ill-conceived wars based on tenuous reasoning. And in time, perhaps, terrorism will fade from view as a notable concern.

Shortly after 9/11 Secretary of Defense Donald Rumsfeld was asked what victory in the "war" against terrorism would consist of. At one point he defined it as "persuading the American people and the rest of the world that this is not a quick matter that's going to be over in a month, or a year, or even five years." Mission accomplished on that one. A few days later, he published this ringing declaration: "Our victory will come with Americans living their lives day by day, going to work, raising their children and building their dreams as they always have—a free and great people."[47] Okay, fine: we've achieved that one, too.

Stephen Flynn, like others in the terrorism industry, likes to begin articles by dramatically proclaiming that the United States is "living on borrowed time—and squandering it," and to end them with warnings about the "long, deadly struggle against terrorism." He also admits that he often labors under a sense of despair and dread. He suggested in 2004 that officials must assume that terrorists will "soon" launch attacks far more deadly and disruptive than those of 9/11. However, in midcourse he cheers up enough to supply a standard for "how much security is enough" and determines that happy moment will come about when "the American people can conclude that a future attack on U.S. soil will be an exceptional event that does not require wholesale changes in how they go about their lives."[48] Well, actually, it seems reasonable to suggest that they can so conclude right now, though that might require them to stop listening to the terrorism industry.

Hysteria and hysterical overreaction to terrorism are hardly required, and, as shown repeatedly in this book, they can be costly and counterproductive. There are uncertainties and risks out there, and plenty of dangers and threats. But these are hardly likely to prove to be "existential." The sky, as it happens, is not falling, nor is apocalypse lurking just over the horizon. Perhaps we can indeed afford to relax a little.

Concerns about the threats supposedly presented by domestic communists, Japan's economy, ethnic war, Qaddafi, and Castro have waned. Other fears that once enjoyed a period of attention and alarm have also faded from fashion, if not, perhaps, from everyone's consciousness. Among these are radon in the soil, pesticides in apple juice, pins in Halloween candy, mercury in the water, cancer or auto accidents caused by cell phones, alar in apples, and the actual or imagined perils posed by road rage, shark attacks, satanic cults, and what physician Marc Siegel calls "bugs du jour" like SARS—not to mention dragons, witches, ghoulies, ghosties, long-leggedy beasties, and things that go bump in the night.[49]

But the waxing and waning of fears can take puzzling trajectories: as noted earlier, anxieties about thermonuclear war faded at various times even though the weapons themselves continued not only to exist, but to escalate in number and destructive capacity.

There are probably only limited lessons to be learned from comparisons with Pearl Harbor in this respect. Although that event inspired reactions quite similar in many ways to those triggered by 9/11, it was possible to eliminate the threat by conquering Japan and replacing its government. There is no similar clear-cut solution in the case of terrorism: there can never be a V-T Day like the V-J Day that was celebrated when Japan surrendered in 1945.[50]

One possibility is that the "war" on terrorism will in time follow the path of the "war" on drugs. Polls suggest that concerns about drugs very much exercised public opinion at one time.[51] But although illegal drugs seem to remain as prevalent as ever, the urgency of concern about them seems to have faded considerably. On the other hand, this does not mean it has become politically possible to sensibly reevaluate drug policy.

The closest parallel is probably with fears about domestic communism. Even when press attention to the enemy within—domestic communists—dropped to nothing, concerns that the American Communist Party somehow still presented a danger waned only quite slowly even as the Party itself almost entirely ceased to exist. This experience suggests that we are hardly likely to relax any time soon: an internalized fear can persist even when evidence of, and attention to, its existence substantially fades.

Moreover, although the campaign against terrorism, despite overreactive policy and an unnecessary, unwise, and perhaps counterproductive war in Iraq, may be in fairly good shape, the likelihood that official hysteria and overreaction will soon be curbed seems slim. The fears about this particular hobgoblin, however overblown, will continue to be stoked.

The costly governmental enterprises the fears have swept into being have become institutionalized and will be resistant to changing perspectives. The Department of Homeland Security will likely always be there, just like the institutionalized warriors on drugs. When the cold war ended, Defense Department thinkers went on a quest for "force justifiers," with the result that a post–cold war peace dividend never really materialized despite the fact that the threat the armed force was chiefly designed to confront *really did* cease to exist. Things are likely to be even worse in this regard for concerns about terrorism: the cold war cannot be reinstituted by one lonely guy with a bomb, but fears about terrorism can.

At base, then, despite the proposals and suggestions offered here, it may well be that not all that much can be done about imagined threats, massively extrapolated fears, and costly overreaction. As noted earlier, the U.S. State Department has now determined that the Afghan drug trade is "an enormous threat to world stability," a feat of richly imaginative threat-mongering that, rather than being greeted with the skepticism—or, actually, the hilarity and derision—it so richly deserves, is soberly transmitted and accepted as deep revelation. Also selling well are efforts to portray Iran as a threat not only to the Middle East, but to the world, because it could conceivably in the course of time develop nuclear weapons and has elected a populist president who spouts off intemperately. The proclivity—even the need and yearning perhaps—to exaggerate threat therefore seems to be alive and well, and it will doubtless still be here long after we have all gone to dust.

This book ends, then, not so much with a proverbial and much sought-after bang, but with a much more common if equally proverbial whimper. No matter what happens in the campaign against terrorism (and, again, it is quite possible to be reasonably optimistic on this score), fears and fearmongers (or terrors and terrormongers) will continue to persist, whatever the objective evidence. People, even those who proudly sing about how they reside in the Home of the Brave, will always jump at some spooks and bumps in the night (but it is not always predictable which ones); they will imagine them to be far more potent than they are; and they will evaluate some risks perversely and fancy some of them to be increasingly threatening, whether that happens to be true or not. Politicians will be inclined sanctimoniously to play to those fears, become convinced themselves, and expend funds and deploy armed force unwisely, sometimes even counterproductively or self-destructively. Bureaucrats will stoke the same fears because they need, after all, to protect their anatomies, particularly the posterior portions thereof, against any conceivable uncertainty, and they clearly have no incentive to work themselves out of a job. The entrepreneurs of the Current Danger industry may eventually move on to the next governmental cash cow, but they will first work very hard to sustain and milk the one currently within their grasp. And the press, ever true to a central precept, will continue to make sure that what bleeds, leads.

Acknowledgments

There are those who consider it unwise, even foolhardy, to present this book's point of view in public and in print. More than one specialist in the area has helpfully cautioned, "I agree with you, but you just can't, actually, you know, *say* that." The fear is that people, still emotional over 9/11, will be outraged by the argument and, moreover, any suggestion that the threat of terrorism has been inflated will be held to be terminally refuted when some fanatical nut somewhere shoots up a bus, bank, or beauty salon while shouting "God is great!"

But as the observation that exceedingly few lottery ticket buyers will win is not refuted when one of them happens to do so, to argue that a threat has been exaggerated is not, of course, to say that it doesn't *exist*. Indeed, during the writing there was quite a bit of international terrorist activity going on around the globe, albeit none, during that time at least, in the United States.

I am, accordingly, particularly grateful to the audiences—community, student, academic, senior citizen, even, once, an advisory committee of the Department of Homeland Security—who have patiently sat through my efforts to develop and explicate the argument in dozens of talks over the last couple of years. Venturing out under the uncomfortable suspicion that my well-intentioned cautioners might be right, I have been surprised (and a little bit disconcerted since I felt my perspective was decidedly unorthodox) at the degree of agreement with which my message has been greeted. There have been points of disagreement as well, some of them rather sharp. However, although I am sure many went away from the talks unconvinced, I think most at least felt that I was presenting a point of view that ought more widely to be considered. Indeed, a most common question was, "Why isn't anybody else saying this?" To which, I must say, I still have no answer except to point to a few people here and there who have published similar or somewhat similar views—a small but hardy band that includes Benjamin Friedman, Russell Seitz, Gwynne Dyer, Bruce Schneier, James Fallows, Ian Lustick, Milton Leitenberg, Jeffrey Rosen, Clark Chapman, Alan Harris, William Arkin, Luke Mitchell, and a few others. At any rate, the gracious, receptive, and attentive audiences have been important in convincing me that I could formally pursue and present this unconventional point of view with some hope of acceptance and without inordinate concerns about my physical safety.

I thank as well some specific individuals who have provided encouragement and/or comments. Among these are Daniel Byman, James Harper, Rick Herrmann, Ted Hopf, Ron Krebs, Christopher Moore, Karl Mueller, Phyllis Mueller, Christopher Preble, David Rapoport, Bruce Russett, Jeffrey Simon, Dominic Tierney. Thanks, too, to Jill Marsal and Sandy Dijkstra of the Sandra Dijkstra Literary Agency. Finally, I would like to thank the risk-takers at Free Press led by Bruce Nichols who, putting their money where my mouth is and without waving a single flag, have demonstrated that America truly remains the home of the brave.

John Mueller
August 28, 2006

Notes

INTRODUCTION: OVERBLOWN

1. Spicuzza 2005.
2. *60 Minutes* (CBS-TV), 16 February 2003. Bowden remarks on *Tucker Carlson Unfiltered*, PBS, 19 November 2004.
3. About 320 Americans per year drown in bathtubs: Stossel 2004, 77. The posited 9/11s would kill 60,000, which is about .02 percent of 300 million. Harris: personal communication. See also Schneier 2003, 237–42. The process of tallying terrorism's deaths is discussed more fully in the next chapter.
4. A phrase suggested by Leif Wenar of the University of Sheffield.
5. Provoke: "Full transcript of bin Laden's speech," http://english.aljazeera.net/NR/exeres/79C6AF22-98FB-4A1C-B21F-2BC36E87F61E.htm, accessed July 31, 2005. Full of fear: news.bbc.co.uk/2/hi/south_asia/1585501.stm.
6. J. C. Kerr 2003.
7. Office of Homeland Security, "The National Strategy for Homeland Security," July 2002, 1: www.whitehouse.gov/homeland/book/nat_strat_hls.pdf, accessed August 17, 2006. B. Friedman 2004, 33.
8. On the almanac menace, see Eggen 2003.
9. Schilling 1965, 389.
10. See J. Mueller 1989, 57–60. For a discussion of the 1930s, see Schweller 2006.
11. Jervis 1976, 275.
12. Posner 2003, 299.
13. One potential fear the United States government has actively tried to downplay concerns Unidentified Flying Objects. Reports about UFOs, it was feared, might endanger national security by confusing the public were an actual aerial attack to take place and by undermining confidence in the military. See Jacobs 1975, especially ch. 4.

CHAPTER 1. THE LIMITED DESTRUCTIVENESS OF TERRORISM

1. In almost all years fewer than ten Americans die worldwide at the hands of international terrorists: U.S. Department of State, *Patterns of Global Terrorism, 1997* (April 1998), 85. An average of ninety people are killed each year by lightning in the United States: National Safety Council (Chicago), *Accident Facts* (1997), 120.

About 100 Americans die per year from accidents caused by deer (Revkin 1998) and the same number from peanut allergies (http://blogcritics.org/archives/2004/09/19/161029.php, accessed July 25, 2006). About 320 drown yearly in bathtubs and four in toilets: Stossel 2004, 77. On this issue, and on bee stings, see Schneier 2003, 11, 237, 241–42. In recent years, the State Department has changed its definitions so that much domestic terrorism is now included in its count of "international" terrorism. Current numbers, therefore, are not comparable to earlier ones.

2. Some people, notably President George W. Bush, continually refer to what is going on in Iraq as "terror" or as "terrorism." But insurgents and guerrilla combatants very often rely on the hit-and-run tactics employed by the terrorist, and the difference is not in the method, but in the frequency with which it is employed. Thus, the Irish Republican Army was generally taken to be a terrorist enterprise, whereas fighters in Algeria and Sri Lanka in the 1990s were considered to be combatants who were employing guerrilla techniques in a civil war situation. Without this distinction, most "primitive warfare," which also relies mostly on raids rather than on set-piece battles, would tend to lapse into the "terrorist" category. See Keeley 1996. For more on the distinction, see J. Mueller 2004a, 18–20.

3. As pointed out by K. Mueller forthcoming.

4. On worst-case scenarios, see Hoffman 2002, 311–12. For a discussion of the phrase "weapons of mass destruction" and for documentation of its much escalated use in the 1990s, see Carus 2006, 8. For an excellent overview of these issues, see Easterbrook 2002. See also Panofsky 1998; Warrick 2004; Pillar 2003, 21–26. For alarm about WMD terrorism, see, for example, Laqueur 2003, 226–28; Ignatieff 2004b, ch. 6.

5. Gilmore 1999, 31, emphasis in the original. See also Linzer 2004.

6. National Planning Association 1958, 42. Kennedy: Kraus 1962, 394. "Who Has the Bomb: The Threat Is Spreading, and the Phantom Proliferators Lead the Way," *Time*, 3 June 1985. Japan: Layne 1993, 37. Germany: Mearsheimer 1990, 38. On the slowness of the proliferation process more generally, see J. Mueller 1967, 1998; S. M. Meyer 1984; Graham 1991; Reiss 1995; Paul 2000.

7. Oberdorfer 2005. See also Pillar 2003, xxi.

8. Oppenheimer: Allison 2004, 104. Jenkins 1975, 33.

9. Careful assessment: Center for Nonproliferation Studies 2002, 4, 12. Duelfer: testimony before the Senate Select Committee on Intelligence, 6 October 2004. See also Seitz 2004.

10. Allison 2004, 15, 97, 168–71 (Korea), 97–98 (crude model), 14–15 (Buffett). See also Goldstein 2004, 128, 132. Iran bomb: Weisman and Jehl 2005. Buffett response: Bialik 2005.

11. Will 2004, working from the musings of Gregg Easterbrook. Snow 1961, 259, emphasis in the original.

12. For a recognition of this point, see OTA 1993, 9; also 46. See also Betts 1998, 30–31; Panofsky 1998; Gilmore 1999, 29.

13. Meselson 1991, 13. Evacuate: McNaugher 1990, 31. OTA 1993, 54. Gilmore 1999, 28. For a discussion that begins by claiming that a single chemical weapon, like a nuclear one, could kill thousands of people, but then in its analysis of chemical weapons comes up with admittedly "simplified and worst-case" scenarios that might inflict deaths in the hundreds or less, see Falkenrath et al. 1998, 1, 147–51.

14. McNaugher 1990, 19n. For the United States 2 percent of gas casualties died and

24 percent of those incapacitated by other weapons died. The rates for Germany were 2.9 percent and 43 percent, and for the British they were 3.3 percent and 36.6 percent. Overall, the estimates are that there were 1,009,038 gas casualties in the war, of whom 78,390 (7.7 percent) died. Gas fatalities were suffered very disproportionately by the Russians, who were ill-protected against gas. However, even taking that into consideration, their ratio of gas deaths to total gas casualties, 11.7 percent, is so out of line with those found on the Western Front that it seems likely that the number of gas fatalities is exaggerated. Gilchrist 1928, 7–8, 48.

15. Return to combat: McNaugher 1990, 20n. Suffer less: Gilchrist 1928, 47. Ineffective against troops: OTA 1993, 8, 58; Meselson 1991, 13. Kitchen sink: Strobel 2006.

16. Deaths: Gilchrist 1928, 7. Tonnage of gas used: Falkenrath et al. 1998, 75. Official British history: Edmonds and Maxwell-Hyslop 1947, 606. Defense analyst Thomas McNaugher considers this conclusion to be "overly glib," but goes on to suggest that "it is closer to the truth than the contention that chemical weapons are nearly magical devices that invariably cause large casualties and inspire panic": 1990, 21.

17. McNaugher 1990, 19n.

18. Human Rights Watch 1995, 262–64. Single airplane claim: see, for example, Mackey 2002, 262.

19. For Union Carbide's explanation, see http://www.bhopal.com/.

20. Seitz 2004. Japan: OTA 1993, 60; Williams and Wallace 1989, ch. 6; Christopher et al. 1997, 413; Blumenthal and Miller 1999, A10; Mintz 2004. See also Ropeik and Gray 2002, ch. 22.

21. J. B. Tucker and Sands 1999, 51. See also Meselson 1995; Terry 1998; Panofsky 1998; Gilmore 1999, 25. Ruppe 2005, 1221; OTA 1993, 48–49, 62; Easterbrook 2002.

22. Leitenberg 2004, 35–39. See also Leitenberg 2005.

23. Immediate damage: Ferguson et al. 2003, 19. Levi and Kelly 2002.

24. Zimmerman and Loeb 2004, 5. See also Rockwell 2003.

25. Raised radiation good for health: on this "hormesis" hypothesis, see information at the Health Physics Society's web site: http://www.hps.org/publicinformation/ate/q299.html (accessed July 8, 2006). Unacceptable levels: Zimmerman and Loeb 2004, 8. Moving from Gulf coast: Understanding Radiation, National Safety Council: www.nsc.org/issues/rad/exposure.htm (accessed March 21, 2005). Denver: Zimmerman and Loeb 2004, 7.

26. Ferguson et al. 2003, 21–22. Ferguson and Potter 2005, 267. See also Zimmerman and Loeb 2004, 8. Overall, conclude Zimmerman and Loeb, "it is likely that very few Americans would be killed directly, suffer radiation sickness, or even have measurably increased risk of cancer from an attack": 2004, 11.

27. Chernobyl: Finn 2005. Japan: Kristof 1995.

28. Ignatieff 2004b, 62–63. British: Christopher et al. 1997, 412; Mintz 2004.

29. Gilmore 1999, 25; Rapoport 1999, 57; Broad 1998; Mintz 2004; J. B. Tucker and Sands 1999, 51; Falkenrath et al. 1998, 21.

30. J. B. Tucker and Sands 1999, 50–51. For extended expressions of alarm on this issue, see Rees 2003, 47–53; Posner 2005a.

31. Gilmore 1999, 38. See also G. Smith 2001.

32. Rabkin 2000, 4, 12. The Gilmore Commission specifically argued that the approach "may be the least efficacious means of setting budgetary priorities and allocating

resources and indeed assuring the security of the country," in part because it assumes that "any less serious incident can be addressed equally well by planning for the most catastrophic threat—ignoring the fact that higher-probability/lower-consequence attacks might present unique challenges of their own": 1999, 35.

33. Weapons they know: see Rapoport 1999, 51; Gilmore 1999, 37; also Schneier 2003, 236. Suicide: see Pape 2005; Bloom 2005.

34. Lack of progress: Leitenberg 2005, part 3. Zawahiri: Leitenberg 2005, 35; see also Pillar 2003, 21. Pakistani contacts: Albright and Higgins 2003, 54–55; see also Suskind 2006, 69–70, 172.

35. Krauthammer 2004a. Allison 2004, 6. Giuliani: CNN, 22 July 2005. See also Benjamin and Simon 2005, 115. For an early suggestion that 9/11 might fail to inspire a massive sequel, see J. Mueller 2002b, 2002c. Krauthammer apparently missed these items, although they appeared in publications he regularly writes for. See also J. Mueller 2003; Seitz 2004.

36. Tylenol: M. L. Mitchell 2002. Turning point: Gilmore 1999, 40, but see also 37.

37. Jenkins 1975, 15.

38. Seitz 2004. On the raising of the bar, see also Pillar 2003, xi.

CHAPTER 2. OVERREACTING TO TERRORISM

1. See also Pillar 2003, 24–29; Schneier 2003, 235–38.

2. Sivak and Flannagan 2004.

3. Wars made politically possible: Pillar 2003, xv; Lustick 2006, ch. 4. Iraq deaths: see *Economist*, 6–12 November 2004, 81–82.

4. Chernobyl: Finn 2005. 9/11 stress: Silver et al. 2002; see also Bourke 2005, 374–91.

5. Domestic flights: *Financial Times*, 14 September 2004, 8. Las Vegas: Clarke 2005, 63; some Las Vegas casinos report that their fourth-quarter earnings in the last quarter of 2001 were about one third of the year earlier. Lost jobs: Calbreath 2002. One study has investigated Italian cities and towns, most of them small, that experienced a single terrorist attack. Although most of these were minor events and few caused any deaths, they appear to have had a measurable short-term impact on employment, chiefly because marginal firms went out of business earlier and because successful ones temporarily cut back on plans to expand. Greenbaum et al. 2004. Another study finds that businesses hit by a terrorist act such as a bombing or the kidnapping of an executive suffer an average market capitalization drop of $401 million. Karolyi and Martell 2006.

6. Passenger screenings: Fallows 2005a, 82–83. Checked baggage: de Rugy 2005a, 5. Marshal budget: www.dhs.gov. $15 billion and airline profits: Congleton 2002, 62. $8 billion: Véronique de Rugy, quoted in Applebaum 2005. Post Office: Rosen 2004, 68. Visas: Rogoff 2004. Graduate students: Clarke 2005, 65. Joint Economic Committee: de Rugy 2005a, 5. Oil price: Solman 2006. On the $9 billion Los Angeles Airport plan to (marginally) improve security from terrorist bombs, see Goo 2004.

7. Blimes and Stiglitz 2006.

8. Vaccine: Siegel 2005, 177–78. Scientists: Shane 2005a. First responders: Manjoo

2005; more generally, see Cooper and Black 2006. FBI: Lustick 2006, 34–35. Local cops: Belzman 2006.

9. Two analysts: Chapman and Harris 2002, 30. Seat belts: suggested by Karl Mueller. Banks 2002, 10.

10. Rove, 2003: Clines 2003; Gorman 2003b, 2781. Rove, 2006: Balz 2006.

11. Terror warnings: Willer 2004. Thoughts of death: Landau et al. 2004. See also Nacos et al. 2006. Ridge: M. Hall 2005.

12. 10 plots: Goo 2005. Cheney: Beinart 2006a. Idle aspiration: Cole 2006b; Ignatius 2006.

13. Quoted in Lustick 2006, 116. On this issue, see also Dionne 2006.

14. Dyer 2004.

15. Lustick 2006, 116. T. L. Friedman 2004.

16. Leitenberg 2005, 47–48.

17. All examples from de Rugy 2005a, except for the Alaska cameras from Tizon 2006. Congressional report: Witte and Hsu 2006. On pork, see also Peterson 2004, 116–17.

18. Boom: Van Drehle 2006. Counties: Goldstein and Keating 2006. See also Neuman 2006.

19. Office of Homeland Security, "The National Strategy for Homeland Security," July 2002, 1 (www.whitehouse.gov/homeland/book/nat_strat_hls.pdf, accessed August 17, 2006). Lustick 2006, 97.

20. Kosko 2004. See also Rosen 2004, 79; Beinart 2006a.

21. Testimony by Mueller can be found at www.fbi.gov/congress/congress.htm.

22. FBI report: Ross 2005. 5,000 estimate: Gertz 2002. Goss: quoted in Leitenberg 2005, 25, emphasis added.

23. CIA quote: Allison 2004, 28. Yes, Virginia: Church 1897.

24. Similarly, media coverage of accidental gun deaths of children rarely seem to supply information about the total number so killed. The U.S. total for children under ten is around thirty-one per year, of whom less than half are killed by themselves or by other children. Lott 2003, 83, 142. On the issue more generally, see E. Singer and Endreny 1993. On the reporting of crime, see Warr 2000, 469–70.

25. Rothschild 2001. Some of the probability calculations in this article, however, appear to be incorrect.

26. Alerts: Nacos et al. 2006. Rapoport 1999, 50.

27. Ricin: Leitenberg 2005, 27–28; Leitenberg notes that those arrested did have in their possession a readily available book that contained a recipe for making ricin. If followed out, the recipe would have yielded enough poison to kill one person if the substance were *injected*. Mubtakkar: Suskind 2006, 194–98. Waterman 2006. On problems of lack of follow-up in the Vietnam War, see Braestrup 1983. On the problem in the Gulf War of 1991, see J. Mueller 1994, 136–37.

28. Lustick 2006, 98. On the phenomenon of selling fear in other contexts, see Furedi 2002, ch. 7.

29. Allison 2004, 27. Hoaxes: Leitenberg 2005, 21. Allison's source is a *Seattle Times* article which also notes that the magazine report and others inspired "a spate of alarming, unconfirmed and exaggerated news reports" playing off those original reports, and these themselves remain unconfirmed: Port and Smith 2001. For news fit enough to print in the London *Times* suggesting that bin Laden had already collected tactical nuclear weapons by 1998, see Binyon 1998.

30. Lustick 2006, ch. 5.
31. Lipton 2006a, 2006b. In the interests of full disclosure, I should note that I have tried to appropriately posture myself once or twice, but my sales pitch, "Since you are going to throw money away anyway, you might as well throw some of it at me," seems to need further refinement.
32. Brodie 1978, 68.
33. Goldstein 2004, 128, 132. Allison 2004, 1, 171.
34. Brodie 1978, 83.
35. Chapman and Harris 2002, 32; 2003.
36. Gergen 2002. Carafano and Rosenzweig 2005, 93. Lugar: *Fox News Sunday*, June 15, 2003. Krauthammer 2004a. Krauthammer 2006. The threat to Israel from terrorism and from its reaction (or overreaction) to the terrorist challenge, however, could conceivably be "existential," and this is perhaps what Krauthammer means by "civilization." For a suggestion along this line, see Fukuyama 2004, 65. Krauthammer replies, however, by parsing "existential," arguing that what Israel faces is more nearly "Carthaginian extinction" (2004b, 18).
37. Allison 2004, 191. Goldstein 2004, 145, 179. Ignatieff 2004b, 147.
38. Officials: Benjamin and Simon 2002, 398–99, 418. Franks: Shanken 2003. Anonymous 2004, 160, 177, 226, 241, 242, 250, 252, 263. One of the book's many hysterical passages runs

> To secure as much of our way of life as possible, we will have to use military force in the way Americans used it on the fields of Virginia and Georgia, in France and on the Pacific islands, and from skies over Tokyo and Dresden. Progress will be measured by the pace of killing and, yes, by body counts. Not the fatuous body counts of Vietnam, but precise counts that will run to extremely large numbers. The piles of dead will include as many or more civilians as combatants because our enemies wear no uniforms. Killing in large number is not enough to defeat our Muslim foes. With killing must come a Sherman-like razing of infrastructure. Roads and irrigation systems; bridges, power plants, and crops in the field; fertilizer plants and grain mills—all these and more will need to be destroyed to deny the enemy its support base. Land mines, moreover, will be massively reintroduced to seal borders and mountain passes too long, high, or numerous to close with U.S. soldiers. As noted, such actions will yield large civilian casualties, displaced populations, and refugee flows. (241–42)

In the acknowledgments, the author thanks Ms. Christina Davidson, his editor, "who labored mightily to delete from the text excess vitriol" (xiii). Perhaps Ms. Davidson should have labored just a bit more mightily.

39. Beinart 2004. This is the journal that published Easterbrook's impressive, if almost completely ignored, essay in 2002 noting that chemical and biological weapons are incapable of inflicting mass destruction. Apparently, even Easterbrook's editor didn't notice.
40. B. Friedman 2004, 39. Rosen 2004, 64. Myers: J. C. Kerr 2003. For a contrast with such views, see Byman 2003, 160, 163; Seitz 2004.
41. Prediction: Ignatieff 2004a, 48. Apocalypse: Ignatieff 2004b, 146. Not forgive: Ignatieff 2004a, 46–48.
42. Katrina estimate: Dart 2005. 9/11 estimate: The estimate on September 24, for

example, was that nearly 7,000 had died (*New York Times*, 24 September 2001, B2); on this issue, see Lipton 2001.

43. Arkin 2006a. Gilmore 1999, 37. See also Byman 2003, 163.

CHAPTER 3. DATES OF INFAMY: PEARL HARBOR AND 9/11

1. U.S. Congress 1946, 65. Toland 1961, 38. Toland 1970, 237. Morison 1963, 68, 70. Prange et al. 1986, 534. Prange et al. 1988, xiii. Spector 1985, 93. Morton 1962, 144. R. Wohlstetter 1962, 3, 398. Small 1980, 234, 253.

2. For a detailed discussion of this issue, see J. Mueller 1995a, 86–97.

3. Dynamic policy: Schroeder 1958, ch. 8. China aid: Utley 1985, 135–36; Utley notes that U.S. aid authorizations in July 1941 were 821,000 tons for Britain and 16,000 for China (see also Russett 1972, 46). Ambassador: Butow 1961, 341.

4. Schilling 1965, 389. Small 1980, 238–39. Jonathan Utley has a different perspective, but he comes to a similar conclusion: "It was not through a careful review of national policy or the stakes involved in Asia that the United States would place itself in the path of Japanese expansion, but incrementally, without long-range planning, and as often as not as a stopgap measure necessitated, or so the planners thought, by the events in Europe" (1985, 58).

5. Morison 1963, 69. Toland 1961, 37. As Morison also points out, it was Pearl Harbor, not the subsequent, more costly and more important attack on the Philippines that moved American opinion (1963, 77–78). Roberta Wohlstetter agrees: "For some reason the damage done to these other American outposts in the Pacific is not considered in the same category of crime" (1962, 340).

6. Willmott 1982, 55. See also Fujiwara 1990, 155; Butow 1961, 129.

7. Military expenditures: Nakamura 1983, 39. Consumer: Gleason 1965, 436. Production: Barnhart 1987, 91, 96, 200–201, 238, 269.

8. As Willmott observes, "The very morale that sustained the Japanese in the advance gave rise to a casual and blind cruelty at almost every turn, and these actions ensured a lasting enmity on the part of subject peoples who might have been won over with decent treatment" (1982, 91).

9. Willmott 1982, 68–70.

10. Willmott 1982, 88–89, 451.

11. On this issue, see also Russett 1972, 44–62. For another critique of U.S. entry into the war, see Small 1980, 215–67. See also Morison 1963, 45.

12. Fujiwara 1990, 157–59. Butow 1961, 167, 251–52, 332–33.

13. For a somewhat more detailed discussion of this policy option, see J. Mueller 1995a, 103–10. Although the Japanese expansion in Asia cut the United States off from the sources of some important raw materials, these supplies were not crucial, as Roosevelt publicly pointed out in 1940 (and as was to be demonstrated during the war), because the United States could produce synthetic rubber, acquire tin from Bolivia, and produce more manganese at home. See Utley 1985, 85.

14. Schroeder 1958, 209. Morison 1963, 45. Russett 1972, 58–60. Utley sees the China issue as less central, but he agrees it triggered the war: "It was the issue of China that in the final hours stood as an insurmountable obstacle between Japan and the United States" (1985, 177). "The final point of disagreement between the two countries was on the withdrawal of Japanese forces from China. If war was to

be prevented, Japan had to yield on this point" (Fujiwara 1990, 154). "The chief issue between Japan and the United States was the future of China" (Small 1980, 238).

15. An estimate of 3 million military and civilian deaths is given by Sivard 1987, 30; Messenger estimates 2.5 million (1989, 243). Battle deaths for the Nationalist Chinese are said to be 1,310,224; *Encyclopedia Britannica*, 1991 ed., vol. 29, 1023. Some put total Chinese battle deaths as high as 2.2 million: Snyder 1982, 126. *Encyclopedia Americana* accepts this higher estimate and then observes that "Chinese civilian losses are unknown but probably numbered several million" (1988 ed., vol. 29, 530).

16. First three years: Meisner 1986, 81; demographer John S. Aird notes that, though estimates generally range from 1 to 3 million, some are much higher: one Hong Kong source puts the death toll at 10 million and quotes a 1981 Chinese journal that claims 20 million people were executed or died of unnatural causes during what it calls the "anti-rightist" and "people's communication" periods (1990, 2, 111n3). Famine: Ashton et al. 1984.

17. These estimates of military and civilian deaths are from Sivard 1987, 31. Battle deaths alone have been estimated at 2 million for Korea and 1.2 million for Vietnam: see J. D. Singer 1991, 60–61.

18. Prange et al. 1981, 582.

19. Cantril and Strunk 1951, 756.

20. Roundup: Stone 2004, 285. Massive escalation, Hoover: Stone 2004, 287, 289, 293. Attorney general: Biddle 1962, 226. For the argument that there were at least a few bad or questionable characters in the bunch, see Malkin 2004.

21. For this process more generally, see Stone 2004. Reactions to terrorism have often led to massive persecution. The Jewish pogroms in Russia at the end of the nineteenth century, for instance, were in major part retaliation against Jews because some of them were notable in terrorist movements at the time: Rapoport 2004, 68; Ignatieff 2004b, 63. On the often deadly and indiscriminate overreaction to anarchist terrorism in the United States and elsewhere, see Jensen 2002.

22. Stone 2004, 302–3.

23. Stone 2004, 290–92.

24. Stone 2004, 292. Lippmann 1942.

25. J. Smith 1980, 90–94. Fujita: Kristof 1997.

26. Willmott 1983, 79. Willmott 1982, 91–93.

27. Seitz 2004.

28. One reason the president supported the Japanese internment, it appears, was to give a bit of a sop to those whose fury was primarily focused on Japan. Stone 2004, 296.

29. Suskind 2004, 187–88. Woodward 2004, 24–27.

30. For the argument that in the case of Pearl Harbor, there were no dots to connect, see D. Kahn 1991–92.

31. National Commission 2004, ch. 13.

32. Seitz 2004.

33. Dower argues that the images initially went from being racist and vicious to racist and patronizing: the Japanese, once pictured as menacing, blood-soaked gorillas, now became appealing little monkeys, for example (1986, 302). But even this is a profound transformation, and it happened almost immediately after the war.

34. Ike 1967, 248, 153. R. Wohlstetter 1962, 355. Prange 1981, 21. Dower 1986, 293. Russett 1972, 55.

35. Sagan 1988, 916. Pearl Harbor was a disaster for the Japanese in another way as well. Together with their other amazing successes in the opening weeks of the war, it contributed substantially to a dangerous overconfidence or "victory disease," as the Japanese dubbed it after the war. At a time when the Japanese should have been changing their tactics to confront enemies who were getting stronger and becoming better prepared, they continued to follow their old modes of operation and committed themselves to a widespread and fragmented effort. See Mueller 1995a, 102–3.

CHAPTER 4. COLD WAR, CONTAINMENT, AND CONSPIRACY

1. Lenin: Burin 1963, 337; Leffler 1994, 17. Stalin: Historicus 1949, 198: Taubman 1982, 224 (as Taubman points out, Stalin was referring to wars *between* capitalist states, something often neglected when the West examined this statement, although, even taking that into account, the declaration clearly remains profoundly threatening to capitalist states; on this issue more generally, see Burin 1963). Khrushchev: Hudson et al. 1961, 214, 196. For the forceful argument that the quoted sentiments reflected real ideological zeal and critically affected policy during the cold war, see Macdonald 1995–96; see also Andrew and Mitrokhin 2003, ch. 1. For an able analysis and discussion of the literature on the ideology-policy connection, see Gould-Davies 1999; also M. Kramer 1999.

2. Kennan 1947, 566–67. Reagan and others: J. Mueller 2004–2005.

3. Kennan 1947, 580–81. As President George H. W. Bush put it in speeches in 1989, the policy of containment required "checking the Soviet Union's expansionist aims, in the hope that the Soviet system itself would one day be forced to confront its internal contradictions" (1990, 602; see also 541).

4. On the importance of the Hitler and Munich analogies in American thinking of the time, see May 1973, ch. 2. On the reactive nature of U.S. policy, see P. Kennedy 1987, 360.

5. Kennan concluded in 1948, "We do not think the Russians, since the termination of the war, have had any serious intentions of resorting to arms." Quoted in Gaddis 1982, 35; see also 366–67, and Gaddis 1987, 41.

6. On this issue, see in particular R. H. Johnson 1994.

7. Even Kennan worried that war might come about if Soviet "political fortunes were to advance too rapidly in Europe and they were to become dizzy with success." Taubman 1982, 169–70. See also Yerkin 1977, 350–54.

8. One event that undercut Communist Party support in the West was the suggestion in 1949 of Maurice Thorez, general secretary of the French Communist Party, that in a war between France and the Soviet Union, the Party would support the Soviet Union. The statement was reprinted by communist parties throughout the world: Shulman 1963, 58–61, 290; Starobin 1972, 209–12.

9. F. Kaplan 1983, 139–40.

10. Unbludgeoned: Callahan 1990, 120–23. Certain: Truman 1956, 333. See also Paige 1968, 137, 174; Taubman 1982, 214; Stueck 2002, 82.

11. Brodie 1973, 63. See also F. Kaplan 1983, 39, 81; Paige 1968, 171, 173. On Gen-

eral Omar Bradley's conviction that Europe was still the "central target," see Paige 1968, 166. Even George Kennan, who had rarely envisioned the Soviet challenge in military terms, speculated that "armed action by German units, along the Korean pattern" was not out of the question, and the Central Intelligence Agency officially feared that Stalin might soon "deliberately provoke" a general war (quoted in Taubman 1982, 201–2). A poll in August 1950 found 57 percent of the public opining that the United States was "now actually in World War III," while only 18 percent held that the fighting "will stop short of another world war" (Gallup 1972, 933).

12. Kennan 1961, 250, 386. See also Khrushchev 1970, 299–301, 308, 311. Moreover, Stalin was given in his last years to believing that he could control nature at will. In 1949 he grandly issued a "Stalin Plan for the Transformation of Nature" which set out extravagant schemes for weather-controlling irrigation and forestation projects; massive dam, canal, and power installations; and the construction of skyscrapers in Moscow to rival those in New York City. He also repudiated Darwin and Mendel, declaring that the evolution of plant and animal life could be fully controlled by environmental manipulation: Bluhm 1974, 301.

13. Callahan 1990, 136–37.

14. See particularly Burin 1963, 337–41; also Taracouzio 1940, 45, 142–44; Brodie 1966, ch. 3. The Soviet regime was born in part because a world war brought about the collapse of the czarist dynasty in Russia, and from this experience, as Taubman has pointed out, the revolutionaries learned the "crucial lesson" that world war "can destroy the Russian regime" (1982, 22).

15. Exploiting conflicts: Taubman 1982, 12; as Richard Pipes concludes, "Soviet interests . . . are to avoid general war with the 'imperialist camp' while inciting and exacerbating every possible conflict within it" (1984, 190–91). Lenin: Nathan Leites has pointed out that three central rules for Soviet leaders were "avoid adventures," "do not yield to provocation," and "know when to stop" (1953, 46–53). Similarly, Pipes stresses the Soviet tactical emphasis on "utmost caution," patience, and prudence (1984, 52–53).

16. Brodie 1966, 71–72; see also F. Kaplan 1983, 339. Jervis 2001, 59. As Nikita Khrushchev remarks in his memoirs, "Our military objectives have always been defensive. That was true even under Stalin. I never once heard Stalin say anything about preparing to commit aggression against another country. His biggest concern was putting up antiaircraft installations around Moscow in case our country came under attack from the West" (1974, 533). Khrushchev is obviously thinking of direct war here, not incursions against South Korea in 1950 or against various border countries in the years before World War II.

17. Khrushchev 1970, 367–70. Simmons 1975, 163. Stueck 2002, 69–77.

18. See also May 1973, 83; Taubman 1982, 225. As discussed more fully below, Soviet military intervention in Afghanistan in 1979 was an effort to prop up a faltering pro-Soviet regime. As such, it was not like Korea, but rather more like U.S. intervention in Vietnam in 1965 or like the Soviet interventions in Hungary in 1956 or Czechoslovakia in 1968.

19. On these international issues, see also Jervis 1980, 579–84.

20. Reactions: F. Kaplan 1983, 135. President's Commission on National Goals 1960, 1–2. CIA: Reeves 1993, 54. On the Soviet Union's apparent economic strength at the time, see Yergin and Stanislaw 1998, 22, 272.

21. Clearly indicates: Callahan 1990, 169. Halperin 1961, 367.
22. F. Kaplan 1983, 165–67, 267, 288–89. See also Preble 2004, 82, 94.
23. Assumption: F. Kaplan 1983, 124, 142–44, 161, 172, 278, 288. Callahan 1990, 160; see also 175, 204. Delicate: A. Wohlstetter 1959. Pearl Harbor: F. Kaplan 1983, 109, 123, and seminars conducted by Wohlstetter at UCLA in the early 1960s. Wife's book: R. Wohlstetter 1962. Retirement: F. Kaplan 1983, 124. Evacuate: F. Kaplan 1983, 225. Schelling: F. Kaplan 1983, 302.
24. Eisenhower on the economy: F. Kaplan 1983, 146–52; Callahan 1990, 172; Halperin 1961, 368, 371; Preble 2004, 77–78. Soviet gamble: Callahan 1990, 174; Preble 2004, 77–78, 95. Liquid fuel: Preble 2004, 80.
25. Kennedy quote: F. Kaplan 1983, 249. Kennedy as president: see Preble 2004, ch. 4; Callahan 1990, 208. Fallout shelters: F. Kaplan 1983, 309–14.
26. Halperin 1961, 364, 369, 384. Vietnam connection: Preble 2004, 16–17.
27. Halberstam 1965, 319. Sheehan 1964.
28. Halberstam 1965, 315. Oddly, none of the passages quoted are included in the 1988 reprint edition of Halberstam's 1965 book. Although Ball's proposal shows exceptional insight, it was based in part on the apparently erroneous judgment that escalation would bring about "a serious danger of intervention by the Chinese" (1982, 400, 505n 10).
29. Nitze: F. Kaplan 1983, 377; see also Callahan 1990, 381. Team B: R. H. Johnson 1994, ch. 6; Garthoff 2001, 328–34. Soviet intentions: Callahan 1990, 379. Nitze was also apparently worried that America's will to stand up to, or to keep up with, the Soviet Union would somehow become sapped: Callahan 1990, 409–10. Cult: Brodie 1966, 93. Fantasies: Brodie 1978, 68.
30. Carter on Nitze: Callahan 1990, 388. Carter on Afghanistan: Hosmer and Wolfe 1983, 240.
31. Garthoff 1994, 1070, emphasis in the original. R. H. Johnson 1994, 166–67, 169.
32. Jervis 2001, 58. See also R. H. Johnson 1994, 168.
33. Porter 1984, 240.
34. Gaddis 1982, 47; Gellman 1984, 53.
35. Breslauer 1987, 436–37. See also Andrew and Mitrokhin 2003, 15–24.
36. East Europe: Bunce 1985. Charles Wolf and his colleagues at the RAND Corporation estimated in 1983 that the cost of the Soviet empire (excluding the costs of maintaining troops in Eastern Europe, but including the costs of the war in Afghanistan) rose enormously between 1971 and 1980, from about 1 percent of its gross national product to nearly 3 percent when measured in dollars, or from under 2 percent to about 7 percent when measured in rubles. (By comparison, insofar as the United States could be said to have had a comparable empire, the costs were less than .5 percent of its GNP.)
37. However, it does not follow that economic and social travail necessarily lead to a mellowing of ideology. Leaders, in this case Gorbachev, had to *choose* that policy route. Faced with the same dilemmas, a conservative leader might have stuck to the faith while suffering gradual decline (as happened to the Ottoman empire), or one might have adopted more modest reforms to maintain the essential quality of the system and the privileges of its well-entrenched elite. Rush 1993. See also Checkel 1997; English 2000; J. Mueller 2004–2005.
38. Kennan should not be given credit, however, for predicting how long this would take or the precise mechanism by which it would come about. He seems to have

expected the contest to last some ten or fifteen years, an estimate that probably stemmed from his belief that a key problem for the Soviet Union lay in "the uncertainty involved in the transfer of power" and was thus unlikely to survive a succession crisis after the death of its leader, Josif Stalin, then nearing seventy (1947, 576–79). See also Gaddis 1982, 49.

39. See also Callahan 1990, 503–4; Garthoff 2001, 389–90; R. H. Johnson 1994, 210.
40. Analysts: D. A. Welch and Blight 1987–88, 27; see also Lebow and Stein 1994, ch. 6; Brodie 1973, 426; Bundy 1988, 453–57, 461–62; Garthoff 2001, 181–82. Khrushchev: Lebow and Stein 1994, 110. A report from a "reliable, well-placed" Soviet source says that the leadership issued a formalized secret directive that it had decided not to go to war even if the United States invaded Cuba: Garthoff 1987, 51. On Khrushchev's mind-set during the crisis, see Taubman 2003, 563, 566–67, 573. Kennedy: R. F. Kennedy 1971, 40, 105; Lukas 1987, 58; Lebow and Stein 1994, 127–28. Luard 1986, 231–33. See also J. Mueller 1988b; J. Mueller 1989, 152–55; Jervis 2001, 57.
41. For a discussion, see Weinstein 1978. See also Stone 2004, 410.
42. State Department officials: see Weinstein 1978, 476–77, 508. Soviet atomic program: Holloway 1994. Rosenbergs: Radosh and Milton 1997.
43. Shannon 1959, 3, 218, 360. American contempt for the Soviet domestic system, however, continued apace: between 1973 and 1982 polls found that the percentage calling communism the worst kind of government rose from 42 to 57 (Niemi et al. 1989). See also J. Mueller 1988a.
44. See Jensen 2002.
45. See also Fukuyama 2004.
46. See Valentino 2004, ch. 4.
47. For reflections on this phenomenon in the communist case, see Stephan 2000.

CHAPTER 5. NUCLEAR FEARS, COLD WAR TERRORISM, AND DEVILS DU JOUR

1. There was also a recurring, and, as it turned out, thoroughly unjustified alarm during the cold war that democracy was doomed or at least stagnated. For a discussion, see J. Mueller 1999, 200–202, 214–15.
2. J. Mueller 1989, 57–60.
3. Toynbee 1950, 4. Stalin: Djilas 1962, 114–15. Grew: Gaddis 1987, 218n. For public opinion data and analysis, see J. Mueller 1979, 303–7.
4. H. Kahn 1960, x.
5. Wells 1968, 67; Wagar 1961, 13n.
6. Einstein 1960, 347, 566. Teller and Russell: Grodzins and Rabinowitch 1963, 101, 124.
7. Snow 1961, 259.
8. Readers' Guide: Paarlberg 1973, 133, 137; see also Weart 1988, 262–69. Polls: J. Mueller 1977, 326–27; see also J. Mueller 1979.
9. Weart 1988, 262.
10. Morgenthau: Boyle 1985, 73. Readers' Guide: McGlen 1986; see also B. M. Kramer et al. 1983; Weart 1988, ch. 19.
11. Smoke 1993, ch. 10. If it takes, say, two bombs to destroy a missile, a target country roughly equal in missilery is reasonably safe from rational attack if all missiles

carry only one warhead because an attacker could count on destroying only half of its retaliatory capacity with a first strike. But if each missile has three warheads, an aggressor would need to use only two-thirds of its missile warheads to destroy the other side's entire force.

12. Smoke 1993, 188–91.

13. Prevail: Smoke 1993, 111–12, 217–21. Reagan on war in Europe: Smoke 1993, 223; H. Mueller and Risse-Kappen 1987, 83. Haig: Gwertzman 1981. See also F. Kaplan 1983, 388–89.

14. H. Mueller and Risse-Kappen 1987, 83–84.

15. Schell 1982, 231. Book index: McGlen 1986. McNeill 1982, 383–84. Bishops: Smoke 1993, 224. Brown: "Atom War 'Suicide Pills' Backed," *New York Times*, 13 October 1984. Polls: J. Mueller 1994, 211.

16. Nor, apparently, did it significantly alter public opinion on the issue: in November 1981 nuclear opponents in Amsterdam pulled off the biggest demonstration in Holland's history, yet popular opposition to the new missiles changed hardly at all: DeBoer 1985, 128; Smoke 1993, 223. See also Schuman et al. 1986.

17. Schell 2003.

18. Jervis 1984, 156–57.

19. Campbell 1967, 24–27.

20. Eden 1960, 480–81, 519.

21. McMahon 1999, 123. See also Taylor 1976, 94 97; Hilsman 1967, part 8.

22. Taylor 1976, 98–101, 104–9. For a 1965 assessment that "the odds are" that the communists "will come to power in Indonesia," see Pauker 1965, 285.

23. L. B. Johnson 1971, 335, 606; see also Shaplen 1970, 84.

24. See Taylor 1976, 113–19; Shaplen 1970, 91–148; McMahon 1999, 119–24.

25. McMahon 1999, 120.

26. Takeyh 2001, 63.

27. Isolated, national security: Simon 2001, 196–97. Qaddafi rhetoric: Wills 2003, 194.

28. Simon 2001, 199.

29. Takeyh 2001, 64. Qaddafi reaction: Simon 2001, 187–200. Shultz: Simon 2001, 200.

30. Simon 2001, 233–34.

31. Takeyh 2001, 63–67.

32. Qaddafi on Bush: Takeyh 2001, 70. 1999: Indyk 2004. See also Stevenson 2004, 11; Jentleson and Whytock 2005–2006.

33. Wills 2003, 1–2. Slogan: see Goodman 1989.

34. Carter 1982, 3.

35. Vance 1983, 380.

36. Over in a few weeks: Carter 1982, 458; Brzezinski 1983, 478. Military approaches: Brzezinski 1983, 485.

37. Carter 1982, 4.

38. J. Mueller 2002a, 156–57.

39. P. Kennedy 1987, 461–67, emphasis in the original.

40. J. Mueller 1994, table 205.

41. Continuation of war: Huntington 1991, 8, 10. The concept of economic war comes close to being oxymoronic. There are times when it may make some sense, as when the world coordinated to embargo Iraq in 1990, but war is substantially zero (or negative) sum, whereas economic exchange, although not always fully fair

or equal, is generally positive sum: both parties gain. See Jervis 1993, 57–58. Professors: Huntington 1993a, 77, 80. Coming war: G. Friedman and LeBard 1991. Yearn: Layne 1993, 37. Uninterested: Berger 1993; Katzenstein and Okawara 1993, 115–16.

42. Huntington 1993b, 1993c, 1996. P. Kennedy 1993.
43. Simon 2001, ch. 3.
44. Simon 2001, 182. See also Wills 2003, 3–4, 213.
45. Reagan 1983, 1096. Public: J. Mueller 2002a, 165–67.
46. J. Mueller 1984.
47. J. Mueller 1984.

CHAPTER 6. DISORDERLINESS IN THE NEW WORLD ORDER

1. Truman 1966, 378.
2. Woolsey 1993.
3. Gates 1993. Hoffmann 1992, 37. For an extended discussion of this issue, see J. Mueller 1995a, ch. 1.
4. Woolsey 1993. T. L. Friedman 1992.
5. Hoffman 1992, 37.
6. R. D. Kaplan 1993b. In 1991, he confidently predicted that it was Macedonia that was going to "erupt": "The various popular convulsions in the Balkans are inexorably converging on Macedonia. . . . Rarely has the very process of history been so transparent and cyclical" (1991, 104). Even later, when war had sprung up not in Macedonia, but in Slovenia, Croatia, and Bosnia, Kaplan continued to see Macedonia as "ground zero for the coming century of culture clash" (1993c, 15). Although Macedonia has had problems, it never really got around to erupting. See also R. D. Kaplan 1991 and 1993a and, for his later doomsaying, now focused, with due agility, on Africa, R. D. Kaplan 1994. For a devastating critique of the argument, see Malcolm 1993, as well as Gagnon 1994–95, 133–34; Hardin 1995, ch. 6; Sadowski 1998; B. Hall 1996, 83. Kaplan paints an extreme picture in a poorly understood area like the Balkans by selective perception: in the words of Noel Malcolm, "As magpies make collections of shiny objects, so Mr. Kaplan goes through national histories, picking out the gory bits" (1993, 85).
7. Engulfing: Kober 1993, 82. Epidemic: Hamburg 1993. Breakdown: Job 1993, 71. Escalating: Huntington 1993a, 71. War is renewed: Huntington 1996, 259, 291. See also R. D. Kaplan 1991, 1993a, 1993b; Mearsheimer 1990; Moynihan 1993; Brzezinski 1993.
8. Thus, waxing eloquent about the Bosnian conflict on national television in 1995, Vice President Al Gore allowed as how the tragedy had been unfolding, "some would say, for five hundred years." President Bill Clinton, not to be outdone, opined in the same interview that "their enmities go back five hundred years, some would say almost a thousand years" (Roger Cohen 1998, 397–98). The exact identity of the hyperbolic "some" was not specified, but one source, perhaps, was Henry Kissinger, who noted authoritatively that "ethnic conflict has been endemic in the Balkans for centuries" (as opposed to gentle, troublefree Western Europe, presumably), and, patronizingly and absurdly, that "none of the populations has any experience with—and essentially no belief in—Western concepts of toleration"

(Kissinger 1999). On Somalia, see Western 2002, 113, 119–21, 131–33. On Clinton's seduction by Kaplan's book, see Drew 1994, 157; on his belated, regretful, public recantation in 1999 of the Kaplan perspective, see Seelye 1999. For Kaplan's professed amazement that anybody should take his work that seriously, see R. D. Kaplan 1999.

9. B. Hall 1994, 68. Thugs, policing: see J. Mueller 2000a, 2000b, 2004b, ch. 6; Fearon and Laitin 2003; Collier 2000.

10. For an early suggestion along this line, see J. Mueller 1996, 113–14. See also Gurr 2000.

11. www.un.org/events/tenstories. On the apparent decline of war, see J. Mueller 2004a, forthcoming; Marshall and Gurr 2005; Easterbrook 2005; Mack 2005.

12. Secretary of State Madeleine Albright, *Today* show, NBC, 19 February 1998.

13. Another rogue, even more mini, was Haiti. President George H. W. Bush imaginatively proclaimed that an antidemocratic coup there in 1991 (but not the near-simultaneous one in a much more important country, Algeria) posed "an unusual and extraordinary threat to the national security, foreign policy and economy of the United States," a phrase his successor, Bill Clinton, chose to repeat when sending troops there to set things right in 1994 (*Washington Post*, 16 September 1994, A31). When what passed for democracy crumbled again in Haiti a decade later, however, the administration of Bush's son scarcely noticed.

14. For data: J. Mueller 1994, 221.

15. Johns and Johnson 1994, 59–60.

16. Woodward 1991, 86 (campaign), 116 (unpleasant symbol), 129 (wimp), 164 (forces).

17. Sigal 1998. Harrison 2002. Kang 2003. Fallows 1994–95.

18. Oberdorfer 2001, 314.

19. Oberdorfer 2001, 307. Harrison 2002, 213.

20. Oberdorfer 2001, 308, 316 (prepared for war), 318 (sanctions), 329 (preemptive), 324 (cost of war; see also Harrison 2002, 117–18).

21. Extortion: Oberdorfer 2001, 305, 336; see also Eberstadt 1999. Pleased by Carter: Oberdorfer 2001, 327. 1994 deal: Sigal 1998, chs. 6–7; Harrison 2002, ch. 18. Expect collapse: Harrison 2002.

22. Famine toll: Oberdorfer 2001, 399; Natsios 2001, 215. U.S. efforts: Natsios 2001, 147–48.

23. Perle: interview for *Frontline*, PBS, conducted March 27, 2003, http://www.pbs.org/wgbh/pages/frontline/shows/kim/interviews/perle.html. Allison 2004, 168–71.

24. See also Arkin 2006c.

25. Conquer, incorporate: Gray 2004, 252. Further aggression: *U.S. News* 1992, 98; Simpson 1991, 197.

26. Sanctions effect: Cortright and Lopez 2000, 43–44. Reelectability: Barnes 1991a, 11.

27. Tested by fire: Frost 1991. As one of his aides observed, Bush was "totally into World War II analogies": Barnes 1991b. A White House official put it to a sympathetic journalist, "Who would have predicted Bush would act like this after a career of compromise? Bush went nuts. It's amazing" (Barnes 1991c, 17). In his book, *The Commanders*, which details the observations of White House intimates in the runup to war, journalist Bob Woodward repeatedly stressed Bush's emotional

mind-set: Bush was "betraying the traits of a cornered man," became "emotional," was "deeply, even emotionally, concerned," made a "personal and emotional declaration," was "personally moved," displayed an "obvious emotional attachment," was "visibly riled up" with "tension showing in the muscles of his neck," "became very emotional," "was stiff," and his "eyes looked scary" (1991, 229, 255, 260, 298, 302, 317, 318, 337, 350). Elizabeth Drew's informants use similar language: Bush "is unlike he is on any other issue. . . . Usually he sees the complexities, and doesn't care all that much. . . . But this touches some deep inner core." And a congressman said "a good many people" were concerned about Bush's "obsession" with Iraq, his "fixation" on it, "to the exclusion of everything else" (1991, 82–83). See also R. W. Tucker and Hendrickson 1992, 91; Simpson 1991, 215–16.

28. See also R. W. Tucker and Hendrickson 1992, 114–19. The nuclear argument was emphasized after Bush's pollsters discovered that the nuclear issue was one that particularly aroused public concerns (J. Mueller 1994, 118). For all his efforts, however, Bush was unable to increase public support for military action during the runup to the war (J. Mueller 1994, 31–34, 118–21).

29. Hitler: Freedman and Karsh 1993, 462n. Important: Frost 1991. New world order: Bush 1991, 314. Bush was not the only person caught up in the drama of the moment. The five-month runup to the impending war was often tense and dramatic, and when it came about it seemed all-consumingly important to many people: one reporter told a friend, "This is the biggest story of my life" (Drew 1991, 90), and a top reporter for the *New York Times* speculated that the war "could change the face of domestic politics, the map of the Middle East, the realities of big-power relationships and the world economy for years or decades to come" (Apple 1991). On the eve of the war half of the people told pollsters they thought about the crisis in the Gulf at least once an hour. J. Mueller 1994, 159–60. For an assessment of the venture's historical importance, or lack thereof, see J. Mueller 1994, chs. 8, 9.

30. Bush demands: R. W. Tucker and Hendrickson 1992, 91; *U.S. News* 1992, 199–200. Drew 1991, 85. As columnist Fred Barnes observed at the time, in the first fifteen minutes of one television interview, "Bush ruled out compromise nineteen separate times" (1991b, 8). Public humiliation: Karsh and Rautsi 1991, 263; R. W. Tucker and Hendrickson 1992, 86. Punitive containment: see especially R. W. Tucker and Hendrickson 1992, 95; also Brzezinski 1990; J. Mueller 1990.

31. J. Mueller 1994, 36–37. The opinion dynamic that probably helped Bush most was a growing fatalism about war: as time went by the public became increasingly convinced not that war was particularly wise, but that it was inevitable. This was reflected in official thinking as well: J. Mueller 1994, 47–48, 56–58. Bush's chief ally in bringing about the war, Saddam Hussein, apparently also became increasingly convinced that war was inevitable: Karsh and Rautsi 1991, 240–41; Freedman and Karsh 1991, 9n. To a considerable extent, it was war by mutual self-entrapment.

32. Kick: Barnes 1991b, 9; Drew 1991, 83; White House press secretary Marlin Fitzwater, however, insisted that this "wasn't macho talk" (Barnes 1991b, 9). Iraqi defenders: J. Mueller 1995b.

33. As Bush put it a few weeks after the war, "With this much turmoil it seems to me that Saddam cannot survive . . . people are fed up with him. They see him for the brutal dictator he is" (quoted in Freedman and Karsh 1993, 417). In its first Sun-

day edition after the war, the *New York Times* published in adjacent columns two confident predictions. In one, James E. Atkins, a career foreign service officer and Middle East specialist, asserted, "There is little reason to concern ourselves with Saddam. He has been defeated and humiliated and will soon be dead at the hands of his own people unless some unlikely country gives him refuge" (Atkins 1991). In the other, *Times* columnist Anna Quindlen predicted with "reasonable" sureness that "George Bush will be re-elected President in 1992" (Quindlen 1991). Gergen 1992, 183; see also Freedman and Karsh 1993, 425.

34. Bush and Albright: Cockburn and Cockburn 1999, 43, 263; also 98; see also Melby 1998, 118, 123. British: Aburish 2000, 342.

35. UN report: United Nations 1999, paras. 43, 49. Sanctions effects: Garfield 1997, 1999; Stahl 1996; O'Kane 1996; "War on Sanctions," *The NewsHour with Jim Lehrer*, PBS, 13 March 1998; UNICEF Report, "Situation Analysis of Children and Women in Iraq," 30 April 1998; Cockburn and Cockburn 1999, ch. 5; J. Mueller and Mueller 2000, 170–71; Cortright and Lopez 2000, 45–51; M. Welch 2002; Pollack 2002, 125–40; Rieff 2003, 43; J. Gordon 2002. One article repeatedly hails the sanctions as a success while noting in passing that they "helped spur a severe humanitarian crisis that resulted in hundreds of thousands of preventable deaths among children." If a policy with collateral damage like that is judged a success, it would be interesting to know what death count must be achieved for it to be considered a failure (Lopez and Cortright 2004).

36. Albright: Stahl 1996. Arab world: Cockburn and Cockburn 1999, 263.

37. For example, defense department adviser Richard Perle, one of the most ardent proponents of war in 2003, published an article in 2000 that, though strongly advocating a policy hostile toward Saddam, recommended only protecting and assisting resistance movements within Iraq, not outright invasion by American troops (2000, 108–9). Public opinion on Saddam: Larson and Savych 2005, 132–38.

38. Suskind 2004, 204; Woodward 2004.

39. Grave and growing: Bush State of Union Address 2002. Fearmonger connections: see Halper and Clarke 2004; also R. H. Johnson 1994, ch. 6.

40. Jervis 2006.

41. For the prewar argument that Iraq presented little threat, see Mearsheimer and Walt 2003; J. Mueller with Lindsey 2003. For a detailed discussion of threat exaggeration in the runup to the Iraq War, see Kaufmann 2004.

42. Weiner 1999a, 1999b; Lippman and Gellman 1999. See also Jervis 2006.

43. Last man: J. Mueller 1995b, 102. Ammunition: Fallows 2005b, 72. Heavy weapons: O'Kane 1998. Even war advocate Perle had written a few years earlier that "Saddam's grip on the regular army . . . has always been tenuous" (2000, 109). For an extended discussion of Saddam's obsessive worries about a military coup, see M. R. Gordon and Trainor 2006, 55–66, 505. War advocates often claimed that "containment" wasn't working because Iraq was able partly to evade some of the sanctions and engage in some modest rearmament (for example, Pollack 2002, ch. 7). This is a bizarre redefinition of the concept. In the cold war, containment meant keeping the enemy from expanding, not keeping it from developing economically or militarily or from conducting trade.

44. For an example of such a prediction, see J. Mueller with Lindsey 2003, 45.

45. Fukuyama 2005. Whatever the argument, support among the public for military

action against Iraq did not increase during the runup to the war, repeating the experience of Bush's father for the 1991 war. J. Mueller 1994, 31–34; J. Mueller 2005a, 48; Jacobson 2006, ch. 5.

46. Mearsheimer and Walt 2003. J. Mueller with Lindsey 2003. The case for going to war is very extensively put forward in Pollack 2002; L. F. Kaplan and Kristol 2003; Frum and Perle 2003.

47. On the monumental inadequacy and incompetence of the Iraq military and its leadership during the 2003 war, see Wilson 2003; Zucchino 2003; Shanker 2004; M. R. Gordon and Trainor 2006.

48. 1991 planning: J. Mueller 1995b, 97. 2003 planning: Bensahel 2006. On the Iraq venture in comparative perspective, see also J. Mueller 2005b.

49. On this phenomenon more generally, see J. Mueller 1995a, ch. 1.

50. Memorial Service speech at the National Cathedral, 14 September 2001. One, of course, wishes him luck. Bush's proclamation about his ambitious mission occasioned almost no commentary in the press at the time, though the New Orleans *Times–Picayune* did suggest in an editorial that "perhaps the president overpromised" (16 September 2001). Interestingly, the chief earlier recorded effort to expunge evil from the world was carried out some years ago by God who drowned every living being on the planet except for one arkload of people and paired animals, a venture that, subsequent history strongly suggests, failed. George W. Bush therefore seems to have taken on the remarkable burden of seeking to outdo *both* his fathers: his earthly one, by ridding Iraq of Saddam, his heavenly one, by ridding the world of evil.

CHAPTER 7. AN ALTERNATIVE TERRORISM POLICY

1. "Full transcript of bin Laden's speech," http://english.aljazeera.net/NR/exeres/ 79C6AF22-98FB-4A1C-B21F-2BC36E87F61F.htm, accessed July 31, 2005.

2. B. Friedman 2004, 32.

3. As paraphrased by columnist George Will. Ironically, Will applies the quotation (or near quotation) in a 1994 column about the "threat" supposedly presented at the time by North Korea's potential nuclear weapons development. The United States, proclaimed Will, had only two alternatives: "confrontation, with the clear risk of war" and "capitulation, with the near certainty of waning U.S. influence in an increasingly anarchic world." Neither happened. Coolidge's actual statement apparently is: "Never go out of your way to meet trouble. If you will just sit still, nine cases out of ten someone will intercept it before it reaches you."

4. Hoffman: Gorman 2003a, 1463. See also Schneier 2003, ch. 15.

5. Targets: M. Hall 2004b; Thomas 2004. Waterpark: Spicuzza 2005.

6. Lieberman: de Rugy 2005a, 28. Statistics: M. Hall 2004b. Terrorism industry and port security: see, interestingly, Lipton 2006b; also de Rugy 2005a, 18. Shoe boxes: Schneier 2003, 246.

7. de Rugy 2005a, 26. 2005 city list at www.ojp.usdoj.gov/odp/docs/fy05hsgp.pdf.

8. Schneier 2003, 243, 253.

9. de Rugy 2005a, 34. Pentagon: MacGillis 2006.

10. Kunreuther 2002, 662–63.

11. Cox: de Rugy 2005a, 25. On international cooperation, see Pillar 2003, xxviii–xxix.

12. Hoffman 2002, 313. Sunstein 2003, 132.
13. On real estate, see Betts 2005, 508. Columbia study: National Center for Disaster Preparedness 2003; see also Gorman 2003b. CEO: M. Hall 2004a. McCarthy era: Stouffer 1955, ch. 3. Fallout shelters: Weart 1988, 258–60.
14. Glass and Schoch-Spana 2002, 214–15. Fischoff 2005.
15. Defensive behavior: as Sunstein notes, "In the context of terrorism, fear is likely to make people reluctant to engage in certain activities, such as flying on airplanes and appearing in public places," and "the resulting costs can be extremely high" (2003, 132). Travel industry, assessment of potential missile problem: Chow et al. 2005, 1.
16. Official: Shields 2005. Sunstein 2003, 124. Flight insurance: E. J. Johnson et al. 1993, 39; the effect was clear, although, because the number of subjects in the experiment was small, it did not achieve statistical significance.
17. Statistician: Gorman 2003a, 1461–62. Kunreuther 2002, 663. For rare attempts at what Kunreuther suggests, see Dyer 2004; Schneier 2003, ch. 15. Almanacs: Eggen 2003.
18. McCain with Salter 2004, 35–36. An e-mail inquiring about the alert problem was sent to Senator McCain's office in August 2004, but it has yet to generate a reply.
19. Sivak and Flannagan 2003, 6–9.
20. Banks 2002, 10; see also Applebaum 2005, but also Schneier 2003, 273–74. Previous hijackings: Schneier 2003, 4. Chechen hijacking: M. Kramer 2004–2005, 58. De Rugy argues that "reinforcing cockpit doors would have most likely prevented most of the deaths" on 9/11 (2005a, 31). But that would only have been the case if the pilots knew to refuse to open the doors no matter what mayhem was taking place in the cabin.
21. On this issue more broadly, see J. Mueller 2004b.
22. Mencken 1949, 29.
23. Rosenthal 1993. For data showing that crime peaked in New York in 1990 and declined steadily thereafter, see *New York Times*, 19 February 1998, A16. For a discussion of the fear of crime, see Warr 2000. On crime and fears in the 1990s, see Glassner 1999, xi.
24. Applebaum 2003; Glass and Schoch-Spana 2002, 219; Rosen 2004, 72. See also Furedi 2002, 68–70.
25. Sunstein 2003, 128.
26. Slovic 1986, 403–15. It has also been found that even health professionals are considerably less likely to recommend discharging a mental patient when the odds the patient will commit violence are expressed as 20 out of 100 than when they are expressed as 20 percent or 2 chances in 10 (Slovic et al. 2000, 288). Authoritative source: Viscusi 1997, 1669.
27. Sunstein 2003, 122. See also Lowenstein et al. 2001.
28. Sunstein 2003, 128.
29. For the French and Romanian studies and for further discussion, see Rohrmann and Renn 2000. See also Douglas and Wildavsky 1982.
30. Asteroid danger: Chapman and Morrison 1989, ch. 19; see also Posner 2005a. Nuclear energy: Weart 1988.
31. Wells 1914; Wells 1968, 67. On the Y2K effect, see also Gorman 2003a, 1464.
32. Sunstein 2003, 122, 131.
33. Schneier 2003, 249. Posner 2005b.
34. For a discussion of the effects of such "signs of incivility," see Warr 2000, 477.

35. De Rugy 2005a, 31. On security theater in dealing with fears about crime, see Warr 2000, 480.
36. Applebaum 2005.
37. Rosen 2004, 79.
38. Lerner et al. 2003.
39. Grosskopf 2006.
40. De Rugy 2005a, 4.
41. Goo 2004.
42. Sober pronouncement: Rothkopf 2003. Ignatieff 2004a, 48.
43. "Transcript: Ashcroft, Mueller Discuss Terrorist Threat," 26 May 2004, washingtonpost.com. Cicada invasion: L. Myers 2004.
44. Johnston and Van Natta 2004.
45. Klaidman 2004.
46. After election: Gorman 2004, 3534. Inauguration: Ornstein 2005. Clarke 2005.
47. Rohrmann and Renn 2000, 31.
48. Engineer: Rockwell 2003. Other specialists: Ferguson and Potter 2005, 335. Fischoff 2005. See also Glanz and Revkin 2002; Allison 2004, 8, 59, 220; Linzer 2004.
49. Zimmerman and Loeb 2004, 10.
50. Wald 2005; see also Wald 2006. For an excellent discussion, see Eraker 2004.
51. Sudan: Daum 2001, 19; William Cohen, defense secretary at the time, has admitted that information was so inadequate that policymakers did not even know that the plant was producing medicine (Stern 1998–99, 178–79). Years later, the United States refused to apologize or offer compensation and had still not ruled out the possibility that the plant did have some "link" to the production of chemical weapons: Lacey 2005. On Afghanistan: Burke 2003, 167–68; Cullison and Higgins, 2002; Coll 2004, 400–402, 414–15; Kepel 2002, 420 n. 50; see also Gerges 2005, 176, 188. On the Chechen war, see M. Kramer 2004–2005, 7–8, 56. In a similar vein, the success of terrorists seeking to sabotage talks that could lead to peace settlements have often been the result of the overreaction they inspire; thus, Palestinian bombings led Israelis to react by electing prime ministers hostile to the peace process in 1996 and 2001, just as the terrorists wanted. On this process more generally, see Lake 2002.
52. M. Kramer 2004–2005, 54–55.
53. See also Howard 2002; Pillar 2003, xxvi.
54. J. Mueller 1989, 83.
55. There may be, in this regard, some advantage to a presidential system, where the leader cannot quickly be removed from office, over a parliamentary system—or for that matter, a dictatorial one—where instant removal is possible and rather common. For example, in 1982 Argentina invaded Britain's Falkland Islands, a desolate, nearly barren territory populated by fewer than 2,000 souls. The British might have responded, "Okay, you can have the islands, but we get to keep the sheep." Objectively, given the low value of the stakes, this might have made some sense, but instead a war ensued, one characterized by an Argentine writer as "two bald men fighting over a comb" (quoted in Norpoth 1987, 957). Although fewer than 1,000 people died in the ten-week war, this cost, proportionate to the value of the stakes, made the war one of the most brutal in history. Moreover, in the aftermath of that

war, the British felt it necessary to send over a protective force larger than the civilian population, and the combined cost of the war and of the postwar defensive
buildup through the 1980s alone came to over $3 million for every liberated Falk-
lander (Freedman 1988, 116). "Far from proving that aggression does not pay,"
observed one American official, "Britain has only proved that resisting it can be
ridiculously expensive" (Hastings and Jenkins 1983, 339). But the British people
were outraged by the invasion; had Margaret Thatcher's government simply surrendered, as the Portuguese did when India abruptly took over their colony of Goa
in 1961, she would very likely have been abruptly removed from that top office.
She was, it seems clear, never so tempted, but the parliamentary system, with its
capacity to visit instant political defeat upon leaders in moments of emotional crisis, did not allow her to consider the less costly alternative, whereas the presidential system would afford that luxury.

56. J. Mueller 2005a, 48. Jacobson 2006, ch. 5.

CHAPTER 8. TERRORISM AND TERROR

1. Chapman and Harris 2002, 2003.
2. Kepel 2002, 19–20, 375–76. See also Gerges 2005, 151.
3. Gerges 2005, 1 3, 27 28, also 161–62. Richard Cohen 2005.
4. Gerges 2005, 175–76, 188.
5. Anticipated damage: Arkin 2006b. Image: B. R. Myers 2004, 142.
6. See also Hoffman 2002, 311–12.
7. *The NewsHour with Jim Lehrer*, PBS, 7 February 2006. See also Benjamin and
   Simon 2005, 115.
8. On government incompetence over Katrina, see, for example, Posner 2005b,
   Cooper and Block 2006. FBI: Gorman 2005. NSA: Gorman 2006. See also L.
   Mitchell 2004; Seitz 2004; Lustick 2006, ch. 3.
9. Bad apples: Shane 2005b. Planners: Arkin 2006b. 300 million: Carafano and
   Rosenzweig 2005, 92.
10. Illegal Islamic immigrants: Beinart 2006b. On the dozens of well used tunnels
    under the U.S.-Mexican border that are continually being discovered, see W. M.
    Welch 2006.
11. Benjamin and Simon 2005, 7. On Madrid: Benjamin and Simon 2005, ch. 1;
    Haven 2006. On the Afghanistan argument: Shane 2005b.
12. Stevenson 2004, 7.
13. Arkin 2006b. See also Gerges 2005, 44.
14. On the patience argument: Shane 2005b; Benjamin and Simon 2005, 116. Two
    years for 9/11: Gerges 2005, 41; Sageman 2004, 164–65; National Commission
    2004, 149. Madrid: Benjamin and Simon 2005, 16. Hashish: Haven 2006.
15. Stevenson 2004, 7.
16. No operatives: Arkin 2006b. 5000: Gertz 2002. Terrorist cells: Ross 2005. See also
    Benjamin and Simon 2005, 116–18.
17. Lustick 2006, ch. 5. Siegel 2005, 63–64. Testimony by Mueller can be found at
    www.fbi.gov/congress/congress.htm.
18. Warrantless surveillance: Gellman et al. 2006. 80,000 immigrants and national
    security letters: Cole 2006a. Credit card: B. Kerr 2006.

219

19. For detailed accountings of convictions, see Cole 2006a; Lustick 2006, ch. 3.
20. Suskind 2006, 99–101, 111, 115, 121.
21. Lipton 2005. See also Pillar 2004, 102, 106.
22. See K. Mueller forthcoming.
23. For an able discussion of the Taliban-Pakistan connections before 9/11, see Rashid 2000. Scientists: Albright and Higgins 2003, 54–55; Suskind 2006, 69–70, 122.
24. Gerges 2005, 232, and, for a tally, 318–19. See also Pillar 2003, xxviii–xxix; Lynch 2006, 54–55.
25. Gerges 2005, 27, 228, 233, also 270; shamateh: 245.
26. Lipton 2005. Rood 2005.
27. Gerges 2005, 153. Sageman 2004, 47.
28. Indonesia: Sageman 2004, 53, 142, 173. Saudi Arabia: Gerges 2005, 249; Sageman 2004, 53, 144; J. Meyer 2006. Morocco: Sageman 2004, 53–54. In sum, although al-Qaeda may retain local affiliates in Saudi Arabia, Yemen, Jordan, Pakistan, and elsewhere, "they are shrinking by the hour and bleeding profusely from the blows of the security services with substantial logistical support from the United States" (Gerges 2005, 249). See also Pillar 2003, xxiv.
29. Jordan polls: Pew Global Attitudes Project, "The Great Divide: How Westerners and Muslims View Each Other," 22 June 2006, http://pewglobal.org/reports/display.php?ReportID=253. See also Lynch 2006, 54–55.
30. Kepel 2002, 371. See also Seitz 2004. Similarly, Olivier Roy traces the growing post-9/11 isolation of Islamic radicals in Europe—though, as Muslim riots in France in 2005 showed, there may be other reasons for Muslim discontent in Europe (2004, 83).
31. For the argument that a Clinton-like administration, even under the impetus of 9/11, might have refrained from "any form of decisive operations involving ground troops in areas of high risk," including Afghanistan, see Feaver 2004. Actually, as it happened, the campaign that toppled the Taliban did not rely much on U.S. ground troops, though there were definite plans to send them in if necessary. Instead, about 110 CIA officers and 316 from Special Forces entered the country, hiring local combatants, supplying leadership and tactical direction, and coordinating precision, and sometimes massive, bombardment from the air. After eight years of chaotic and often brutal rule, the Taliban had become deeply unpopular in the war-exhausted country, and its poorly trained forces mostly disintegrated under the onslaught. Many al-Qaeda members did stand and fight, but few Afghans seemed to be willing to battle alongside these foreigners except under duress. The country was secured in two months at a cost to the CIA of some $70 million. For a discussion, see J. Mueller 2004a, 134–36.
32. Stevenson 2004, 6. See also Gerges 2005, 247, 252.
33. Watson 2005. America forgets: C. Tucker 2003.
34. Gerges 2005, 188, 190–91.
35. Gerges 2005, 254–65, 272.
36. Gerges 2005, 252–53, 256–59.
37. Priest 2005. Gerges 2005, 264. As the International Institute for Strategic Studies put it succinctly in its 2004 report, al-Qaeda "recruitment [is] accelerating on account of Iraq" (Stevenson 2004, 6).
38. For a discussion of this point, see J. Mueller 2005a, 51. See also MacFarquhar 2003. The Soviet withdrawal from Afghanistan was "orderly" in the sense that it

left behind a government that managed to continue to hang on for another three years.

39. Pew Global Attitudes Project, "A Year after Iraq War: Mistrust of America in Europe Ever Higher, Muslim Anger Persists," 16 March 2004. www .pewtrusts.com/pdf/pew_global_attitudes_year_war_031604.pdf.

40. Gerges 2005, 57, 264.

41. Gerges 2005, 274.

42. Lind 2003. Roy 2003.

43. Reilly 2005. On the potential Iraq syndrome, see J. Mueller 2005a.

44. On such targeting (except for the last two), see Podhoretz 2002, 28.

45. Efron and Wallace 2005.

46. Pape 2005, ch. 12. Walt 2005. In the meantime, in a process that antedates America's war in Iraq, monarchs in a number of Middle Eastern countries may gradually be coming to the realization that they are out of date—rather in the way Latin American militarists more or less voluntarily decided over the past quarter century to relinquish control to democratic forces (J. Mueller 1999, 224–25). If this does happen, however, the process will be impelled, as in Latin America, primarily by domestic forces, not outside ones. One potentially beneficial result of the war in Iraq, if perhaps only temporary, was that it may have helped reduce at least some of the tensions between Muslims in non-Muslims in Europe. As Olivier Roy has pointed out, both groups have strongly opposed the American venture, and, as a result, "Muslims did not feel isolated or targeted; rather they felt as though they belonged to mainstream public opinion" (2004, 88). Later local developments, however, tended again to exacerbate tensions.

47. *The NewsHour with Jim Lehrer*, PBS, 20 September 2001. Rumsfeld 2001. At the same time, however, Secretary of State Colin Powell issued a definition that may be impossible: "Victory in this campaign against terrorism ultimately is for all of our societies to be safer, to feel that they don't have the same kind of threat from terrorists that may have existed in the past" (*This Week*, ABC News, 23 September 2001).

48. Flynn 2004a, 20, 33, 27; Flynn 2004b, 15, 164, 169.

49. Siegel 2005; see also Lustick 2006, 30. Actually, a Halloween poll in 2005 did discover that nearly half of all Americans actually do claim to believe in ghosts, and that nearly half of those feel they have been in the presence of one. ("Ghosts and the Afterlife," CBS News Poll, 30 October 2005). Perhaps there is a difference in that, unlike in the era of witch hunts, no one today seems to be terribly threatened by these presumed spooks.

50. For all the initial shock, however, the "war" against terrorism after September 11 may not prove to be as preoccupying or as fully and urgently embraced as was the war against Japan after December 7. For analysis, it would be useful to be able to compare the events' impact on the frequently asked poll question, "What do you think is the most important problem facing this country today?" As it happens, however, comparisons can be only tentative because, although the question had been asked quite a few times before Pearl Harbor, it was completely neglected during World War II and was revived again only after the war: it was so obvious that winning the war was the most important problem that pollsters apparently concluded that the question lost all meaning. The most-important-problem question has been repeatedly posed in the wake of September 11, however, and although

terrorism remained an important issue, its salience declined considerably as economic and other concerns came to command more attention. Another massive terrorist attack in the United States could abruptly reverse this decline, of course—as did, temporarily, the terrorist attacks in London in 2005. But, like concern over crime and unlike the preoccupying concern that was apparently sustained after the Japanese attack that launched World War II, alarm about terrorism is likely to wax and wane with events. Nonetheless, as noted in the introduction, concerns about its likelihood and consequences seem not to have declined very much since 2001.

51. J. Mueller 1994, 212.

Bibliography

Aburish, Saïd K. 2000. *Saddam Hussein: The Politics of Revenge*. New York: Bloomsbury.

Aird, John S. 1990. *Slaughter of the Innocents*. Washington, DC: AEI Press.

Albright, David, and Holly Higgins. 2003. A Bomb for the Ummah. *Bulletin of the Atomic Scientists* March/April: 49–55.

Allison, Graham. 2004. *Nuclear Terrorism: The Ultimate Preventable Catastrophe*. New York: Times Books.

Andrew, Christopher, and Vasili Mitrokhin. 2003. *The World Was Going Our Way: The KGB and the Battle for the Third World*. New York: Basic Books.

Anonymous [Michael Scheuer]. 2004. *Imperial Hubris: Why the West Is Losing the War on Terror*. Dulles, VA: Brassey's.

Apple, R. W., Jr. 1991. Stake for Bush: Presidency and Politics. *New York Times* 16 January: A1.

Applebaum, Anne. 2003. Finding Things to Fear. *Washington Post* 24 September: A29.

———. 2005. Airport Security's Grand Illusion. *Washington Post* 15 June: A25.

Arkin, William M. 2006a. Goodbye War on Terrorism, Hello Long War. *http://blogs.washingtonpost.com/earlywarning* 26 January.

———. 2006b. What the 9/11 Plotter Tells Us. *http://blogs.washingtonpost.com/early warning* 30 March.

———. 2006c. What to Do about North Korea. *http://blogs.washingtonpost.com/early warning* 5 July.

Ashton, Basil, Kenneth Hill, Alan Piazza, and Robin Zeitz. 1984. Famine in China. *Population and Development Review* 10(4) December: 613–45.

Atkins, James E. 1991. Hooray? The Gulf May Not Be Calm for Long. *New York Times* 3 March: 4, 17.

Aviv, Juval. 2004. *Staying Safe*. New York: HarperResource.

Ball, George W. 1982. *The Past Has Another Pattern*. New York: Norton.

Balz, Dan. 2006. Rove Offers Republicans a Battle Plan for Elections. *Washington Post* 21 January: A1.

Banks, David L. 2002. Statistics for Homeland Defense. *Chance* 15(1): 8–10.

Barnes, Fred. 1991a. The Wimp Factor. *New Republic* 7 & 14 January: 10–11.

———. 1991b. The Hawk Factor. *New Republic* 28 January: 8–9.

———. 1991c. The Unwimp. *New Republic* 18 March: 17–18.

Barnhart, Michael A. 1987. *Japan Prepares for Total War: The Search for Economic Security, 1919–1941*. Ithaca, NY: Cornell University Press.

Beinart, Peter. 2004. The Good Fight. *New Republic* 20 December.

————. 2006a. Elevated Threat. *New Republic* 6 February.

————. 2006b. The Wrong Place to Stop Terrorists. *Washington Post* 4 May: A25.

Belzman, Josh. 2006. Communities Grapple with Rise in Violence. *MSNBC.COM* 30 August: www.msnbc.com/id/14137625.

Benjamin, Daniel, and Steven Simon. 2002. *The Age of Sacred Terror.* New York: Random House.

————. 2005. *The Next Attack: The Failure of the War on Terror and a Strategy for Getting It Right.* New York: Times Books.

Bensahel, Nora. 2006. Mission Not Accomplished: What Went Wrong with Iraqi Reconstruction. *Journal of Strategic Studies* 29(3) June: 453–73.

Berger, Thomas U. 1993. From Sword to Chrysanthemum: Japan's Culture of Anti-Militarism. *International Security* 17(4) Spring: 119–50.

Betts, Richard K. 1998. The New Threat of Mass Destruction. *Foreign Affairs* 77(1) January/February: 26–41.

————. 2005. Maybe I'll Stop Driving. *Terrorism and Political Violence* 17(4) Autumn: 507–10.

Bialik, Carl. 2005. The Numbers Guy: Pondering the Chances of a Nuclear Attack. *Wall Street Journal* 17 July.

Biddle, Francis. 1962. *In Brief Authority.* Garden City, NY: Doubleday.

Binyon, Michael. 1998. Bin Laden "Now Has Nuclear Arsenal." *Times (London)* 7 October.

Blimes, Linda, and Joseph Stiglitz. 2006. War's Stunning Price Tag. *Los Angeles Times* 17 January: B13.

Bloom, Mia. 2005. *Dying to Kill: The Allure of Suicide Terror.* New York: Columbia University Press.

Bluhm, William T. 1974. *Ideologies and Attitudes: Modern Political Culture.* Englewood Cliffs, NJ: Prentice-Hall.

Blumenthal, Ralph, and Judith Miller. 1999. Japanese Germ-War Atrocities: A Half-Century of Stonewalling the World. *New York Times* 4 March: A10.

Bourke, Joanna. 2005. *Fear: A Cultural History.* London: Virago.

Boyle, Francis Anthony. 1985. *World Politics and International Law.* Durham, NC: Duke University Press.

Braestrup, Peter. 1983. *Big Story: How the American Press and Television Reported and Interpreted the Crisis of Tet 1968 in Vietnam and Washington.* New Haven, CT: Yale University Press.

Breslauer, George W. 1987. Ideology and Learning in Soviet Third World Policy. *World Politics* 39(3) April: 429–48.

Broad, William J. 1998. How Japan Germ Terror Alerted World. *New York Times* 26 May: A1.

Brodie, Bernard. 1966. *Escalation and the Nuclear Option.* Princeton, NJ: Princeton University Press.

————. 1973. *War and Politics.* New York: Macmillan.

————. 1978. The Development of Nuclear Strategy. *International Security* 2(4) Spring: 65–83.

Brzezinski, Zbigniew. 1983. *Power and Principle: Memoirs of the National Security Adviser 1977–1981.* New York: Farrar, Straus & Giroux.

————. 1990. Patience in the Persian Gulf, Not War. *New York Times* 7 October: 4–19.

———. 1993. *Out of Control: Global Turmoil on the Eve of the 21st Century.* New York: Scribner.

Bunce, Valerie. 1985. The Empire Strikes Back: The Evolution of the Eastern Bloc from a Soviet Asset to a Soviet Liability. *International Organization* 39(1) Winter: 1–46.

Bundy, McGeorge. 1988. *Danger and Survival: Choices about the Bomb in the First Fifty Years.* New York: Random House.

Burin, Frederic S. 1963. The Communist Doctrine of the Inevitability of War. *American Political Science Review* 57(2) June: 334–54.

Burke, Jason. 2003. *Al-Qaeda: Casting a Shadow of Terror.* New York: Tauris.

Bush, George H. W. 1990. *Public Papers of the Presidents of the United States: George Bush, 1989.* Washington, DC: U.S. Government Printing Office.

———. 1991. The Liberation of Kuwait Has Begun. In *The Gulf War Reader: History, Documents, Opinions,* ed. Micah L. Sifry and Christopher Cerf. New York: Times Books/Random House, 311–14.

Butow, Robert J. C. 1961. *Tojo and the Coming of the War.* Stanford: Stanford University Press.

Byman, Daniel L. 2003. Al-Qaeda as an Adversary: Do We Understand Our Enemy? *World Politics* 56(1) October: 139–63.

Calbreath, Dean. 2002. Attacks to Cost 1.6 Million Jobs. *San Diego Union-Tribune* 12 January: C-2.

Callahan, David. 1990. *Dangerous Capabilities: Paul Nitze and the Cold War.* New York: HarperCollins.

Campbell, John C. 1967. *Tito's Separate Road: America and Yugoslavia in World Politics.* New York: Harper & Row.

Cantril, Hadley, and Mildred Strunk. 1951. *Public Opinion 1935–1946.* Princeton, NJ: Princeton University Press.

Carafano, James, and Paul Rosenzweig. 2005. *Winning the Long War: Lessons from the Cold War for Defeating Terrorism and Preserving Freedom.* Washington, DC: Heritage Books.

Carter, Jimmy. 1982. *Keeping Faith: Memoirs of a President.* New York: Bantam.

Carus, W. Seth. 2006. *Defining "Weapons of Mass Destruction."* Washington, DC: National Defense University Press.

Center for Nonproliferation Studies. 2002. *"Suitcase Nukes": A Reassessment.* Monterey, CA: Monterey Institute of International Studies, 22 September.

Chapman, Clark R., and Alan W. Harris. 2002. A Skeptical Look at September 11th: How We Can Defeat Terrorism by Reacting to It More Rationally. *Skeptical Inquirer* September/October: 29–34.

———. 2003. Response. *Skeptical Inquirer* January/February: 65.

Chapman, Clark, and David Morrison. 1989. *Cosmic Catastrophes.* New York: Plenum Press.

Checkel, Jeffrey T. 1997. *Ideas and International Political Change: Soviet/Russian Behavior and the End of the Cold War.* New Haven, CT: Yale University Press.

Chow, James, et al. 2005. *Protecting Commercial Aviation against the Shoulder-Fired Missile Threat.* Occasional Paper. Santa Monica, CA: RAND Corporation.

Christopher, George W., T. J. Cieslak, J. A. Pavlin, and E. M. Eitzen Jr. 1997. Biological Warfare: A Historical Perspective. *Journal of the American Medical Association* 278(5) 6 August: 412–17.

Bibliography

Church, Francis P. 1897. Yes, Virginia, There Is a Santa Claus. *New York Sun* 21 September.

Clarke, Richard A. 2005. Ten Years Later. *Atlantic* January/February: 61–77.

Clines, Francis X. 2003. Karl Rove's Campaign Strategy Seems Evident: It's the Terror, Stupid. *New York Times* 10 May: A28.

Cockburn, Andrew, and Patrick Cockburn. 1999. *Out of the Ashes: The Resurrection of Saddam Hussein.* New York: HarperCollins.

Cohen, Richard. 2005. Truth for the Troops. *Washington Post* 8 December: A33.

Cohen, Roger. 1998. *Hearts Grown Brutal: Sagas of Sarajevo.* New York: Random House.

Cole, David. 2006a. Are We Safer? *New York Review of Books* 9 March: 15–18.

———. 2006b. Are We Safer? An Epilogue. *New York Review of Books* 23 March: 43.

Coll, Steve. 2004. *Ghost Wars: The Secret History of the CIA, Afghanistan, and Bin Laden, from the Soviet Invasion to September 10, 2001.* New York: Penguin.

Collier, Paul. 2000. Doing Well out of War: An Economic Perspective. In *Greed and Grievance: Economic Agendas in Civil Wars*, ed. Mats Berdal and David M. Malone. Boulder, CO: Lynne Rienner, 91–111.

Congleton, Roger D. 2002. Terrorism, Interest-Group Politics, and Public Policy. *Independent Review* 7(1) Summer: 47–67.

Cooper, Christopher, and Robert Block. 2006. *Disaster: Hurricane Katrina and the Failure of Homeland Security.* New York: Times Books.

Cortright, David, and George A. Lopez. 2000. *The Sanctions Decade: Assessing UN Strategies in the 1990s.* Boulder, CO: Lynne Rienner.

Cullison, Alan, and Andrew Higgins. 2002. Strained Alliance: Al Qaeda's Sour Days in Afghanistan. *Wall Street Journal* 2 August: A1.

Dart, Bob. 2005. Leak Plugged: Toll Estimate Rises as Water Begins to Fall. *Atlanta Journal-Constitution* 6 September: 1A.

Daum, Werner. 2001. Universalism and the West: An Agenda for Understanding. *Harvard International Review* Summer: 19–23.

de Rugy, Véronique. 2005a. *What Does Homeland Security Spending Buy?* Working Paper #107. Washington, DC: American Enterprise Institute for Public Policy Research, 1 April.

———. 2005b. Bad News for Homeland Security. *Tech Central Station* 8 June.

DeBoer, Connie. 1985. The Polls: The European Peace Movement and Development of Nuclear Missiles. *Public Opinion Quarterly* 49 Spring: 119–32.

Dionne, E. J., Jr. 2006. Rove's Early Warning. *Washington Post* 24 January: A17.

Djilas, Milovan. 1962. *Conversations with Stalin.* New York: Harcourt, Brace.

Douglas, Mary, and Aaron Wildavsky. 1982. *Risk and Culture: An Essay on the Selection of Technical and Environmental Dangers.* Berkeley: University of California Press.

Dower, John W. 1986. *War without Mercy: Race and Power in the Pacific War.* New York: Pantheon.

Drew, Elizabeth. 1991. Letter from Washington. *New Yorker* 4 February: 82–90.

———. 1994. *On the Edge: The Clinton Presidency.* New York: Simon & Schuster.

Dyer, Gwynne. 2004. Politicking Skews Needed Perspective on Terror War. *Columbus (Ohio) Dispatch* 6 September: A11.

Easterbrook, Gregg. 2002. Term Limits: The Meaninglessness of "WMD." *New Republic* 7 October: 22–25.

———. 2005. The End of War? *New Republic* 30 May: 18–21.

Bibliography

Eberstadt, Nicholas. 1999. The Most Dangerous Country. *National Interest* Fall: 45–54.

Eden, Anthony. 1960. *Full Circle*. Boston: Houghton Mifflin.

Edmonds, James E., and R. Maxwell-Hyslop, eds. 1947. *Military Operations: France and Belgium, 1918*. Vol. 5. London: HMSO.

Efron, Sonni, and Bruce Wallace. 2005. North Korea Escalates Its Nuclear Threat. *Los Angeles Times* 11 February: A1.

Eggen, Dan. 2003. Almanacs May Be Tool for Terrorists, FBI Says. *Washington Post* 30 December: A2.

Einstein, Albert. 1960. *Einstein on Peace*, ed. Otto Nathan and Heinz Norden. New York: Simon & Schuster.

English, Robert D. 2000. *Russia and the Idea of the West: Gorbachev, Intellectuals, and the End of the Cold War*. New York: Columbia University Press.

Eraker, Elizabeth. 2004. Cleanup after a Radiological Attack: U.S. Prepares Guidance. *Nonproliferation Review* 11(3) Fall/Winter: 167–85.

Falkenrath, Richard A., Robert D. Newman, and Bradley A. Thayer. 1998. *America's Achilles' Heel: Nuclear, Biological, and Chemical Terrorism and Covert Attack*. Cambridge, MA: MIT Press.

Fallows, James. 1994–95. The Panic Gap: Reactions to North Korea's Bomb. *National Interest* Winter: 40–45.

———. 2005a. Success without Victory. *Atlantic* January/February: 80–90.

———. 2005b. Why Iraq Has No Army. *Atlantic* December: 60–77.

Fearon, James D., and David D. Laitin. 2003. Ethnicity, Insurgency, and Civil War. *American Political Science Review* 97(1) February: 75–90.

Feaver, Peter D. 2004. The Clinton Mind-Set. *Washington Post* 24 March: A21.

Ferguson, Charles D., Tahseen Kazi, and Judith Perera. 2003. *Commercial Radioactive Sources: Surveying the Security Risks*. Monterey, CA: Center for Nonproliferation Studies, Monterey Institute of International Studies.

Ferguson, Charles D., and William C. Potter. 2005. *The Four Faces of Nuclear Terrorism*. New York: Routledge.

Finn, Peter. 2005. Chernobyl's Harm Was Far Less than Predicted, U.N. Report Says. *Washington Post* 6 September: A22.

Fischoff, Baruch. 2005. A Hero in Every Seat. *New York Times* 7 August: 4–13.

Flynn, Stephen. 2004a. The Neglected Home Front. *Foreign Affairs* September/October: 20–33.

———. 2004b. *America the Vulnerable: How Our Government Is Failing to Protect Us from Terrorism*. New York: HarperCollins.

Freedman, Lawrence. 1988. *Britain and the Falklands War*. Oxford: Basil Blackwell.

Freedman, Lawrence, and Efraim Karsh. 1991. How Kuwait Was Won: Strategy in the Gulf War. *International Security* 16(2) Fall: 5–41.

———. 1993. *The Gulf Conflict, 1990–1991: Diplomacy and War in the New World Order*. Princeton, NJ: Princeton University Press.

Friedman, Benjamin. 2004. Leap before You Look: The Failure of Homeland Security. *Breakthroughs* 13(1) Spring: 29–40.

Friedman, George, and Meredith LeBard. 1991. *The Coming War with Japan*. New York: St. Martin's.

Friedman, Thomas L. 1992. It's Harder Now to Figure Out Compelling National Interests. *New York Times* 31 May: E5.

———. 2004. Addicted to 9/11. *New York Times* 14 October: A29.

Frost, David. 1991. *Talking with David Frost: An Interview with President and Mrs. Bush.* PBS, 2 January.

Frum, David, and Richard Perle. 2003. *An End to Evil: How to Win the War on Terror.* New York: Random House.

Fujiwara, Akira. 1990. The Road to Pearl Harbor. In *Pearl Harbor Reexamined: Prologue to the Pacific War,* ed. Hilary Conroy and Harry Wray. Honolulu: University of Hawaii Press.

Fukuyama, Francis. 2004. The Neoconservative Moment. *National Interest* Summer: 57–68.

———. 2005. America's Parties and Their Foreign Policy Masquerade. *Financial Times* 8 March: 21.

Furedi, Frank. 2002. *Culture of Fear: Risk-Taking and the Morality of Low Expectations,* revised ed. London: Continuum.

Gaddis, John Lewis. 1982. *Strategies of Containment.* New York: Oxford University Press.

———. 1987. *The Long Peace: Inquiries into the History of the Cold War.* New York: Oxford University Press.

Gagnon, V. P., Jr. 1994–95. Ethnic Nationalism and International Conflict: The Case of Serbia. *International Security* 19(3) Winter: 130–66.

Gallup, George H., ed. 1972. *The Gallup Poll: Public Opinion 1935–1971.* New York: Random House.

Garfield, Richard. 1997. The Impact of Economic Embargoes on the Health of Women and Children. *Journal of the American Medical Women's Association.* 52(4) Fall: 181–85.

———. 1999. *Morbidity and Mortality among Iraqi Children from 1990 to 1998.* South Bend, IN: Kroc Institute for International Peace Studies, University of Notre Dame.

Garthoff, Raymond L. 1987. *Reflections on the Cuban Missile Crisis.* Washington, DC: Brookings.

———. 1994. *Détente and Confrontation: American-Soviet Relations from Nixon to Reagan,* revised ed. Washington, DC: Brookings Institution.

———. 2001. *A Journey through the Cold War: A Memoir of Containment and Coexistence.* Washington, DC: Brookings Institution Press.

Gates, Robert M. 1993. No Time to Disarm. *Wall Street Journal* 23 August: A10.

Gellman, Barton. 1984. *Contending with Kennan: Toward a Philosophy of American Power.* New York: Praeger.

Gellman, Barton, Dafna Linzer, and Carol D. Leonnig. 2006. Surveillance Net Yields Few Suspects. *Washington Post* 5 February: A1.

Gergen, David. 1992. The Unfettered Presidency. In *After the Storm: Lessons from the Gulf War,* ed. Joseph S. Nye, Jr. and Roger K. Smith. Lanham, MD: Madison Books, 169–93.

———. 2002. A Fragile Time for Globalism. *U.S. News and World Report* 11 February: 41.

Gerges, Fawaz A. 2005. *The Far Enemy: Why Jihad Went Global.* New York: Cambridge University Press.

Gertz, Bill. 2002. 5,000 in U.S. Suspected of Ties to al Qaeda; Groups Nationwide under Surveillance. *Washington Times* 11 July: A1.

Gilchrist, H. L. 1928. *A Comparative Study of World War Casualties from Gas and Other Weapons.* Edgewood Arsenal, MD: Chemical Warfare School.

Gilmore Commission (Advisory Panel to Assess Domestic Response Capabilities for Terrorism Involving Weapons of Mass Destruction). 1999. *First Annual Report to the President and the Congress: Assessing the Threat,* 15 December. Washington, DC: U.S. Government Printing Office.

Glanz, James, and Andrew C. Revkin. 2002. Some See Panic as Main Effect of Dirty Bombs. *New York Times* 7 March: A1.

Glass, Thomas A., and Monica Schoch-Spana. 2002. Bioterrorism and the People: How to Vaccinate a City against Panic. *CID* 34 15 January: 217–23.

Glassner, Barry. 1999. *The Culture of Fear: Why Americans Are Afraid of the Wrong Things.* New York: Basic Books.

Gleason, Alan H. 1965. Economic Growth and Consumption in Japan. In *The State and Economic Enterprise in Japan,* ed. William W. Lockwood. Princeton, NJ: Princeton University Press.

Goldstein, Amy, and Dan Keating, D.C. Suburbs Top List of Richest Counties. *Washington Post* 30 August: A1.

Goldstein, Joshua S. 2004. *The Real Price of War: How You Pay for the War on Terror.* New York: New York University Press.

Goodman, Walter. 1989. Day 3,650: Looking Back at the Hostage Crisis. *New York Times* 7 November: C22.

Goo, Sara Kehaulani. 2004. Going the Extra Mile. *Washington Post* 9 April: E1.

———. 2005. List of Foiled Plots Puzzling to Some. *Washington Post* 23 October: A6.

Gordon, Joy. 1999. A Peaceful, Silent, Deadly Remedy: The Ethics of Economic Sanctions. *Ethics and International Affairs* 13: 123–42.

———. 2002. Cool War: Economic Sanctions as a Weapon of Mass Destruction. *Harper's* November: 43–49.

Gordon, Michael R., and Bernard E. Trainor. 2006. *Cobra II: The Inside Story of the Invasion and Occupation of Iraq.* New York: Pantheon.

Gorman, Siobhan. 2003a. Fear Factor. *National Journal* 10 May: 1460–64.

———. 2003b. Shaken, Not Stirred. *National Journal* 13 September: 2776–81.

———. 2004. War on Terror, Phase Two. *National Journal* 20 November: 3530–34.

———. 2005. FBI Might Lack Terror Threat Data. *Baltimore Sun* 14 September.

———. 2006. 2 Technology Programs, Weapons for the War on Terrorism, Have Proved Duds. *Baltimore Sun* 26 February.

Gould-Davies, Nigel. 1999. Rethinking the Role of Ideology in International Politics During the Cold War. *Journal of Cold War Studies* 1(1) Winter: 90–109.

Graham, Thomas W. 1991. Winning the Nonproliferation Battle. *Arms Control Today* September: 8–13.

Gray, Christine. 2004. *International Law and the Use of Force.* 2nd ed. Oxford: Oxford University Press.

Greenbaum, Robert, Gary LaFree, and Laura Dugan. 2004. *The Impact of Terrorism on Economic Development: The Case of Italy.* Paper presented at the American Society of Criminology annual meeting. Nashville, TN, November.

Grodzins, Morton, and Eugene Rabinowitch, eds. 1963. *The Atomic Age: Scientists in National and World Affairs.* New York: Basic Books.

Grosskopf, Kevin R. 2006. Evaluating the Societal Response to Antiterrorism Measures. *Journal of Homeland Security and Emergency Management* 3(2).

Gurr, Ted Robert. 2000. Ethnic Warfare on the Wane. *Foreign Affairs* 79(3) May/June: 52–64.

Gwertzman, Bernard. 1981. Allied Contingency Plan Envisions a Warning Shot, Says Haig. *New York Times* 5 November: A1.

Hackett, John. 1979. *The Third World War: August 1985.* New York: Macmillan.

Halberstam, David. 1965. *The Making of a Quagmire.* New York: Random House.

———. 1988. *The Making of a Quagmire,* revised ed. New York: Knopf.

Hall, Brian. 1994. *The Impossible Country.* New York: Penguin.

———. 1996. Rebecca West's War. *New Yorker* 15 April: 74–83.

Hall, Mimi. 2004a. Most Not Prepared for Attack. *USA Today* 31 March: 1A.

———. 2004b. Terror Security List Way Behind. *USA Today* 9 December: 1A.

———. 2005. Ridge Reveals Clashes on Alerts. *USA Today* 11 May: A1.

Halper, Stefan, and Jonathan Clarke. 2004. *America Alone: The Neo-Conservatives and the Global Order.* New York: Cambridge University Press.

Halperin, Morton. 1961. The Gaither Committee and the Policy Process. *World Politics* 13(3) 3 April: 360–84.

Hamburg, David A. 1993. *Preventing Contemporary Intergroup Violence.* New York: Carnegie Corporation of New York.

Hardin, Russell. 1995. *One for All: The Logic of Group Conflict.* Princeton, NJ: Princeton University Press.

Harrison, Selig S. 2002. *Korean Endgame: A Strategy for Reunification and U.S. Disengagement.* Princeton, NJ: Princeton University Press.

Hastings, Max, and Simon Jenkins. 1983. *The Battle for the Falklands.* New York: Norton.

Haven, Paul. 2006. Madrid Bombings Show No al-Qaida Ties. 9 March. washingtonpost.com.

Hilsman, Roger. 1967. *To Move a Nation: The Politics of Foreign Policy in the Administration of John F. Kennedy.* New York: Delta.

Historicus [George Allen Morgan]. 1949. Stalin on Revolution. *Foreign Affairs* 27(2) January: 175–214.

Hoffman, Bruce. 2002. Rethinking Terrorism and Counterterrorism Since 9/11. *Studies in Conflict and Terrorism* 25: 303–16.

Hoffmann, Stanley. 1992. Delusions of World Order. *New York Review of Books* 9 April: 37–43.

Holloway, David. 1994. *Stalin and the Bomb: The Soviet Union and Atomic Energy, 1939–1956.* New Haven, CT: Yale University Press.

Hosmer, Stephen T., and Thomas W. Wolfe. 1983. *Soviet Policy and Practice toward Third World Countries.* Lexington, MA: Lexington.

Howard, Michael. 2002. What's in a Name? How to Fight Terrorism. *Foreign Affairs* 81(1) January/February: 8–13.

Hudson, G. F., Richard Lowenthal, and Roderick MacFarquhar, eds. 1961. *The Sino-Soviet Dispute.* New York: Praeger.

Human Rights Watch/Middle East. 1995. *Iraq's Crime of Genocide: The Anfal Campaign Against the Kurds.* New Haven, CT: Yale University Press.

Huntington, Samuel P. 1991. America's Changing Strategic Interests. *Survival* January/February: 3–17.

———. 1993a. Why International Primacy Matters. *International Security* 17(4) Spring: 68–83.

———. 1993b. The Clash of Civilizations? *Foreign Affairs* 72(3) Summer: 22–49.

———. 1993c. If Not Civilizations, What? Paradigms of the Post–Cold War World. *Foreign Affairs* 72(5) November/December: 186–94.

———. 1996. *The Clash of Civilizations and the Remaking of the World Order.* New York: Touchstone.

Ignatieff, Michael. 2004a. Lesser Evils: What It Will Cost Us to Succeed in the War on Terror. *New York Times Magazine* 2 May: 44ff.

———. 2004b. *The Lesser Evil: Political Ethics in an Age of Terror.* Princeton, NJ: Princeton University Press.

Ignatius, David. 2006. An Arrogance of Power. *Washington Post* 15 February: A21.

Ike, Nobutaka. 1967. *Japan's Decision for War: Records of the 1941 Policy Conferences.* Stanford: Stanford University Press.

Indyk, Martin. 2004. The Iraq War Did Not Force Gadaffi's Hand. *Financial Times* 9 March: 21.

Jacobs, David Michael. 1975. *The UFO Controversy in America.* Bloomington: Indiana University Press.

Jacobson, Gary C. 2006. *A Divider, Not a Uniter: George W. Bush and the American People.* New York: Pearson.

Jenkins, Brian Michael. 1975. International Terrorism: A New Mode of Conflict. In *International Terrorism and World Security,* ed. David Carlton and Carolo Schaerf. New York: Wiley, 13–49.

Jensen, Richard Bach. 2002. The United States, International Policing and the War against Anarchist Terrorism, 1900–1914. *Terrorism and Political Violence* 13(1) Spring: 15–46.

Jentleson, Bruce W., and Christopher A. Whytock. 2005–2006. Who "Won" Libya? The Force-Diplomacy Debate and Its Implications for Theory and Policy. *International Security* 30(3) Winter: 47–86.

Jervis, Robert. 1976. *Perception and Misperception in International Politics.* Princeton, NJ: Princeton University Press.

———. 1980. The Impact of the Korean War on the Cold War. *Journal of Conflict Resolution* 24(4) December: 563–92.

———. 1984. *The Illogic of American Nuclear Strategy.* Ithaca, NY: Cornell University Press.

———. 1993. International Primacy: Is the Game Worth the Candle? *International Security* 17(4) Spring: 52–67.

———. 2001. Was the Cold War a Security Dilemma? *Journal of Cold War Studies* 3(1) Winter: 36–60.

———. 2006. Reports, Politics, and Intelligence Failures: The Case of Iraq. *Journal of Strategic Studies.* 29(1) February: 3–52.

Job, Cvijeto. 1993. Yugoslavia's Ethnic Furies. *Foreign Policy* Fall: 52–74.

Johns, Christina Jacqueline, and P. Ward Johnson. 1994. *State Crime, the Media, and the Invasion of Panama.* Westport, CT: Praeger.

Johnson, E. J., J. Hershey, J. Meszaros, and Howard Kunreuther. 1993. Framing, Probability Distortions, and Insurance Decisions. *Journal of Risk and Uncertainty* 7: 35–41.

Johnson, Lyndon Baines. 1971. *The Vantage Point: Perspectives of the Presidency 1963–1969*. New York: Holt, Rinehart and Winston.

Johnson, Robert H. 1994. *Improbable Dangers: U.S. Conceptions of Threat in the Cold War and After*. New York: St. Martin's.

Johnston, David, and Don Van Natta Jr. 2004. Little Evidence of Qaeda Plot Timed to Vote. *New York Times* 24 October: 1.1.

Kahn, David. 1991–92. The Intelligence Failure of Pearl Harbor. *Foreign Affairs* 70(5) Winter: 136–52.

Kahn, Herman. 1960. *On Thermonuclear War*. Princeton, NJ: Princeton University Press.

Kang, David C. 2003. International Relations Theory and the Second Korean War. *International Studies Quarterly* 47(3) September: 301–24.

Kaplan, Fred. 1983. *The Wizards of Armageddon*. New York: Simon & Schuster.

Kaplan, Lawrence F., and William Kristol. 2003. *The War over Iraq: Saddam's Tyranny and America's Mission*. San Francisco: Encounter Books.

Kaplan, Robert D. 1991. History's Cauldron. *Atlantic* June: 93–104.

———. 1993a. *Balkan Ghosts: A Journey through History*. New York: St. Martin's.

———. 1993b. A Reader's Guide to the Balkans. *New York Times Book Review* 18 April: 1, 30–32.

———. 1993c. Ground Zero: Macedonia: The Real Battleground. *New Republic* 2 August: 15–16.

———. 1994. The Coming Anarchy. *Atlantic* February: 44–76.

———. 1999. Reading Too Much into a Book. *New York Times* 13 June: 4. 17.

Karolyi, G. Andrew, and Rodolfo Martell. 2006. Terrorism and the Stock Market. ssrn.com/abstract=823465.

Karsh, Efraim, and Inari Rautsi. 1991. *Saddam Hussein: A Political Biography*. New York: Free Press.

Katzenstein, Peter J., and Nobuo Okawara. 1993. Japan's National Security: Structures, Norms, and Policies. *International Security* 17(4) Spring: 84–118.

Kaufmann, Chaim. 2004. Threat Inflation and the Failure of the Marketplace of Ideas: The Selling of the Iraq War. *International Security* 29(1) Summer: 5–48.

Keeley, Lawrence H. 1996. *War before Civilization: The Myth of the Peaceful Savage*. New York: Oxford University Press.

Kennan, George F. 1947. The Sources of Soviet Conduct. *Foreign Affairs* 25(4) July: 566–82.

———. 1961. *Russia and the West under Lenin and Stalin*. Boston: Little, Brown.

Kennedy, Paul. 1987. *The Rise and Fall of the Great Powers*. New York: Random House.

———. 1993. *Preparing for the Twenty-First Century*. New York: Random House.

Kennedy, Robert F. 1971. *Thirteen Days: A Memoir of the Cuban Missile Crisis*. New York: Norton.

Kepel, Gilles. 2002. *Jihad: The Trail of Political Islam*. Trans. Anthony F. Roberts. Cambridge, MA: Harvard University Press.

Kerr, Bob. 2006. Pay Too Much and You Could Raise the Alarm. *Providence Journal* 28 February: B1.

Kerr, Jennifer C. 2003. Terror Threat Level Raised to Orange. *Associated Press* 21 December.

Khrushchev, Nikita. 1970. *Khrushchev Remembers*, ed. Edward Crankshaw and Strobe Talbott. Boston: Little, Brown.

Bibliography

——. 1974. *Khrushchev Remembers: The Last Testament*, ed. Strobe Talbott. Boston: Little, Brown.

Kissinger, Henry A. 1999. No U.S. Ground Forces for Kosovo. *Washington Post* 22 February: A15.

Klaidman, Daniel. 2004. If Terror Strikes the Polls. *Newsweek* 18 October: 36.

Kober, Stanley. 1993. Revolutions Gone Bad. *Foreign Policy* Summer: 63–83.

Kosko, Bart. 2004. Terror Threat May Be Mostly a Big Bluff. *Los Angeles Times* 13 September: B11.

Kramer, Bernard M., S. Michael Kalick, and Michael A. Milburn. 1983. Attitudes toward Nuclear Weapons and Nuclear War: 1945–1982. *Journal of Social Issues* 39(1): 7–24.

Kramer, Mark. 1999. Ideology and the Cold War. *Review of International Studies* 25(4) October: 539–76.

——. 2004–2005. The Perils of Counterinsurgency: Russia's War in Chechnya. *International Security* 29(3) Winter: 5–63.

Kraus, Sidney, ed. 1962. *The Great Debates: Kennedy vs. Nixon, 1960*. Bloomington: University of Indiana Press.

Krauthammer, Charles. 2004a. Blixful Amnesia. *Washington Post* 9 July: A19.

——. 2004b. In Defense of Democratic Realism. *National Interest* Fall: 15–25.

——. 2006. Emergency Over, Saith the Court. *Washington Post* 7 July: A17.

Kristof, Nicholas D. 1995. The Bomb. *New York Times* 6 August: 1.

—— 1997. Nobuo Fujita, 85, Dead; Only Foe to Bomb America. *New York Times* 3 October: C20.

Kunreuther, Howard. 2002. Risk Analysis and Risk Management in an Uncertain World. *Risk Analysis* 22(4) August: 655–64.

Lacey, Marc. 2005. Look at the Place! Sudan Says, "Say Sorry," but U.S. Won't. *New York Times* 20 October: A4.

Lake, David A. 2002. Rational Extremism: Understanding Terrorism in the Twenty-First Century. *Dialog-IO* Spring: 15–29.

Landau, Mark J., et al. 2004. Deliver Us from Evil: The Effects of Mortality Salience and Reminders of 9/11 on Support for President George W. Bush. *Personality and Social Psychology Bulletin* 30(9) September: 1136–50.

Laqueur, Walter. 2003. *No End to War: Terrorism in the Twenty-First Century*. New York: Continuum.

Larson, Eric V., and Godgan Savych. 2005. *American Public Support for U.S. Military Operations from Mogadishu to Baghdad*. Santa Monica, CA: RAND Corporation.

Layne, Christopher. 1993. The Unipolar Illusion: Why New Great Powers Will Rise. *International Security* 17(4) Spring: 5–51.

Lebow, Richard Ned, and Janice Gross Stein. 1994. *We All Lost the Cold War*. Princeton, NJ: Princeton University Press.

Leffler, Melvyn P. 1994. *The Specter of Communism*. New York: Hill and Wang.

Leitenberg, Milton. 2004. *The Problem of Biological Weapons*. Stockholm: Swedish National Defence College.

——. 2005. *Assessing the Biological Weapons and Bioterrorism Threat*. Carlisle, PA: Strategic Studies Institute, U.S. Army War College.

Leites, Nathan. 1953. *A Study of Bolshevism*. Glencoe, IL: Free Press.

Lerner, Jennifer, Roxana M. Gonzalez, Deborah A. Small, and Baruch Fischoff. 2003.

Effects of Fear and Anger on Perceived Risks of Terrorism. *Psychological Science* 14(2) March: 144–50.

Levi, Michael A., and Henry C. Kelly. 2002. Weapons of Mass Disruption. *Scientific American* November.

Lind, Michael. 2003. The Weird Men behind George W Bush's War. *New Statesman* 7 April: 10–13.

Linzer, Dafna. 2004. Attack with Dirty Bomb More Likely, Officials Say. *Washington Post* 29 December: A6.

Lippman, Thomas W., and Barton Gellman. 1999. U.N. "Helped U.S. to Spy on Saddam." *Guardian Weekly* 17 January: 17.

Lippmann, Walter. 1942. The Fifth Column on the Coast. *Washington Post* 12 February: 9.

Lipton, Eric. 2001. The Toll: Numbers Vary in Tallies of the Victims. *New York Times* 25 October: B2.

———. 2005. Homeland Report Says Threat from Terror-List Nations Is Declining. *New York Times* 31 March: A5.

———. 2006a. Former Antiterror Officials Find Industry Pays Better. *New York Times* 18 June: A1.

———. 2006b. Company Ties Not Always Noted in Push to Tighten U.S. Security. *New York Times* 19 June: A1.

Lopez, George A., and David Cortright. 2004. Containing Iraq: Sanctions Worked. *Foreign Affairs* 83(4) July/August: 90–113.

Lott, John R., Jr. 2003. *The Bias against Guns: Why Almost Everything You've Heard about Gun Control Is Wrong*. Washington, DC: Regnery.

Lowenstein, George F., Elke U. Weber, Christopher K. Hsee, and Ned Welch. 2001. Risk as Feelings. *Psychology Bulletin* 127(2): 267–86.

Luard, Evan. 1986. *War in International Society*. New Haven, CT: Yale University Press.

Lukas, J. Anthony. 1987. Class Reunion: Kennedy's Men Relive the Cuban Missile Crisis. *New York Times Magazine* 30 August: 22ff.

Lustick, Ian S. 2006. *Trapped in the War on Terror*. Philadelphia: University of Pennsylvania Press.

Lynch, Marc. 2006. Al-Qaeda's Media Strategies. *National Interest* Spring: 50–56.

Macdonald, Douglas J. 1995–96. Communist Bloc Expansion in the Early Cold War: Challenging Realism, Refuting Revisionism. *International Security* 20(3) Winter: 152–88.

MacFarquhar, Neil. 2003. Rising Tide of Islamic Militants See Iraq as Ultimate Battlefield. *New York Times* 13 August: A1.

MacGillis, Alec. 2006. Paralyzed Roads Envisioned Near Belvoir: Army Move Requires Many Improvements That Lack Funding. *Washington Post* 1 August: A1.

Mack, Andrew. 2005. *Human Security Report 2005*. New York: Oxford University Press.

Mackey, Sandra. 1989. *Lebanon: Death of a Nation*. New York: Congdon & Weed.

Malcolm, Noel. 1993. Seeing Ghosts. *National Interest* Summer: 83–88.

Malkin, Michelle. 2004. *In Defense of Internment: The Case for "Racial Profiling" in World War II and the War on Terror*. Washington, DC: Regnery.

Manjoo, Farhad. 2005. Why FEMA Failed. www.salon.com, 7 September.

Marshall, Monty G., and Ted Robert Gurr. 2005. *Peace and Conflict, 2005: A Global Survey of Armed Conflicts, Self-Determination Movements, and Democracy*. College Park, MD: Center for International Development and Conflict Management, University of Maryland.

Bibliography

May, Ernest R. 1973. *"Lessons" of the Past: The Use and Misuse of History in American Foreign Policy*. New York: Oxford University Press.

McCain, John, with Mark Salter. 2004. *Why Courage Matters: The Way to a Braver Life*. New York: Random House.

McGlen, Nancy E. 1986. *The Sources of Support of the Freeze Movement*. Niagara University, NY, Department of Political Science.

McMahon, Robert J. 1999. *The Limits of Empire: The United States and Southeast Asia Since World War II*. New York: Columbia University Press.

McNaugher, Thomas L. 1990. Ballistic Missiles and Chemical Weapons: The Legacy of the Iran-Iraq War. *International Security* 15(2) Fall: 5–34.

McNeill, William H. 1982. *The Pursuit of Power: Technology, Armed Force, and Society Since A.D. 1000*. Chicago: University of Chicago Press.

Mearsheimer, John J. 1990. Back to the Future: Instability in Europe after the Cold War. *International Security* 15(1) Summer: 5–56.

Mearsheimer, John J., and Stephen M. Walt. 2003. Iraq: An Unnecessary War. *Foreign Policy* January/February: 50–59.

Meisner, Maurice. 1986. *Mao's China and After*. New York: Free Press.

Melby, Eric D. K. 1998. Iraq. In *Economic Sanctions and American Diplomacy*, ed. Richard N. Haass. New York: Council on Foreign Relations Press.

Mencken, H. L. 1949. *A Mencken Chrestomathy*. New York: Knopf.

Meselson, Matthew. 1991. The Myth of Chemical Superweapons. *Bulletin of the Atomic Scientists* April: 12–15.

———. 1995. *How Serious Is the Biological Weapons Threat?* Massachusetts Institute of Technology: Defense & Arms Control Studies Program Seminar, 29 November.

Messenger, Charles. 1989. *The Chronological Atlas of World War Two*. New York: Macmillan.

Meyer, Josh. 2006. U.S. Faults Saudi Efforts on Terrorism. *Los Angeles Times* 15 January: A1.

Meyer, Stephen M. 1984. *The Dynamics of Nuclear Proliferation*. Chicago: University of Chicago Press.

Mintz, John. 2004. Technical Hurdles Separate Terrorists from Biowarfare. *Washington Post* 30 December: A1.

Mitchell, Luke. 2004. A Run on Terror: The Rising Cost of Fear Itself. *Harper's* March: 79–81.

Mitchell, Mark L. 2002. The Impact of External Parties on Brand-Name Capital: The 1982 Tylenol Poisonings and Subsequent Cases. In *Risk, Media and Stigma: Understanding Public Challenges to Modern Science and Technology*, ed. James Flynn, Paul Slovic, and Howard Kunreuther. London: Earthscan, 203–17.

Morison, Samuel Eliot. 1963. *The Two-Ocean War: A Short History of the United States Navy in the Second World War*. Boston: Little, Brown.

Morton, Louis. 1962. *The United States Army in World War II: The War in the Pacific, Vol. 10. Strategy and Command: The First Two Years*. Washington, DC: Department of the Army, Office of the Chief of Military History.

Moynihan, Daniel Patrick. 1993. *Pandaemonium: Ethnicity in International Politics*. New York: Oxford University Press.

Mueller, Harold, and Thomas Risse-Kappen. 1987. Origins of Estrangement: The Peace Movement and the Changed Image of America in West Germany. *International Security* 12(1) Summer: 52–88.

Mueller, John. 1967. Incentives for Restraint: Canada as a Nonnuclear Power. *Orbis* 11(3) Fall: 864–84.

———. 1977. Changes in American Public Attitudes toward International Involvement. In *The Limits of Military Intervention*, ed. Ellen Stern. Beverly Hills, CA: Sage, 323–44.

———. 1979. Public Expectations of War During the Cold War. *American Journal of Political Science* 23(2) May: 301–29.

———. 1984. Lessons Learned Five Years After the Hostage Nightmare. *Wall Street Journal* 6 November: 28.

———. 1987. Presidents and Terrorists Should Not Mix. *Wall Street Journal* 31 March: 36.

———. 1988a. Trends in Political Tolerance. *Public Opinion Quarterly* 52(1) Spring: 1–25.

———. 1988b. The Essential Irrelevance of Nuclear Weapons: Stability in the Postwar World. *International Security* 13(2) Fall: 55–79.

———. 1989. *Retreat from Doomsday: The Obsolescence of Major War.* New York: Basic Books.

———. 1990. The Art of a Deal: No Rewards for Iraqi Aggression. *Arizona Republic* 16 December: C1.

———. 1994. *Policy and Opinion in the Gulf War.* Chicago: University of Chicago Press.

———. 1995a. *Quiet Cataclysm: Reflections on the Recent Transformation of World Politics.* New York: HarperCollins.

———. 1995b. The Perfect Enemy: Assessing the Gulf War. *Security Studies* 5(1) Autumn: 77–117.

———. 1996. Democracy, Capitalism and the End of Transition. In *Post-Communism: Four Views*, ed. Michael Mandelbaum. New York: Council on Foreign Relations, 102–67.

———. 1998. The Escalating Irrelevance of Nuclear Weapons. In *The Absolute Weapon Revisited: Nuclear Arms and the Emerging International Order*, ed. T. V. Paul, Richard J. Harknett, and James J. Wirtz. Ann Arbor: University of Michigan Press, 73–98.

———. 1999. *Capitalism, Democracy, and Ralph's Pretty Good Grocery.* Princeton, NJ: Princeton University Press.

———. 2000a. The Banality of "Ethnic War." *International Security* 25(1) Summer: 42–70.

———. 2000b. *The Banality of "Ethnic War": Yugoslavia and Rwanda.* Paper Presented at the annual meeting of the American Political Science Association. Washington, DC, 2 September.

———. 2002a. American Foreign Policy and Public Opinion in a New Era: Eleven Propositions. In *Understanding Public Opinion*, ed. Barbara Norrander and Clyde Wilcox. Washington, DC: CQ Press, 149–72.

———. 2002b. Harbinger or Aberration? A 9/11 Provocation. *National Interest* Fall: 45–50.

———. 2002c. False Alarms. *Washington Post* 29 September: B7.

———. 2003. *Blip or Step Function?* Paper presented at the annual convention of the International Studies Association. Portland, OR, 27 February.

———. 2004a. *The Remnants of War.* Ithaca, NY: Cornell University Press.

———. 2004b. Why Isn't There More Violence? *Security Studies* 13(3) Spring: 191–203.

———. 2004–2005. What Was the Cold War About? Evidence from Its Ending. *Political Science Quarterly* 119(4) Winter: 609–31.

———. 2005a. The Iraq Syndrome. *Foreign Affairs* 84(6) November/December: 44–54.

———. 2005b. Force, Legitimacy, Success, and Iraq. *Review of International Studies* 31(S1) December: 109–25.

———. Forthcoming. Ideas, Thugs, and the Decline of War. In *Handbook of War Studies III*, ed. Manus I. Midlarsky. Ann Arbor, MI: University of Michigan Press.

Mueller, John, with Brink Lindsey. 2003. Should We Invade Iraq? *Reason* January: 40–48. (Also on reason.com.)

Mueller, John, and Karl Mueller. 2000. The Methodology of Mass Destruction: Assessing Threats in the New World Order. In *Preventing the Use of Weapons of Mass Destruction*, ed. Eric Herring. London: Frank Cass, 163–87.

Mueller, Karl P. Forthcoming. The Paradox of Liberal Hegemony: Globalization and U.S. National Security. In *Globalization and National Security*, ed. Jonathan Kirshner. New York: Routledge.

Myers, B. R. 2004. Mother of All Mothers: The Leadership Secrets of Kim Jong Il. *Atlantic* September: 133–42.

Myers, Lisa. 2004. Terror Threat Source Called into Question. *NBC News*, 28 May. msnbc.com/5087301/.

Nacos, Brigette L., Yaeli Bloch-Elkon, and Robert Y. Shapiro. 2006. *The Threat of International Terrorism After 9/11: News Coverage and Public Perceptions.* Paper presented at the annual meeting of the American Political Science Association, Philadelphia, 31 August.

Nakamura, Takafusa. 1983. *Economic Growth in Prewar Japan.* New Haven, CT: Yale University Press.

National Center for Disaster Preparedness. 2003. *How Americans Feel about Terrorism and Security: Two Years after 9/11.* New York: Mailman School of Public Health, Columbia University.

National Commission on Terrorist Attacks upon the United States. 2004. *The 9/11 Report.* Washington, DC: U.S. Government Printing Office.

National Planning Association. 1958. *1970 without Arms Control.* Washington, DC: National Planning Association.

Natsios, Andrew S. 2001. *The Great North Korean Famine.* Washington, DC: United States Institute of Peace Press.

Neuman, Johanna. 2006. A Reversal of Fortunes Transforms Washington. *Los Angeles Times* 15 January: A22.

Niemi, Richard G., John Mueller, and Tom W. Smith. 1989. *Trends in Public Opinion: A Compendium of Survey Data.* Westport, CT: Greenwood.

Norpoth, Helmut. 1987. Guns and Butter and Government Popularity in Britain. *American Political Science Review* 81(3) September: 949–59.

Oberdorfer, Don. 2001. *The Two Koreas: A Contemporary History,* revised and updated ed. New York: Basic.

———. 2005. *Dealing with the North Korean Nuclear Threat.* Philadelphia, PA: Foreign Policy Research Institute (www.fpri.org).

Office of Technology Assessment, U.S. Congress. 1993. *Proliferation of Weapons of Mass Destruction: Assessing the Risks, OTA-559, August.* Washington, DC: U.S. Government Printing Office.

O'Kane, Maggie. 1996. The Wake of War. *Guardian (London)* 18 May: T34.

———. 1998. Saddam Wields Terror—and Feigns Respect. *Guardian (London)* 25 November: 3.

Ornstein, Norman. 2005. Why Inauguration Day Is Dangerous. *New Republic* 17 January.

Paarlberg, Rob. 1973. Forgetting about the Unthinkable. *Foreign Policy* Spring: 132–40.

Paige, Glenn D. 1968. *The Korean Decision, June 24–30, 1950.* New York: Free Press.

Panofsky, Wolfgang K. H. 1998. Dismantling the Concept of "Weapons of Mass Destruction." *Arms Control Today* April.

Pape, Robert A. 2005. *Dying to Win: The Strategic Logic of Suicide Terrorism.* New York: Random House.

Pauker, Guy J. 1965. Indonesia: The PKI's "Road to Power." In *The Communist Revolution in Asia: Tactics, Goals, and Achievements,* ed. Robert A. Scalapino. Englewood Cliffs, NJ: Prentice-Hall, 256–89.

Paul, T. V. 2000. *Power versus Prudence: Why Nations Forgo Nuclear Weapons.* Montreal: McGill-Queen's University Press.

Perle, Richard N. 2000. Iraq: Saddam Unbound. In *Present Dangers: Crisis and Opportunity in American Foreign and Defense Policy,* ed. Robert Kagan and William Kristol. San Francisco: Encounter Books, 99–110.

Peterson, Peter G. 2004. Riding for a Fall. *Foreign Affairs* September/October: 111–25.

Pillar, Paul R. 2003. *Terrorism and U.S. Foreign Policy.* Washington, DC: Brookings Institution Press.

———. 2004. Counterterrorism after Al Qaeda. *Washington Quarterly* Summer: 101–13.

Pipes, Richard. 1984. *Survival Is Not Enough.* New York: Simon & Schuster.

Podhoretz, Norman. 2002. In Praise of the Bush Doctrine. *Commentary* 114(2) September: 19–28.

Pollack, Kenneth M. 2002. *The Threatening Storm: The Case for Invading Iraq.* New York: Random House.

Port, Bob, and Greg B. Smith. 2001. "Suitcase Bomb" Allegedly Sought: Bin Laden Eyes Russian Stockpile. *Seattle Times* 3 October: A3.

Porter, Bruce D. 1984. *The USSR in Third World Conflicts: Soviet Arms and Diplomacy in Local War 1945–1980.* New York: Cambridge University Press.

Posner, Richard A. 2003. *Law, Pragmatism, and Democracy.* Cambridge, MA: Harvard University Press.

———. 2005a. *Catastrophe: Risk and Response.* New York: Oxford University Press.

———. 2005b. Our Incompetent Government. *New Republic* 14 November.

Prange, Gordon W. with Donald M. Goldstein and Katherine V. Dillon. 1981. *At Dawn We Slept: The Untold Story of Pearl Harbor.* New York: McGraw-Hill.

———. 1986. *Pearl Harbor: The Verdict of History.* New York: McGraw-Hill.

———. 1988. *December 7, 1941: The Day the Japanese Attacked Pearl Harbor.* New York: McGraw-Hill.

Preble, Christopher. 2004. *John F. Kennedy and the Missile Gap.* DeKalb: Northern Illinois Press.

President's Commission on National Goals. 1960. *Goals for Americans.* New York: Prentice-Hall.

Priest, Dana. 2005. Iraq New Terror Breeding Ground: War Created Haven, CIA Advisers Report. *Washington Post* 14 January: A1.

Quindlen, Anna. 1991. The Microwave War. *New York Times* 3 March: 4. 17.

Bibliography

Rabkin, Norman J. 2000. *Combating Terrorism.* GAO/T-NSIAD-00-145. Washington, DC: U.S. General Accounting Office, 6 April.

Radosh, Ronald, and Joyce Milton. 1997. *The Rosenberg File.* New Haven, CT: Yale University Press.

Rapoport, David C. 1999. Terrorists and Weapons of the Apocalypse. *National Security Studies Quarterly* 5(1) Summer: 49–67.

———. 2004. The Four Waves of Modern Terrorism. In *Attacking Terrorism: Elements of a Grand Strategy,* ed. Audrey Kurth Cronin and James M. Ludes. Washington, DC: Georgetown University Press, 46–73.

Rashid, Ahmed. 2000. *Taliban: Militant Islam, Oil and Fundamentalism in Central Asia.* New Haven, CT: Yale University Press.

Reagan, Ronald. 1983. *Public Papers of the Presidents of the United States.* Washington, DC: U.S. Government Printing Office.

Rees, Martin. 2003. *Our Final Hour.* New York: Basic Books.

Reeves, Richard. 1993. *President Kennedy: Profile of Power.* New York: Simon & Schuster.

Reilly, Sean. 2005. Poll Shows Alabamians Still Support President. *Mobile Register* 22 May.

Reiss, Mitchell. 1995. *Bridled Ambition: Why Countries Constrain Their Nuclear Capabilities.* Washington, DC: Woodrow Wilson Center Press.

Revkin, Andrew C. 1998. Coming to the Suburbs: A Hit Squad for Deer. *New York Times* 30 November: A1.

Rieff, David. 2003. Were Sanctions Right? *New York Times Magazine* 27 July: 41–46.

Rockwell, Theodore. 2003. Radiation Chicken Little. *Washington Post* 16 September: A19.

Rogoff, Kenneth. 2004. The Cost of Living Dangerously. *Foreign Policy* November/December.

Rohrmann, Bernd, and Ortwin Renn, eds. 2000. *Cross-Cultural Risk Perception: A Survey of Empirical Studies.* Dordrecht, The Netherlands: Kluwer Academic.

Rood, Justin. 2005. Animal Rights Groups and Ecology Militants Make DHS Terrorist List, Right-Wing Vigilantes Omitted. *CQ.com* 25 March.

Ropeik, David, and George Gray. 2002. *Risk: A Practical Guide for Deciding What's Really Safe and What's Really Dangerous in the World Around You.* Boston: Houghton Mifflin.

Rosen, Jeffrey. 2004. *The Naked Crowd.* New York: Random House.

Rosenthal, A. M. 1993. New York to Clinton. *New York Times* 1 October: A31.

Ross, Brian. 2005. Secret FBI Report Questions al Qaeda Capabilities: No "True" al Qaeda Sleeper Agents Have Been Found in U.S. *ABC News* 9 March: abcnews.go.com/WNT/Investigation/story?id=566425&page=1.

Rothkopf, David J. 2003. Terrorist Logic: Disrupt the 2004 Election. *Washington Post* 23 November: B1.

Rothschild, Michael L. 2001. Terrorism and You: The Real Odds. *Washington Post* 25 November: B07.

Roy, Olivier. 2003. Europe Won't Be Fooled Again. *New York Times* 13 May: A31.

———. 2004. The Challenge of Euro-Islam. In *A Practical Guide to Winning the War on Terrorism,* ed. Adam Garfinkle. Stanford: Hoover Institution Press, 77–88.

Rumsfeld, Donald H. 2001. A New Kind of War. *New York Times* 27 September: A25.

Ruppe, David. 2005. Threat-Mongering? *National Journal* 23 April: 1218–25.

Rush, Myron. 1993. Fortune and Fate. *National Interest* Spring: 19–25.

Russett, Bruce. 1972. *No Clear and Present Danger: A Skeptical View of the United States' Entry into World War II*. New York: Harper & Row.

Sadowski, Yahya. 1998. *The Myth of Global Chaos*. Washington, DC: Brookings.

Sagan, Scott. 1988. Origins of the Pacific War. *Journal of Interdisciplinary History* 18(4) Spring: 893–922.

Sageman, Marc. 2004. *Understanding Terror Networks*. Philadelphia: University of Pennsylvania Press.

Schell, Jonathan. 1982. *The Fate of the Earth*. New York: Knopf.

———. 2003. *The Unconquerable World: Power, Nonviolence, and the Will of the People*. New York: Metropolitan Books.

Schilling, Warner R. 1965. Surprise Attack, Death, and War. *Journal of Conflict Resolution* 9(3) September: 285–90.

Schneier, Bruce. 2003. *Beyond Fear: Thinking Sensibly about Security in an Uncertain World*. New York: Copernicus.

Schroeder, Paul W. 1958. *The Axis Alliance and Japanese-American Relations, 1941*. Ithaca, NY: Cornell University Press.

Schuman, Howard, Jacob Ludwig, and Jon A. Krosnick. 1986. The Perceived Threat of Nuclear War, Salience, and Open Questions. *Public Opinion Quarterly* 50(4) Winter: 519–36.

Schweller, Randall L. 2006. *Unanswered Threats: Political Constraints on the Balance of Power*. Princeton, NJ: Princeton University Press.

Seelye, Katharine Q. 1999. Clinton Blames Milosevic, Not Fate, for Bloodshed. *New York Times* 14 May: A12.

Seitz, Russell. 2004. Weaker Than We Think. *American Conservative* 6 December.

Shane, Scott. 2005a. U.S. Germ-Research Policy Is Protested by 758 Scientists. *New York Times* 1 March: A14.

———. 2005b. London, Madrid, Bali. And Yet Nothing Here. *New York Times* 11 September: 4.4.

Shanken, Marvin R. 2003. General Tommy Franks: An Exclusive Interview with America's Top General in the War on Terrorism. *Cigar Aficionado* December.

Shanker, Thom. 2004. Regime Thought War Unlikely Iraqis Tell U.S. *New York Times* 12 February: A1.

Shannon, David A. 1959. *The Decline of American Communism: A History of the Communist Party of the United States Since 1945*. New York: Harcourt, Brace.

Shaplen, Robert. 1970. *Time out of Hand*. New York: Harper Colophon.

Sheehan, Neil. 1964. Much Is at Stake in Southeast Asian Struggle. *New York Times* 16 August: E4.

Shields, Katheryn J. 2006. Braving the Culture of Fear. *National Catholic Reporter* 3 February.

Shulman, Marshall D. 1963. *Stalin's Foreign Policy Reappraised*. New York: Atheneum.

Siegel, Marc. 2005. *False Alarm: The Truth about the Epidemic of Fear*. New York: Wiley.

Sigal, Leon V. 1998. *Disarming Strangers: Nuclear Diplomacy with North Korea*. Princeton, NJ: Princeton University Press.

Silver, Roxane Cohen, E. Alison Holman, Daniel N. McIntosh, Michael Poulin, and Virginia Gil-Rivas. 2002. Nationwide Longitudinal Study of Psychological Responses to September 11. *Journal of the American Medical Association*. 288(10) September: 1235–44.

Bibliography

Simmons, Robert R. 1975. *The Strained Alliance: Peking, Pyongyang, Moscow and the Politics of the Korean Civil War.* New York: Free Press.

Simon, Jeffrey D. 2001. *The Terrorist Trap: America's Experience with Terrorism.* 2nd ed. Bloomington: Indiana University Press.

Simpson, John. 1991. *From the House of War: John Simpson in the Gulf.* London: Arrow Books.

Singer, Eleanor, and Phyllis M. Endreny. 1993. *Reporting on Risk: How the Mass Media Portray Accidents, Diseases, Disasters, and Other Hazards.* New York: Russell Sage Foundation.

Singer, J. David. 1991. Peace in the Global System: Displacement, Interregnum, or Transformation? In *The Long Postwar Peace: Contending Explanations and Projections,* ed. Charles W. Kegley Jr. New York: HarperCollins, 56–84.

Sivak, Michael, and Michael J. Flannagan. 2003. Flying and Driving after the September 11 Attacks. *American Scientist* 91(1) January–February: 6–9.

———. 2004. Consequences for Road Traffic Fatalities of the Reduction in Flying Following September 11, 2001. *Transportation Research Part F:* 301–5.

Sivard, Ruth Leger. 1987. *World Military and Social Expenditures 1987–88.* Washington, DC: World Priorities.

Slovic, Paul. 1986. Informing and Educating the Public about Risk. *Risk Analysis* 6(4): 403–15.

Slovic, Paul, John Monahan, and Donald G. MacGregor. 2000. Violence Risk Assessment and Risk Communication: The Effects of Using Actual Cases, Providing Instruction, and Employing Probability versus Frequency Formats. *Law and Human Behavior* 24(3): 271–96.

Small, Melvin. 1980. *Was War Necessary? National Security and U.S. Entry into War.* Beverly Hills, CA: Sage.

Smith, George. 2001. Gas Peddled: Exaggerating the Chemical and Biological Terrorism Threat. *Village Voice* 3–9 October.

Smith, Jack. 1980. *Jack Smith's L.A.* New York: McGraw-Hill.

Smoke, Richard. 1993. *National Security and the Nuclear Dilemma: An Introduction to the American Experience in the Cold War.* 3rd ed. New York: McGraw-Hill.

Snow, C. P. 1961. The Moral Un-Neutrality of Science. *Science* 27 January: 255–59.

Snyder, Louis L. 1982. *Louis L. Snyder's Historical Guide to World War II.* Westport, CT: Greenwood.

Solman, Paul. 2006. Moving the Markets. *Newshour with Jim Lehrer,* PBS, 21 July.

Spector, Ronald H. 1985. *Eagle against the Sun: The American War with Japan.* New York: Vintage.

Spicuzza, Mary. 2005. Weeki Wachee Mermaids in Terrorists' Cross Hairs? *St. Petersburg Times* 22 April.

Stahl, Leslie. 1996. Punishing Saddam: Sanctions against Iraq Not Hurting Leaders of the Country, but the Children Are Suffering and Dying. *60 Minutes,* CBS, 12 May.

Starobin, Joseph R. 1972. *American Communism in Crisis, 1943–1957.* Cambridge, MA: Harvard University Press.

Stephan, Alexander. 2000. *"Communazis."* New Haven, CT: Yale University Press.

Stern, Jessica. 1998–99. Apocalypse Never, but the Threat Is Real. *Survival* 40(4) Winter: 176–79.

Stevenson, Jonathan, ed. 2004. *Strategic Survey 2003–4: An Evaluation and Forecast of*

World Affairs. London: Oxford University Press for the International Institute for Strategic Studies.

Stone, Geoffrey R. 2004. *Perilous Times: Free Speech in Wartime*. New York: Norton.

Stossel, John. 2004. *Give Me a Break*. New York: HarperCollins.

Stouffer, Samuel A. 1955. *Communism, Conformity, and Civil Liberties*. Garden City, NY: Doubleday.

Strobel, Warren P. 2006. New Arms Report Fails to Back Bush on Iraq War Basis. *Pittsburgh Post-Gazette* 23 June: A5.

Stueck, William. 2002. *Rethinking the Korean War: A New Diplomatic and Strategic History*. Princeton, NJ: Princeton University Press.

Sunstein, Cass R. 2003. Terrorism and Probability Neglect. *Journal of Risk and Uncertainty* 26(2/3) March–May: 121–36.

Suskind, Ron. 2004. *The Price of Loyalty: George W. Bush, the White House, and the Education of Paul O'Neill*. New York: Simon & Schuster.

———. 2006. *The One Percent Doctrine: Deep Inside America's Pursuit of Its Enemies Since 9/11*. New York: Simon & Schuster.

Takeyh, Ray. 2001. The Rogue Who Came in from the Cold. *Foreign Affairs* 80(3) May/June: 62–72.

Taracouzio, T. A. 1940. *War and Peace in Soviet Diplomacy*. New York: Macmillan.

Taubman, William. 1982. *Stalin's American Policy*. New York: Norton.

———. 2003. *Khrushchev: The Man and His Era*. New York: Norton.

Taylor, Jay. 1976. *China and Southeast Asia: Peking's Relations with Revolutionary Movements*. New York: Praeger.

Terry, Don. 1998. Treating Anthrax Hoaxes with Costly Rubber Gloves. *New York Times* 29 December: A10.

Thomas, Pierre. 2004. Department Struggling to Rank 80,000 Sites, Including Miniature Golf Courses. *ABC News* 9 December: abcnews.go.com/WNT/print?id-316360 (accessed November 8, 2005).

Tizon, Tomas Alex. 2006. 80 Eyes on 2,400 People. *Los Angeles Times* 28 March: A1.

Toland, John. 1961. *But Not in Shame: The Six Months after Pearl Harbor*. New York: Random House.

———. 1970. *The Rising Sun: The Decline and Fall of the Japanese Empire, 1936–1945*. New York: Random House.

Toynbee, Arnold J. 1950. *War and Civilization*. New York: Oxford University Press.

Truman, Harry S. 1956. *Years of Trial and Hope*. Garden City, NY: Doubleday.

———. 1966. *Public Papers of the Presidents of the United States: Harry S. Truman, 1952–1953*. Washington, DC: U.S. Government Printing Office.

Tucker, Cynthia. 2003. If Afghanistan Stays Forgotten, It Won't Forget. *Atlanta Journal-Constitution* 27 April: 10E.

Tucker, Jonathan B., and Amy Sands. 1999. An Unlikely Threat. *Bulletin of Atomic Scientists* July/August: 46–52.

Tucker, Robert W., and David C. Hendrickson. 1992. *The Imperial Temptation: The New World Order and America's Purpose*. New York: Council on Foreign Relations Press.

U.S. Congress, Joint Committee on the Investigation of the Pearl Harbor Attack. 1946. *Report*. Washington, DC: U.S. Government Printing Office.

U.S. News and World Report. 1992. *Triumph without Victory: The Unreported History of the Persian Gulf War*. New York: Times Books/Random House.

242

Bibliography

United Nations. 1999. *Report of the Second Panel Established Pursuant to the Note by the President of the Security Council of 30 January 1999 (S/1999/100), Concerning the Current Humanitarian Situation in Iraq.* New York: United Nations, 30 March. http://www.un.org/Depts/oip/panelrep.html.

Utley, Jonathan G. 1985. *Going to War with Japan, 1937–1941.* Knoxville: University of Tennessee Press.

Valentino, Benjamin. 2004. *Final Solutions: Mass Killing and Genocide in the 20th Century.* Ithaca, NY: Cornell University Press.

Van Drehle, David. 2006. Rallying 'Round the Flag. *Washington Post* 9 April: W10.

Van Evera, Stephen. 1990–91. Primed for Peace: Europe after the Cold War. *International Security* 15(3) Winter: 7–57.

Vance, Cyrus. 1983. *Hard Choices: Critical Years in America's Foreign Policy.* New York: Simon & Schuster.

Viscusi, W. Kip. 1997. Alarmist Decisions with Divergent Risk Information. *Economic Journal* 107 November: 1657–70.

Wagar, W. Warren. 1961. *H. G. Wells and the World State.* New Haven, CT: Yale University Press.

Wald, Matthew L. 2005. Agency Seeks Broad Standard for "Dirty Bomb" Exposure. *New York Times* 8 November: A20.

———. 2006. Proposal on "Dirty Bomb" Attack Would Accept Higher Exposure. *New York Times* 5 January: A15.

Walt, Stephen. 2005. *Taming American Power: The Global Response to U.S. Primacy.* New York: Norton.

Warr, Mark. 2000. Fear of Crime in the United States: Avenues for Research and Policy. *Criminal Justice* 4:451–89.

Warrick, Joby. 2004. An Easier, but Less Deadly, Recipe for Terror. *Washington Post* 31 December: A1.

Waterman, Shaun. Cyanide Gas Device "Probably Didn't Work." 25 June: www.upi.com/Security_Terrorism/view.php?StoryID=20060621-084527-8972r.

Watson, Paul. 2005. The Lure of Opium Wealth Is a Potent Force in Afghanistan. *Los Angeles Times* 29 May: A1.

Weart, Spencer R. 1988. *Nuclear Fear: A History of Images.* Cambridge, MA: Harvard University Press.

Weiner, Tim. 1999a. U.S. Spied on Iraq under U.N. Cover, Officials Now Say. *New York Times* 7 January: A1.

———. 1999b. U.S. Used U.N. Team to Place Spy Device in Iraq, Aides Say. *New York Times* 8 January: A1.

Weinstein, Allen. 1978. *Perjury: The Hiss-Chambers Case.* New York: Knopf.

Weisman, Steven R., and Douglas Jehl. 2005. Estimate Revised on When Iran Could Make a Nuclear Bomb. *New York Times* 3 August: A8.

Welch, David A., and James G. Blight. 1987–88. The Eleventh Hour of the Cuban Missile Crisis: An Introduction to the ExComm Transcripts. *International Security* 12(3) Winter: 5–29.

Welch, Matt. 2002. The Politics of Dead Children. *Reason* 2 March: 53–58.

Welch, William M. 2006. In Age of Terror, U.S. Fears Tunnels Pose Bigger Threat. *USA Today* 2 March: 9A.

Wells, H. G. 1914. *The War That Will End War.* New York: Duffield.

———. 1968. *The Last Books of H. G. Wells.* London: H. G. Wells Society.

Western, Jon. 2002. Sources of Humanitarian Intervention: Beliefs, Information, and Advocacy in the U.S. Decisions on Somalia and Bosnia. *International Security* 26(4) Spring: 112–42.

Will, George. 1994. The Tenth Problem: The Dangerous Reticence of Clinton the UnCoolidge. *Newsweek* 27 June: 62.

———. 2004. Global Warming? Hot Air. *Washington Post* 23 December: A23.

Willer, Robb. 2004. The Effects of Government-Issued Terror Warnings on Presidential Approval. *Current Research in Social Psychology* 10(1) 30 September.

Williams, Peter, and David Wallace. 1989. *Unit 731: Japan's Secret Biological Warfare in World War II*. New York: Free Press.

Willmott, H. P. 1982. *Empires in the Balance*. Annapolis, MD: Naval Institute Press.

———. 1983. *The Barrier and the Javelin: Japanese and Allied Pacific Strategies, February to June 1942*. Annapolis, MD: Naval Institute Press.

Wills, David C. 2003. *The First War on Terrorism: Counter-Terrorism Policy During the Reagan Administration*. Lanham, MD: Rowman & Littlefield.

Wilson, George C. 2003. Why Didn't Saddam Defend His Country? *National Journal* 19 April: 1222.

Witte, Griff, and Spencer S. Hsu. 2006. Homeland Security Contracts Abused: Report Finds Extensive Waste. *Washington Post* 27 July: A1.

Wohlstetter, Albert. 1959. The Delicate Balance of Terror. *Foreign Affairs* 27(2) January: 211–34.

Wohlstetter, Roberta. 1962. *Pearl Harbor: Warning and Decision*. Stanford: Stanford University Press.

Wolf, Charles, Jr., K. C. Yeh, Edmund Brunner Jr., Aaron Gurwitz, and Marilee Lawrence. 1983. *The Costs of Soviet Empire*. Santa Monica, CA: RAND Corporation.

Woodward, Bob. 1991. *The Commanders*. New York: Simon & Schuster.

———. 2002. *Bush at War*. New York: Simon & Schuster.

———. 2004. *Plan of Attack*. New York: Simon & Schuster.

Woolsey, R. James, Jr. 1993. Testimony before the Senate Intelligence Committee, 2 February. Washington, DC: U.S. Government Printing Office.

Yergin, Daniel, and Joseph Stanislaw. 1998. *The Commanding Heights: The Battle between Government and the Marketplace That Is Remaking the Modern World*. New York: Simon & Schuster.

Yerkin, Daniel. 1977. *Shattered Peace: The Origins of the Cold War and the National Security State*. Boston: Houghton Mifflin.

Zimmerman, Peter D., and Cheryl Loeb. 2004. Dirty Bombs: The Threat Revisited. *Defense Horizons* January: 1–11.

Zucchino, David. 2003. Iraq's Swift Defeat Blamed on Leaders. *Los Angeles Times* 11 August: A1.

Index

Index

Hurricane Katrina, 32, 47, 176, 177, 204*n*

Hussein, Saddam, 63, 126–37, 187, 214*n*–15*n*, 216*n*

hydrogen bomb, 95

identity thieves, 146

ideology, 4, 27, 34, 35, 57–58, 67–69, 93, 100–103, 117, 143, 149, 174, 176, 178–79, 207*n*, 209*n*

Ignatieff, Michael, 23–24, 45, 46, 162

immigration, 61, 177, 181

imperialism, 53, 56–57, 58, 68

India, 111, 219*n*

indirect aggression, 70, 71, 79–80

Indochina, 119

Indonesia, 102–3, 114, 115, 136, 147, 211*n*

infidels, 175

influenza vaccine, 32

informants, 88

intelligence agencies, 16, 64, 124, 161–64, 170, 176–77, 180

see also Central Intelligence Agency

intercontinental ballistic missiles (ICBMs), 76–77, 78, 97–98, 210*n*–11*n*

intermediate-range missiles, 97–98

international community, 95–96, 121–22, 128, 134–35, 148

International Institute for Strategic Studies, 178, 186, 220*n*

Internet, 178

Iran:

earthquake in (2003), 147

Islamic government of, 105–9, 113, 114, 126, 136, 175, 183–85, 195

nuclear program of, 17

U.S. relations with, 112, 136, 173, 191–92, 195

Iran-Contra scandal, 113–14

Iran hostage crisis, 8, 33, 105–9, 111, 167–68, 170

Iran-Iraq War, 19–20, 126–27, 130, 132

Iraq:

authoritarian regime of, 63, 122, 126–37, 187, 214*n*, 216*n*

in "axis of evil," 126

biological weapons in, 129

chemical weapons in, 19, 126, 129

democratization of, 133–34

economics sanctions against, 127, 128, 129–30, 211*n*, 215*n*

inspection teams in, 129, 132

Kuwait invaded by, 127–29, 132

military forces of, 129, 134, 215*n*

no-fly zones over, 129

nuclear weapons of, 127–28, 129, 131–32, 214*n*

oil exports of, 127, 128, 130, 131, 188

terrorism supported by, 133, 134–35

WMDs in, 19, 105, 126, 127–35, 214*n*

Iraq Syndrome, 189–92

Iraq War, 187–92

Bush's strategy in, 105, 131, 134, 136–37, 171, 190, 200*n*, 213*n*–14*n*

cost of, 31

hostages in, 170

insurgency in, 13, 173, 178, 179, 184, 187–89, 190, 200*n*

media coverage of, 132

public reaction to, 122, 171, 190–91, 221*n*

reconstruction after, 134

September 11th attacks and, 30, 59, 131, 136–37, 167

U.S. invasion in, 215*n*

U.S. withdrawal in, 189–92

war on terrorism and, 133, 134–35, 195, 200*n*, 220*n*

WMDs as issue in, 105, 131–35

Irish Republican Army (IRA), 200*n*

Islamic fundamentalism, 105–9, 113, 114, 126, 136, 175, 178–79, 183–85, 195

isolationism, 54

Israel, 25, 65, 102, 103, 119, 124, 131, 167, 175, 176, 184, 188–90, 192, 204*n*, 218*n*

Istanbul bombings (2006), 178

Italy, 69–72, 179, 202*n*

Japan, 51–66

atomic bomb used against, 23, 90, 108

China invaded by, 19, 21, 53–54, 56, 60, 205*n*–6*n*

251

About the Author

John Mueller holds the Woody Hayes Chair of National Security Studies, Mershon Center, and is a political science professor at Ohio State University.